LANGUAGE RE̶̶̶̶̶̶̶̶̶̶̶̶̶̶̶̶̶ INTERESTS, OUR IN-
VENTIONS, OUR PASSIONS. AND IT HAPPENS FIRST
IN SLANG. DO YOU KNOW THE MEANING OF . . .

1. At loggerheads.
2. Spin control.
3. Voiceover.
4. Number cruncher.
5. Deep space.
6. Infomercial.

1. In strong, seemingly unsolvable opposition. 2. A person or
group's effort to keep an issue or event regarded and reported with a certain slant. 3. A narration over a visual
image. 4. An accountant or other math grind. 5. Beyond
Pluto. 6. Extended-length commercial advertisement for a
product. Different from other commercials in length and format, which mimics a talk show, often with a studio audience
and celebrity guests enthusiastically discussing the product.

TO COMMUNICATE EFFECTIVELY AND TO UNDER-
STAND OUR FAST-PACED WORLD, YOU NEED A
RELIABLE, HELPFUL RESOURCE THAT IS CRE-
ATED SPECIFICALLY FOR OUR TIMES—

21ST CENTURY
DICTIONARY OF SLANG

—21ST— CENTURY DICTIONARY OF SLANG

EDITED BY THE PRINCETON LANGUAGE INSTITUTE

KAREN WATTS,
COMPILER

Produced by The Philip Lief Group, Inc.

A LAUREL BOOK

Published by
Dell Publishing
a division of
Bantam Doubleday Dell Publishing Group, Inc.
1540 Broadway
New York, New York 10036

Published by arrangement with
The Philip Lief Group, Inc.
6 West 20th Street
New York, NY 10011

ISBN: 0-440-21551-X

Printed in the United States of America

Published simultaneously in Canada

February 1994

OPM   12   11   10   9   8   7   6   5   4   3

Contents

Introduction

The *21st Century Dictionary of Slang* is a valuable contemporary language reference featuring some 5,000 American-English slang terms and phrases. This comprehensive collection reflects a wide range of interests, from up-to-the-minute street talk to the cryptic code used by computer people to the enduring idiomatic expressions common to almost all native English speakers. The *21st Century Dictionary of Slang* offers a rich inclusive mix of the mysterious private lingos of the most notable microcosms in this country—including teenagers, criminals and lawyers, doctors, Wall Streeters, athletes and sports fans, and the military. The book also contains a selection of widely used and longstanding idiomatic phrases that continue to be the backbone of the spoken shorthand that is slang. The *21st Century Dictionary of Slang* forms a practical guide to contemporary language in a time when effective communication depends upon an accurate knowledge of terms that range from the clever and precise to the obtuse and obfuscating.

Slang's appeal is enduring and undeniable—wherever there is formal, conventional language, there has been a lively and provocative shadow of this language used by various people, whether they share an interest, occupation or hobby, or speak across cultural barriers to tap into a common well of verbal intercourse. Writers and speakers could survive without slang, but this colorful and imaginative vocabulary adds vividness to descriptions, punch to the daily badinage that makes up our interactions with acquaintances, coworkers, and confidants. Over time, elements of private languages bridge their areas of origin to make their way into the general language, providing evidence of the way language reflects the shifting contours of our culture.

Slang serves the spoken language in a number of ways, providing conversational shortcuts, rallying cries, catch phrases, and functional codes for everyone who speaks. The purpose of this book is to give the reader a tool to understand slang and its significance in the smaller orbs of speaking culture. If a speaker or writer understands the language used by diverse subsets of our culture, he or she can more ably navigate the fluctuating landscape of language.

How to use the
21st Century Dictionary of Slang

The *21st Century Dictionary of Slang* has been written and compiled to ensure ease of use. Terms are alphabetically arranged: each entry features the word, phrase, or expression, its part of speech, and a category notation pointing to the term's origin or area of prevalent use. A definition follows, with the word or phrase then used in a sample sentence to illustrate its meaning and use.

Examples:
bug juice 1. (*noun phrase*) Kids: a generic term for any sort of fruit flavored beverage served at sleep-away camp
When it was hot, Warren downed pitchers of bug juice like they were water.
2. (*noun*) Medical: antibiotics
Let's get this patient fixed up with some bug juice to knock out that infection.

greenwashing (*verb phrase*) Press: a company's extensive public relations efforts to convince consumers or investors that it is operating in a manner that is environmentally sensitive
Acme's costly greenwashing program was beginning to pay off; sales figures were picking up again.

Use the dictionary by looking up a specific term that interests or puzzles you, consider synonymous terms noted in many entries, or simply browse through the text. Another approach is to peruse the lists of words grouped by category in the index at the back of the dictionary.

These lists provide a cross section of the slang vocabulary of the subcultures represented here. The categories include the following:

Advertising	Military
Auction World	News
Bars	Office Talk
Business	PC (politically correct)
Bartalk	Press
Computerspeak	Psychology
Crime & Law	Public Relations
Drug World	Real Estate
Ecology	Salespeople
Education	Sci-fi
Entertainment	Seafarers
Fantasy	Social
Fashion	Sports
Food	Street
Foreign	Surferspeak
General	Technology
Government and	Teen & College
Politics	Traffic
Health & Fitness	Travel
Kids	Wall Street
Medicine	Word Biz

A NOTE ON USAGE

The *21st Century Dictionary of Slang* features a wide, roundly representative array of American slang terms. It does not, however, include terms of a certain type, namely those that describe the sex act, parts of the human anatomy, or any that refer to sexual preference, ethnic background, or size. The purpose of this book is to provide a compilation of practical, useful terms employed every day in business and popular language.

For foreign speakers of English and for those dubious about the context of unfamiliar terms, times and situations where certain words are appropriate for use can be baffling. Most slang terms are for use in informal conversations. As meanings are subtle and implications depend on circumstances, it is best to avoid using any slang term or phrase unless you are sure of its finer delineations. Know your audience. Slang terms are lively and can pack a punch—powerful words can go off the mark as well as delight.

Reflecting contemporary language, the 21ST CENTURY DICTIONARY OF SLANG is a valuable addition to any personal reference library. The key to understanding the difference between a *fashion victim* and a *fashion criminal*, to listening as your computer consultant *gritches* about *kludge*, or to deciphering the code of real estate brokers talking about *BANANAs* while they show you a *doghouse* can unlock a whole new world of opportunity for insider knowledge and communication. To know that *stink* is good and *groovy* is bad, that the train leaves in five *micks,* and not to be taken in by *flash and trash* is the sign of a well-rounded, informed citizen of the 21st century.

10 (*noun*) General: superb specimen; from the movie 10, extolling the perfect woman
This revised version looks like a 10! You'll definitely win with this.

24-7 (*adverbial phrase*) Teen & College: all the time; short for 24 hours a day, 7 days a week
I've been writing this paper 24-7 for two weeks.

56 (*noun*) Crime & Law: police term for time off from work
"I've got about two weeks of 56 coming to me," the cop noted wearily, "and I'm ready."

86 1. (*verb*) General: to get rid of
Let's 86 the extra bags we're carrying.
2. (*verb*) Food: to be out of an item
"Eighty-six on blackened tuna," the chef called to the waiter.

110 percent (*noun phrase*) Sports: an inspirational sports term referring to the extra effort often required to win a difficult contest
We may have lost but I'm proud to say that everyone on this team gave 110 percent.

180-out (*adj. phrase*) Military: false
All the details in that soldier's report are 180-out, sir.

411 (*noun*) Teen & College, Street: latest information or gossip
What's the 411 on the foreign exchange student in your trig class?

A

a___ and a half (*noun phrase*) Teen & College: extreme version of something
Morton is a brain and a half, so everybody asks him for help with their assignments.

a cold day in hell (*noun phrase*) General: never
It'll be a cold day in hell before I ever go out with you again.

A.A. (*noun phrase*) Government & Politics: initialism for administrative assistant, the senior staffer under a legislator
Senator Dogood's A.A. was a familiar face in the circles of power on the Hill.

A-okay (*expression*) Air & Space: superb
All engines are fine; We're A-okay.

abb (*noun*) Surferspeak: short for abnormal person
I can't believe I ever went out with that abb.

above the line (*prep. phrase*) Entertainment: describing costs accrued in making a movie even before filming begins
The action film's above-the-line costs were enormous because of all the special effects.

accelerated death benefits (*noun phrase*) Business: insurance industry term referring to a policyholder's option to use cash benefits from life insurance to finance medical care during serious illness

Dave was relieved to find out that he could pay for chemotherapy with his accelerated death benefits.

ace (*verb*) Teen & College: to conquer or do extremely well

I aced my French final this afternoon.

ace hurler (*noun phrase*) Sports; Baseball: team's best pitcher

Melido spent five years in the minor leagues, then suddenly became the Redbirds' ace hurler.

ace in the hole (*noun phrase*) General: final surprise which will likely guarantee success, from card playing, an ace dealt to a player face down

The candidate believed that the labor union endorsement was an ace in the hole in the final week before the election.

across the board (*prep. phrase*) General: all-inclusive

Management announced that there would be an increase in the employees' insurance premiums across the board.

across the river (*prep. phrase*) Military: White House and Congress, from the point of view of the Pentagon

"I'm tired of those folks across the river demanding military budget cuts right when we're sitting on an international crisis,"

the general complained to the reporter.

actcom (*noun*) Entertainment: television action comedy, where every episode is based on a disruption of the status quo, followed by humorous efforts to bring the situation back to normal

The network's new actcom took a refreshing, if extremely irreverent, look at American values.

action (*noun*) Crime & Law: small-scale criminal activities, such as gambling or prostitution

Just out of jail, the ex-cons cruised the rough neighborhood looking for some action.

add fuel to the fire (*verb phrase*) General: to make a bad or intense situation worse

The results of the tax audit just added fuel to the fire of the couple's financial woes.

add insult to injury (*verb phrase*) General: to aggravate an already difficult situation

Just to add insult to injury, the burglars smashed the storefront window as they fled with the contents of the cash register.

addiction medicine (*noun phrase*) Medical: contemporary psychiatric treatment for those who suffer from all manner of addictions, from substances to behaviors

Due to advances in addiction medicine, the writer was finally

able to conquer a long time drug dependency.

Adonis (*noun*) Teen & College: attractive male

Did you see that Adonis in Brenda's study group?

advance directive (*noun phrase*) Medical: a medical patient's written instructions as to what course of treatment should be followed in the event he or she becomes incapable of communicating

Barry signed an advance directive which forbade the use of life support systems in the event that he should become brain dead.

affair (*noun*) Government & Politics: reception held for the purposes of fundraising and/or honoring the achievements of an individual

The lobbyists paid $1,000 each to attend the affair honoring the senator's twenty years in office.

aficionado (*noun*) Spanish: devotee

I'm a real opera aficionado.

afraid of one's shadow (*verb phrase*) General: easily frightened

Old Red's not much of a watchdog; he's afraid of his own shadow.

after one's own heart (*prep. phrase*) General: of like interests or sensibilities

When I saw Eliza interacting with the hamsters, I knew that *she was a woman after my own heart.*

afterboomer (*noun*) Press: person born between the years of 1965 and 1974, after the Baby Boom of 1946–1964

The advertisers targeted the afterboomers, who had plenty of disposable income.

-age (*suffix*) Teen & College: presence of something

Do you have any coinage in your pocket?

ahead of the game (*prep. phrase*) General: in an advantageous position

I figure if I get half of the assignment done by tomorrow I'm ahead of the game.

airball (*noun*) Sports (Basketball): shot that completely misses the rim of the basket

Rowena was embarrassed at the number of airballs she threw in the game that afternoon.

aircraft carrier (*noun phrase*) Sports (Basketball): player whose driving force can carry the team to victory

The center suddenly became the team's aircraft carrier, scooping up points that shot them right to the lead.

air dirty laundry (*verb phrase*) General: to let others know of private conflicts or problems

We felt uncomfortable when Uncle Maury began airing the family's dirty laundry at the dinner table.

airhead (*noun*) Teen & College: dizzy, empty-headed individual; *see also:* space cadet *and* trip-out

Vince proved too much of an airhead to be class treasurer when he lost all the money.

air support (*noun phrase*) Military: bombing that occurs in conjunction with a land assault

We need some air support now or we'll have to retreat by sundown.

albatross (*noun*) **1.** General: an encumbrance; something that causes anxiety

"I'll be happy to be rid of this albatross," said the author as she placed the 400 page manuscript on the editor's desk.

2. Medical: patient who never seems to get better, or who is regularly ill with a new ailment, and who sticks with one physician for seemingly endless treatment

It was discouraging to the internist to realize that many patients could not be cured and would be albatrosses returning again and again for treatment.

ALF (*acronym*) Sci-fi: alien life form

The cruel neighborhood rowdies loved to call the new kid ALF.

all bets are off (*expression*) General: situation is entirely different than in the beginning

The premier was assassinated after the economic summit, so as far as the international trade policy proposal is concerned, all bets are off.

all day and night (*expression*) Crime & Law: life sentence in prison; *see also:* book

The kidnappers knew that if they were apprehended they'd be in jail all day and night.

all ears (*adj. phrase*) General: completely attentive

Judy was all ears when the subject of promotions came up.

all hands (*noun phrase*) Seafarers: ship's full crew

The captain ordered all hands on deck for inspection.

all of one's dogs aren't barking (*expression*) General: not in one's right mind; scatter-brained

It was clear that the sitcom writers went overboard in showing that all of the new character's dogs weren't barking.

all systems go (*noun phrase*) General: everything ready for action; from an early space radio

The car is packed, all systems go.

all the rage (*noun phrase*) General: most current fashion

Those leopard-print scarves are all the rage in the city.

all the way (*phrase*) Food: descriptive term for a sandwich or dish served with all possible extras, such as mustard, mayonnaise, lettuce, onions, etc.

Give me a hotdog, all the way.

all wet (*adj. phrase*) General: mistaken

Georgia did not check her facts before interviewing the doctor, and as a result she came up all wet on television.

allegro (*adv.*) Italian: lively, referring to the pace of music

Okay campus, let's practice the fire drill again—this time, make it allegro.

alley oop (*noun phrase*) Sports (Basketball): a pass that is lobbed far through the air and tipped in by a player waiting near the basket

The game was decided in the last few seconds by the forward's nifty alley oop.

alligator (*noun*) Real Estate: investment property that does not bring in enough income to cover expenses, a condition that devours the property's capital like an alligator

Since the agent could only rent the island condominium for half the year, the property became an alligator to its owner.

alligator spread (*noun*) Wall Street: deal where the commissions are equal to, or larger than, the profit

*The young brokers daydreamed about alligator spreads while they made their **cold calls** to prospective customers.*

along for the ride (*prep. phrase*) General: unofficially associated with

I'm not a member of this delegation; I'm just along for the ride.

also ran (*noun phrase*) Sports; Horseracing: horse who doesn't place anywhere near the top in a race

Vincent was tired of being described as an "also ran" in the mayoral race.

alternative dentation (*noun phrase*) Medical: dentures

My dentist told me that with my advanced gum disease I should consider alternative dentation.

alternative rock (*noun phrase*) Entertainment: form of rock music at the cutting edge of trends, often blending techno, heavy metal, and mainstream pop music with avant-garde flavors

My brother is the drummer in an alternative rock band in Portland.

amateur night (*noun phrase*) Bars: any special occasion celebrated traditionally by imbibing liquor, as referred to by big drinkers

I'll be staying in this New Year's Eve. That's amateur night and I'm not interested.

amped up (*adj. phrase*) Teen & College, Street: very excited

What are you all amped up about?

anchor 1. (*noun*) Seafarers: lowest-ranking class member at the United States Naval Academy

It was no honor to be the anchor, even at Annapolis.

2. (*noun*) Real Estate: main component of a shopping mall or complex

Daley's Department Store was the anchor at the Hillside Mall.

angel (*noun*) Entertainment: primary financial backer of a theatrical production

The play is first-rate, but we're still lucky to have found an angel.

angel dust (*noun phrase*) Drug World: nickname for the drug PCP; also known as: dummy, juice, loveboat, lovely, rocket fuel, and water

They vowed to kick angel dust after a really bad trip.

animal companion (*noun phrase*) PC: pet

My client would like to make arrangements for the transportation of her animal companion to Europe.

animalist (*noun*) PC: animal rights advocate

Brigitte Bardot has been an animalist for years.

ankle (*verb*) Entertainment: to quit

The star decided to ankle the play when attendance began to drop drastically.

ankle slapper (*noun phrase*) Surferspeak: tiny wave not worth riding

I'm not wasting my time on those ankle slappers today.

antenna shop (*noun phrase*) Business, Advertising: store that displays prototype products to test consumer reaction; a Japanese concept

I saw this cool audio-visual headset at an antenna shop in Tokyo.

anticipointment (*noun*) Entertainment: the result of a network raising expectations and generating hype on its programming, then falling far short of the anticipated success; this is the collective reaction of viewers, network affiliates, and network executives

The network, touting the young comic as the next Lucille Ball, launched her in an expensive sitcom, only to create widespread anticipointment when it became clear the show was a failure.

antidote (*noun*) Computerspeak: a program used to protect a computer from computer viruses

The virus scare sent everyone to the software store to get an antidote.

antipersonnel (*adj.*) Military: designed to eliminate life; usually refers to weapons that target people rather than locations or equipment

The supervising officer requested extra antipersonnel weapons for the pending assault on the coastal villages.

anti-stalking law (*noun*

phrase) Crime & Law: law that forbids one person from following or harassing

The private detective was careful not to follow his client too closely as he did not want to break the state's anti-stalking law.

any Tom, Dick, or Harry (*noun phrase*) General: any person at all

I'm not just inviting any Tom, Dick, or Harry to my party.

apple of one's eye (*noun phrase*) General: most beloved

His first grandchild was the apple of his eye.

apple-pie order (*noun phrase*) General: neat and tidy

The office was in apple-pie order for the annual inspection.

apple polish (*verb phrase*) General: to flatter someone to gain an advantage or favor; *see also:* brownnose, kiss up, suck up

I can't believe you would apple polish like that, just to get a better assignment at the convention!

apples and oranges (*noun phrase*) General: completely different things

Comparing Proust and Prince is like comparing apples and oranges.

applying a band-aid (*verb phrase*) Government: inadequate solution to a difficult situation

The conservatives have long believed that providing welfare is just applying a band-aid to the

larger problems plaguing the community.

appointment television (*noun phrase*) Entertainment: television industry term for the viewing habits of those who do not watch TV indiscriminately, but rather plan in advance to watch only certain programs

*The documentary series was in a bad **time slot**, but benefited from a following among appointment television viewers.*

apron (*noun*) Bars: bartender

Leave the apron a decent tip, eh? He's taken good care of us.

arc (*noun*) Entertainment: television series format that allows for the development of characters and storylines over the course of several episodes, rather than just within a 30- or 60-minute program.

The networks discovered that many television viewers enjoyed arc programs and tuned in weekly to keep up on the stories.

area denial weapon (*noun phrase*) Military: bomb that causes great damage within a specific area

Portions of the city had been destroyed by the enemy's area denial weapons.

armchair quarterback (*noun phrase*) Sports: sports fan who thinks he or she could have made better decisions affecting the outcome of a game

Bryce was such an obnoxious

armchair quarterback that we hated to watch the Super Bowl with him.

armor (*noun*) Crime & Law: criminal's term for weapons

The gang's huge stash of armor was the biggest discovery in the police raid.

arrest (*verb*) Teen & College: to accuse someone of dressing out of style

Someone should arrest that kid for wearing socks with sandals.

artificial reality (*noun phrase*) Computerspeak: computer technology that allows the user to engage in a three-dimensional computer experience; the use of a helmet or goggles, headphones, and gloves is required to immerse the user in this computer-generated environment; also known as: virtual reality

Quint had been among the first to participate in the artificial reality experiments at the university's computer lab.

artsy fartsy (*adj. phrase*) Teen & College: describing one who is pretentiously artistic

Her clothes are a little artsy fartsy, but underneath she's just a girl from the suburbs.

artware (*noun*) Computerspeak: advanced software and hardware that allows the user to generate art using a variety of elements (sound, color, multi-dimensions, etc.)

The new cola advertisements on

television were created with the help of a sophisticated artware system.

ask for the moon (*verb phrase*) General: request the impossible

Asking to be famous within a year of being in Hollywood is like asking for the moon.

asleep on the job (*adj. phrase*) General: not alert

I was embarrassed to miss that error because it looked like I was asleep on the job.

ass out (*noun phrase*) Teen & College: in trouble

I'm ass out at home because of my report card, so I don't think I can go to the dance tonight.

as the crow flies (*adverbial phrase*) General: in a straight measure between tow points

My mother lives only about a mile from me as the crow flies.

at death's door (*prep. phrase*) General: near death

I couldn't believe they would ask him for money when he was lying there at death's door.

at heart (*prep. phrase*) General: in reality

Even though we live out in the country, I'm a city person at heart.

at large (*prep. phrase*) Crime & Law: mingling among the population while being sought by the police

The escaped convict was at large for several months before

being recaptured in Tulsa.

at loggerheads (*prep. phrase*)
General: in strong, seemingly
unresolvable opposition
*The President's budget director
and housing secretary had long
been at loggerheads over domestic policy spending.*

at one's beck and call (*prep.
phrase*) General: ready to serve
at the least notice
*I don't know why Sandy thinks I
should be at her beck and call.*

at one's fingertips (*prep.
phrase*) General: very nearby
*I always have a dictionary at my
fingertips when I work.*

at pains (*prep. phrase*)
General: with careful effort
*Maddy was at pains not to hurt
her sister's feelings.*

at sea (*prep. phrase*) General:
in a state of confusion
*I'll admit I'm a bit at sea over
the new tax law.*

at sixes and sevens (*prep.
phrase*) General: confused, un-
decided
*I'm really at sixes and sevens
over taking this new job.*

at the drop of a hat (*prep.
phrase*) General: at a moment's
notice, for the slightest reason
*Sheila was ready to move to
California at the drop of a hat.*

attitude (*noun*) Teen &
College, Street: hostile or high-
handed behavior
*I asked the waitress nicely for a
bottle of mustard and she gave*

*me an attitude and didn't bring
it for fifteen minutes.*

auction fever (*noun phrase*)
Auction World, Advertising: the
shopper or bidder's mistaken
belief that everything being auc-
tioned or sold is a bargain
*Auction fever caused by the
"limited-time offer" advertisements, certainly inspired auction fever and we made a lot of
sales.*

audible (*noun*) Sports (Football): play that is called out loud
by the quarterback after the teams
have assumed their positions
*The game turned on the outcome
of the audible the quarterback
called in the fourth quarter.*

Aunt Flo (*proper noun*) Teen
& College: woman's menstrual
period; also known as: the dot,
monthly bill, on the rag, and the
big x.
*I don't feel like going out tonight
because Aunt Flo is here and
I've got a headache*

automall (*noun*) Cartalk: complex of car, van, or truck dealer-
ships clustered together to offer
the consumer convenience and
a wide selection
*Doug and Kumi spent the entire
day at the automall comparing
the new family vans.*

automated attendant (*noun*)
Technology: a prerecorded voice
which answers telephones, takes
messages, and offers directory
assistance

The voice of the automated attendant used by the company's elaborate telephone system was computer-generated.

avant garde (*adj.*) Foreign (French): ahead of the current trends or styles

Barbara has joined that avant garde theater troupe downtown.

awesome (*adj.*) Teen & College: great, and in a more current incarnation, just okay

The burger is awesome but those fries bite.

ax to grind (*noun phrase*) General: personal matter to resolve or promote

I'm only asking you about your mail situation because I've got an ax to grind with the post office.

Aztec two-step (*noun phrase*) Medical, Travel: diarrhea; refers to the tendency to contract the ailment during travel in South America

The tour guide advised us not to buy food from street vendors in order to avoid the Aztec two-step.

B

B (*noun*) Teen & College: short for Frisbee

You should see how my dog can catch the B.

B- (*prefix*) Entertainment: second-rate

The B-movies of the fifties have become cult classics.

babe (*noun*) Teen & College: attractive person (refers to both sexes)

What a babe that new lifeguard is!

babe lair (*noun phrase*) Teen & College: swanky sort of home or apartment that is helpful in attracting women as romantic or physical partners; from the popular skit "Wayne's World," featured on television's "Saturday Night Live"

Audrey giggled when she realized that her date fancied himself a swinging bachelor and his apartment, an effective babe lair.

babe magnet (*noun phrase*) Teen & College: an item or person that should attract members of the opposite sex

Guy, that leather jacket is a total babe magnet.

babelicious (*adj.*) Teen & College: extremely sexy and attractive, referring to a female; from the popular skit "Wayne's World," featured on television's "Saturday Night Live"

Rachel must think she's babelicious to be prancing around those guys like that.

Baby Bells (*proper noun*) Business, Wall Street: nickname for the regional telephone companies created by the break-up of American Telephone and Telegraph

Further antitrust litigation is expected to create Baby Bells in other industries.

baby boomer (*noun phrase*) Press: person who was born between the years 1946 and 1964
Now that the baby boomers were having children of their own, a whole new market was expected to emerge.

baby catcher (*noun*) Medical: obstetrician
There aren't enough baby catchers on call tonight so I'm going to have to work a double shift.

Baby M laws (*noun phrase*) Crime & Law: legislation regarding surrogate motherhood; from Baby M, the child involved in a highly publicized and precedent-setting surrogacy case
Marnie's lawyer needed to do research on Baby M laws when her surrogate decided to keep the baby she carried for Marnie.

baby pop (*noun phrase*) Street: a young man
Who is that baby pop that's been hanging around your house?

babycise class (*noun phrase*) General: parent-baby exercise class involving swimming, massage, and other stimulating physical movement
Ronald, hoping to instill a life-long love of fitness in his daughter, took her to a babycise class.

back (*adj.*) Bars: on the side

The waitress called for a rye and water, back.

back end money (*noun phrase*) Entertainment: a movie's final profits, or true net, after all expenses have been paid
When the screenwriter threatened to sue, the industry accountant claimed that the movie had yielded no back end money.

backer (*noun*) Entertainment: investor
We've got an initial backer for the show and we think she'll be able to attract others.

backgrounder (*noun*) Government, Politics, News: a conversation between a government official and a reporter that takes place only on the condition that the official is not quoted directly or mentioned in the report by name; *see also:* deep background
In a diner during an afternoon break, the Senator gave the two reporters a backgrounder on the tax bill.

back in the box (*prep. phrase*) Drug World: back in business after a drug arrest
The cops were discouraged to see how soon dealers got back in the box after being busted.

backseat driver (*noun phrase*) General: passenger in a car who can't help telling the driver where to go and how to drive
I can't stand going anywhere

with my father because he's a terrible backseat driver.

back-pedal (*verb*) General: to reverse one's position just when reactions appear unfavorable

As soon as the audience's stony silence was apparent, the candidate began to back-pedal on the subject of military base closings.

back to square one (*adv. phrase*) General: at the beginning of the process again

If the seller doesn't accept our offer, we're back to square one.

badass (*adj.*) Teen & College: excellent

What a badass band this is! Let's dance!

bad blood (*noun phrase*) General: longstanding resentment

There has been bad blood between our families for many years.

bad egg (*noun phrase*) General: troublemaker

He's not really a bad egg, just mischievous.

badge (*noun*) Crime & Law: police officer

"Just because the guy's a badge doesn't mean he can come here and shove us around," the neighborhood thugs complained.

bad guy (*noun phrase*) General: dishonest, deceitful, guilty character in a situation; as opposed to the good guy, who is the honest, blameless character

(applies to both sexes); *see also:* black hat

Why do you always make me sound like the bad guy when you recount our conversations?

bad hejab (*noun phrase*) Foreign (Arab): improper Islamic dress

The mosque elders were chagrined to see so much bad hejab among the Moslem youth.

bad-mouth (*verb*) General: to speak badly of, to criticize

You've been bad-mouthing that movie all week, but I didn't think it was that awful.

bag 1. (*verb*) Teen & College: to quit, end, discontinue

Let's bag this movie and try the one next door.

2. (*verb*) Crime & Law: to arrest; *see also:* collar and pinched

The undercover officer finally bagged the dealer she'd been after for a year.

bag and baggage (*noun phrase*) General: everything one owns

If I don't pay the rent soon, my landlord will toss me out, bag and baggage.

bag biter (*noun phrase*) Government & Politics: spoiler or troublemaker

The school board struggled with the bag biters who kept showing up at meetings to dispute the budget discussions.

bag on (*verb phrase*) Teen & College: to chastise

Maura bagged on me for letting her cat out of the house.

bag some rays (*verb phrase*) Teen & College: to sunbathe
Let's bag some rays at the beach this afternoon instead of going to class.

bagger (*noun*) Teen & College: dolt
You left your driver's license at home? What a bagger!

bail 1. (*verb*) Teen & College: to quit, avoid; short for bail out
I bailed my driver's ed class on Saturday and now I can't make it up until next month.
2. (*verb*) Teen & College: to abandon or leave
Let's bail this party and find something else to do.

baked (*adj.*) Bars: hung over; also known as: crispy, fried, and toasted
Ivan was so baked the next day that he didn't get out of bed until four in the afternoon.

bald (*adj.*) Teen & College: bad
What a bald move that was!

baldhead (*noun*) Drug World: disparaging term for an outsider
I don't want to sniff with that baldhead. I've got a bad feeling about him.

ball is in your court, the (*expression*) Sports (tennis), Government, Business: onus is on you to take the next step in an exchange or series of exchanges
Look, I've called to apologize, so the ball is in your court.

ball of fire (*noun phrase*) General: person who possesses plenty of energy
Jackie is a real ball of fire; she should run for office.

balloon (*noun*) Real Estate: final payment due on the type of loan that requires a series of comparatively small early payments and a much larger last payment
The young couple might have to forfeit their mortgage because they had no money for the balloon.

balloon goes up (*expression*) Military: major military confrontation begins
When the dictator refused to withdraw from the occupied territory by the deadline, the balloon went up at midnight.

ball park figure (*noun phrase*) General: rough estimate
Could you give me a ball park figure on how many people you think are coming to the concert on Thursday?

banana (*noun*) Medical: patient with jaundice
We're going to have to keep the banana in Room #201 around for a few days.

BANANA (*acronym*) Real Estate: Build Absolutely Nothing Anywhere Near Anything; refers to a community's disinclination to allow undesirable land use, such as waste disposal or landfill construction

The committee was having trouble deciding on a location for the nuclear waste processing plant, thanks to the BANANA syndrome in most of the preferred communities.

banger (*noun*) Bars: any sort of straight liquor, which the drinker bangs on the bar before imbibing

After his fifth banger, Jimmy was an ugly sight.

bang-up (*adj.*) General: excellent

You did a bang-up job on that presentation!

bank (*noun*) College, Drug World: plenty of money

Lonnie was running around bragging he had bank and buying drinks for everybody.

bankable (*adj.*) Entertainment: descriptive term for a film star whose commitment to a film virtually guarantees the film's success

Because the young athlete-turned-actor was consistently bankable, all the studios fought over him for their projects.

bar (*noun*) Wall Street: one million

At a million a month, Acme weights in as a 12-bar account.

barf 1. (*verb*) Teen & College: to vomit, also known as: blow lunch, boag, boot, decorate one's shoes, drive the porcelain bus, earl, heave, honk, hurl, ralph, reverse gears, shout at one's shoes, spew, toss, yak, yawn in technicolor, and zuke

Trini was so nervous before going on stage that she barfed.

2. (*verb*) Computerspeak: to malfunction

My computer barfed right in the middle of a 40-page document.

barfly (*noun*) Bars: individual who spends more time at a bar drinking than just about anywhere else

The usual barflies were queued up at the door of the Shaggy Lion at opening time.

barhop (*verb*) Bars: to go from bar to bar looking for the most interesting scene

Willis was exhausted from the previous night's barhopping.

bark up the wrong tree (*verb phrase*) General: to choose a course of action that won't reap positive results

If you're going to ask me to help with the spaghetti supper, you're barking up the wrong tree.

barney (*noun*) Surferspeak, Teen & College: idiot; refers to the character of Barney Rubble from television's "The Flintstones"; *see also:* gilligan

Who told this barney he could have a ride with us?

barrel (*verb*) General: to go extremely fast

Mickey barreled around the corner on her bike and ran right into a stop sign.

base (*verb*) Street: to dispute

Don't base with me, man. I know I'm right.

basehead (*noun*) Drug World: person who is addicted to free-basing cocaine
That guy is a total basehead. I don't want him hanging around here.

base on (*verb*) Teen & College: to criticize
Mr. Mooney was basing on me after class today for not applying myself.

basic brown (*noun phrase*) Government & Politics: person who has little or no interest in, or commitment to, environmental issues
The basic browns will resist the higher prices caused by the need to make products environmentally sound.

basket case (*noun phrase*) General: in an overwrought condition
After the car accident, I just became a basket case.

bassing (*adj.*) Teen & College, Street: getting loud; from increasing the bass on a stereo
It's really bassing here. Let's go outside so we can talk.

bat an eye (*verb phrase*) General: to show feeling
She took that money from her mother without batting an eye.

bathtub (*noun*) Sports (Skiing): indentation left in the snow from someone falling on his or her derriere

Riley was embarrassed by the bathtub he left in the soft snow after wiping out.

batten down the hatches (*verb phrase*) Weather: secure everything for a terrible storm
We better batten down the hatches if my sister's kids are coming over today.

batting a thousand (*verb phrase*) Sports (Baseball): to be succeeding in an extraordinary way; literally, to be holding the best possible baseball batting average, which is 1.000
So far I'm batting a thousand on the new people I've hired.

beach, the (*noun*) Seafarers: on shore
The sailors couldn't wait to get to the beach for a little R&R.

beached (*adj.*) Surferspeak: absolutely stuffed with food to the point of being unable to move
I can't surf today. I'm still beached from breakfast this morning.

bo all (*verb phrase*) Teen & College: to say
So I was all, "What do you mean you're going out with Jake?"

be all over (*verb phrase*) Teen & College: to do something earnestly
I was all over that assignment right after I got to the library.

bean counter (*noun phrase*) General: person whose business is to work closely with numbers or statistics; also known as: number cruncher

The President angrily described the skepticism on the budget as overly critical bean counters.

beam up (*verb phrase*) Street: to experience a crack-induced high; from a term used frequently in another context on television's "Star Trek"

Wally's been beaming up all afternoon.

beanball (*noun*) Sports (Baseball): pitch intended to hit the batter's head

The pitcher's beanball caused a bench-clearing brawl that took ten minutes to break up.

beard 1. (*noun*) Surferspeak: veteran surfer

I'm going to ask that beard over there for some tips.

2. (*noun*) Business, Law Enforcement: effort to disguise the actual purpose, activities, or interests of a person or organization, the use of which is usually improper, if not illegal

Prohibited from having holdings in the fiber optic industry, the corporation used one of its smaller subsidiaries as a beard for its secret advancement in that area.

bearhug (*noun*) Business, Wall Street: squeeze a large company puts on a usually smaller, company in the course of a takeover; the "hugger" seems unaware of its own strength and often inadvertently squeezes the life out of the "huggee."

It's clear that the new facilities built for the subsidiary are going to prove to be ChicagCo's bearhug on its new acquisition.

beast (*noun*) Drug World: police

"I'm not buying anything tonight," the addict said nervously. "The beast is all over the place."

beat (*adj.*) Teen & College: bad

That was such a beat movie! I can't believe we paid to see it.

beat a dead horse (*verb phrase*) General: to continue to do something even though it is having no effect

I don't want to beat a dead horse, but I've got to talk to you again about that Henderson account.

beat around the bush (*verb phrase*) General: to avoid the principal matter

Let's not beat around the bush here. How much will these repairs cost?

beat one's brains out (*verb phrase*) General: to try to resolve a difficult question or problem in one's mind

I've been beating my brains out trying to think of a way to get to Baltimore tonight.

beat one's head against a wall (*verb phrase*) General: to struggle with something futilely

I can see that I'm beating my head against the wall trying to get you to come with us.

beat sheet (*noun phrase*)
Entertainment: outline for a television show or film, which describes the project by scene
Where's the beat sheet on that new fall medical drama?

beats me (*expression*) General: I don't know. How should I know?
What time is it? Beats me.

beat the bricks (*verb phrase*)
Crime & Law: to be released from prison
The thief had only beat the bricks a month before being picked up again for a parole violation.

beat to the punch (*verb phrase*) General: to do something before someone else is able to
John wanted to buy Mom a new robe for her birthday but I beat him to the punch.

beautiful people, the (*noun phrase*) social: glamorous people whose lifestyles and escapades are reported in the news; also known as glitterati
Now that you're one of the beautiful people, how does it feel to have the papparazi after you?

be-backs (*noun*) Salespeople: mildly derogatory name for shoppers who say they'll return to purchase an item but obviously have no intention of doing so
Sue didn't even take out the lease papers because she could see her two customers were just a couple of be-backs.

be beat with an ugly stick
(*verb phrase*) Teen & College: to be unattractive
That dog's been beat with an ugly stick.

b-boy/girl (*noun*) Teen & College: rap music fan
Gina's little brother is a b-boy and dresses like a gangsta.

be caught dead (*verb phrase*) General: to be seen in public in a certain condition; usually used in the negative
Mom, no offense, but I wouldn't be caught dead in those shoes.

bed and breakfast 1. (*noun phrase*) Travel: small private home where rooms may be let by the night, usually providing the guest with a bed, shared bath, and breakfast
Jim wanted to stay in a hotel with a pool, but Jackie had her heart set on a cozy bed and breakfast.
2. (*verb phrase*) Wall Street: to sell a security and buy it back directly in order to avoid excessive capital gains taxes
All the brokers in the office bed and breakfasted their securities so they could save taxes.

bedienung (*noun*) Foreign (German): note that appears on a bill indicating that any tip is included in the final price
Marshall was glad to see "bedienung" on his rather large restaurant tab.

bed of roses (*noun phrase*)

General: pleasant situation, usually used in the negative

This may look like a great job, but believe me, it's no bed of roses.

beef 1. (*verb*) Teen & College: to fall on one's rear end when skateboarding

Did you see me beef in front of all the kids in the parking lot!

2. (*verb*) Teen & College, Street: to have a conflict or problem

Donna and I beefed, but we worked it out.

beefcake (*noun*) General: photograph of a man revealing plenty of skin; cheesecake is a similar type of photography of a woman

That picture of Bobby on the beach was real beefcake, wasn't it?

beef up (*verb*) General: to reinforce and strengthen an existing condition

In response to a drop in consumer confidence, the cosmetics tycoon beefed up her advertising campaign efforts.

beergoggles (*noun*) Bars: unclear vision and thinking brought on by excessive drinking

Tamara was wearing beergoggles and couldn't see that the guy she was talking to was a creep.

be hating it (*verb phrase*) Teen & College: to be in bad shape

Jordan got very drunk last night and he's hating it this morning.

behind bars (*prep. phrase*) Crime & Law: in jail

I'm glad to know that kidnapper is finally behind bars.

behind the eight ball (*prep. phrase*) General: in a difficult position

You've really got me behind the eight ball on that issue, Henderson.

be history 1. (*verb phrase*) Teen & College: to be finished

I turned in my last paper and now I'm history.

2. (*verb phrase*) Teen & College: in trouble

If I don't return that uniform on time, I'll be history.

beige (*adj.*) Teen & College: boring

The characters in the film were too beige to keep our interest up for three hours.

belay that (*verb phrase*) Seafarers: put a stop on that

Belay that order to drop anchor. It seems the captain has changed plans.

belch (*verb*) Crime & Law: to inform or testify against another party; *see also:* rat and sing

The small-time hoodlum decided to belch on the fatal robbery he'd witnessed out of fear of being implicated in the crime himself.

be like (*verb phrase*) Teen & College: to say

The guy asks me out and I'm like, "Yeah, sure."

bellhop (*noun*) Seafarers: sailor's term for a Marine in full dress uniform
Did you get a look at the bellhop showing off at the reception?

bells and whistles (*noun phrase*) Computerspeak: fancy features that are attractive but not essential
A serious computer user can see beyond the bells and whistles when buying a system.

bellyache (*verb*) General: to complain
Quit bellyaching and just go clean your room.

be loving it (*verb phrase*) Teen & College: to be in great shape
I turned in my last art assignment and now I'm loving it.

below the line (*prep. phrase*) Entertainment: describing the costs of the actual making of a movie
Beyond the stars' exorbitant salaries, the below the line costs for the film were modest by industry standards.

Beltway bandit (*noun phrase*) Government, Politics: expensive Washington consultant or consulting firm, Beltway refers to the highway loop circling Washington, D.C.
The campaign consultant was widely considered to be a Beltway bandit, having charged outrageous fees for what turned out to be questionable influence and wisdom.

Belushi cocktail (*noun phrase*) Drug World: powerful mix of heroine and cocaine, so named after comedian John Belushi, who died from partaking of the lethal combination; see also speedball
The young dancer knew enough to go home when they started serving Belushi cocktails.

BEM (*acronym*) Sci-fi: Bug-Eyed Monster, a staple character in science fiction
Young Rory was thrilled to receive his monthly science fiction magazine, filled to the brim with stories about BEMs and ALFs.

bench warmer (*noun phrase*) Sports: player who spends most of his or her time on the bench and seldom makes it into a game
Derek was discouraged to have finished the season as a bench warmer, especially since he was in such good shape.

bend over backward (*verb phrase*) General: to try excessively
I bent over backward to schedule this appointment at a convenient time for you and now you're canceling it?

bend someone's ear (*verb phrase*) General: to talk incessantly to someone; see also: talk someone's ear off
It hate it when my seat partner in a train sits there and bends my ear the whole trip.

benny (*noun*) Surferspeak: one who emulates a surfer in dress, behavior, and speech but who does not actually surf at all
This guy's such a pathetic benny he doesn't even know how to swim!

bent (*adj.*) Teen & College: deranged, extremely weird
Stealing that CD was a bent thing to do.

beside oneself (*prep. phrase*) General: extremely excited
I'm beside myself over my job promotion.

best boy (*noun phrase*) Entertainment: all-purpose assistant on a film shoot (applies to both sexes)
Carla was thrilled to see her name on the film's credits as best boy.

best shot (*noun phrase*) General: best or maximum effort
If you're going to try out for the new crew team, at least give it your best shot.

bestseller (*noun*) Word Biz: book that is extremely successful, in terms of the number of copies sold, as measured primarily by the New York Times Book Review's ranking system and the publishing industry's own accounting
The entertainment industry was shocked when Blanch Whiting's memoirs became a bestseller.

best thing since sliced bread (*expression*) General: best to come on the scene in a long time
Doug thinks interactive television is the best thing since sliced bread.

be sword (*verb phrase*) Street: to calm down, relax
Would you be sword, man? You're going to get us in trouble.

be there (*verb phrase*) Teen & College: be at a certain place at a certain time
The movie starts at 7:00 P.M., so be there.

bet on the wrong horse (*verb phrase*) General: to make a misjudgment
I guess I bet on the wrong horse when I thought you would straighten out and fly right.

bet the farm (*verb phrase*) General: to risk everything; also known as: bet the ranch
Don't bet the farm that Clayton is coming back from Europe next month.

betty (*noun*) Teen & College: attractive girl
Josh and his friends all agreed that the new girl was a real betty.

between a rock and a hard place (*expression*) General: in a difficult, seemingly unresolvable situation
The tenants in the condemned building were between a rock and a hard place—if they left immediately they might lose all of their belongings, but if they

tried to save their stuff they were risking their lives.

bias-free (*adj.*) PC: neutral, nonjudgmental, nondiscriminatory

The department prided itself in the use of bias-free language in all official documents and reports.

Bible belt (*noun phrase*) Press: mostly southern region of the United States where large concentrations of fundamentalist Christians live

The conservative candidate was likely to win in the Bible belt but would suffer in the traditionally liberal states.

Big Blue (*proper noun*) Wall Street, Computerspeak: nickname for International Business Machines (IBM), derived from the color of the company's logo

Apple and the others have been giving Big Blue a rough time in the personal computer market.

big board (*noun phrase*) Wall Street: nickname for the New York Stock Exchange

After seeing the big board on her class trip to Wall Street, Alison decided she wanted to be a stockbroker.

big C (*noun phrase*) Medical: cancer

The doctors were saddened to hear that one of their colleagues had been diagnosed with the big C.

big cheese (*noun phrase*)

General: boss; also known as: head honcho, top banana, and top dog

The big cheeses from corporate headquarters are coming to the office today for a meeting.

Big Crunch (*noun phrase*) Science, Sci-fi: imploding contraction of the universe, which is hypothesized to be the inverse theory and historical counterpart of the Big Bang theory of creation

Waldo liked to think that his existence constituted an historically important moment somewhere between the Big Bang and the Big Crunch.

big daddy (*noun phrase*) General: the largest or most important of something; see also mother of all

That particular iguana is the big daddy of the species.

big hair (*noun phrase*) Teen & College: hairstyle that has extraordinary volume

That girl with the big hair over there is smiling at me.

big mama (*noun phrase*) Surferspeak: ocean

Ah, there's big mama, calling my name.

big picture (*noun phrase*) Government, Politics: the larger considerations a situation may require

All these details are interesting, but let's have a look at the big picture.

big rig (*noun phrase*) Traffic:

large (usually 18-wheel) commercial vehicle

Uncle David's been driving a big rig for twenty years.

big shot (*noun phrase*) General: important person

The big shots from the bank came to the office today to talk to the partners about a loan.

big stink (*noun phrase*) General: fuss or scandal

Don't make such a big stink over my being late.

big time (*adv.*) General: in an extreme way

I lost that last tennis match, big time.

bigger than Texas (*adj. phrase*) General: right in front of one's eyes

There were my keys, bigger than Texas, sitting on the counter.

bilge (*noun*) Seafarers: something of a distinctly bad nature; from the nautical term that means "below the water line"

All her efforts to explain her whereabouts Saturday night was just a lot of bilge in disguise.

bilge water (*noun phrase*) Seafarers: soup

This bilge water could use some seasoning.

billing (*noun*) Entertainment: ranking order in which stars' names appear in the credits for a movie

These days some actors won't accept a film role unless they get top billing.

bin, the (*noun*) General: mental health facility; short for the loony bin; also known as: funny farm, nut house, and rubber room

Legend has it that the artist was in the bin for several years after a quick rise to fame.

binder (*noun*) Food: food such as rice and bananas, that thickens digestive waste, sometimes to the point of constipation

When the babe had diarrhea, the doctor encouraged a binder diet.

bindle (*noun*) Drug World: paper wrapper in which a batch of drugs is contained

Fold me a bindle so I can split this blow with you.

biocentrism (*noun*) PC, Ecology: belief that the earth is a resource not just for humans, and that honoring the equal importance of all living things will preserve the balance of nature

As a proponent of biocentrism, the research scientist decided to dedicate her life to preserving the world's rain forests.

biopic (*noun*) Entertainment: film based on the life of a famous person

The beloved singer's life is movingly depicted in the new television biopic.

bird (*noun*) Technology: telecommunications satellite

We sent up a bird to increase our international broadcast capability.

bird farm (*noun phrase*)

Seafarers: aircraft carrier; *see also:* flat top

Morgan was posted to six months at sea on the bird farm.

birdbath (*noun*) Real Estate: unintended indent in the pavement that causes a puddle after the rain

The seller promised the prospective buyer that the birdbath at the end of the driveway would be repaired before the closing.

birthday suit (*noun phrase*) General: total nakedness

I was standing there in my birthday suit when the doorbell rang.

biscuit 1. (*adj.*) Teen & College: easy, effortless

That French exam was biscuit.

2. (*noun*) Teen & College: a gullible person

I told him we'd be right back and he believed me. What a biscuit!

biscuits (*noun*) Drug World: methadone, a drug used to ease individuals away from their heroine addictions

I'm trying to kick the horse so I'm on biscuits.

bit 1. (*noun*) Crime & Law: the term of a prison sentence

"My bit'll be over in October," the inmate bragged to the others on the cellblock.

2. (*noun*) Entertainment: story or joke used by a comedian

The comedian knew the bit was going flat even before he was halfway through with it.

bit part (*noun phrase*) Entertainment: small, hardly noticeable role in a television program or a movie

If you look closely, you can see the director playing a bit part in her own film.

bite 1. (*verb*) Drug World: to arrest; *see also:* bust

Violet got bit on Thursday, but she'll probably be back on the street by Friday.

2. (*verb*) Teen & College: to copy or appropriate an idea

Milo bit my costume idea and now I've got to think of a new one.

3. (*verb*) Teen & College: to be very bad; *see also:* suck

You have to work tonight? That bites.

bite someone's head off (*verb phrase*) General: to attack someone verbally

I only asked for a little help. You don't have to bite my head off.

bite the bullet (*verb phrase*) General: to face something unpleasant but unavoidable

I guess I'll have to bite the bullet and pay the extra insurance.

bite the dust (*verb phrase*) General: to expire

I guess one more restaurant downtown bit the dust last month.

bitter pill (*noun phrase*) General: disappointment

It was hard for Todd to swallow the bitter pill of knowing his father never intended to keep his promise.

Black & Decker (*proper noun*) Teen & College: boring grind; a reference to the power tool manufacturer

That science class was Black & Decker, from start to finish.

black and white (*noun phrase*) Crime & Law: police car

The partners spent their third straight night cruising the neighborhood in their black and white.

black book (*verb phrase*) Business, Wall Street: company's anticipatory defense against a threatened takeover

The small plastics manufacturer didn't have the resources to black book the raider's advance.

black box (*noun phrase*) Air & Space: fireproof container that holds a recording of all cockpit conversations and transmissions occurring during a flight; used by investigators to reconstruct events preceding a crash

A rescuer found the aircraft's black box amidst the wreckage of the cockpit.

black hat (*noun phrase*) General: person who appears to be the villain in a scandal or similarly unfortunate situation; as opposed to the white hat, who is considered the blameless party

I know I'm going to look like the black hat when this campaign contribution controversy comes to light.

black knight (*noun phrase*) Business, Wall Street: individual or company making an unwelcome attempt to takeover another company

Dex Newmarket is corporation's black knight in the takeover deal.

black market (*noun phrase*) Business: an illegal retail enterprise

Diamonds can be purchased on the international black market, but customs inspector's are always on the lookout.

black shoe (*noun phrase*) Seafarers: regular member of the Navy, as distinct from the brown shoes, who are naval aviators

Lisa was a black shoe, but she hoped to attend flight school and make some advancement.

blackball (*verb*) General: to prevent someone from working

Sylvan was convinced he had been blackballed from the big construction job by his union leader.

blacked out (*adj. phrase*) Travel: restricted; referring to a period of time during which special airline or train fares do not apply

I'd like to buy one of those bargain tickets to go home next month but they're blacked out at Thanksgiving.

blacklist (*verb*) General: to smear someone's reputation and prevent him or her from working

Susan had been blacklisted by her former colleagues for sup-

porting the controversial oil drilling project.

blade 1. (*verb*) Teen & College: to skate on rollerblades

I'm blading to school today, Mom, so I don't need a ride.

2. (*noun*) Medical: surgeon

Why don't you just have a blade remove that cyst for you? It's a simple procedure.

blank check (*noun phrase*) General: complete freedom, especially from financial constraints

I've been given a blank check to restaff and computerize the office.

blast 1. (*noun*) Drug World: single helping of cocaine, either a line or a snort

After hearing the doctor's lecture on the effects of cocaine, Carmen knew she would never be tempted to try a few blasts before going dancing.

2. (*noun*) Teen & College: great time

We had a blast at that soccer clinic.

bleedin' (*adj.*) Teen & College, Street: extremely cold; *see also:* jackfrost

I'm not riding my bike down to the store. It's bleedin' out.

blitz 1. (*noun*) General: fast, intensive attack or campaign

The candidate planned a media blitz for the last week of the campaign that included TV and radio spots and billboard ads.

2. (*noun*) Sports, Foreign (Football, German): overwhelming defensive attempt to break through the offensive line and tackle the quarterback

The quarterback was injured in the blitz.

blooper 1. (*noun*) General: a public blunder

When Jonathan spilled wine in the restaurant he knew it was a blooper that might cost him a bundle.

2. (*noun*) Entertainment: a humorous mistake filmed during production of a television show or a movie

Let's watch "Television's Most Priceless Bloopers" tonight.

blow (*noun*) Drug World: cocaine; also known as: candy, coke, evil, jolt, nose candy, nose powder, snow, stardust, White Christmas, Ye Old Peruvian Marching Powder

"Got any blow?" the tourist furtively asked an undercover cop.

blow a fuse (*verb phrase*) General: to become enraged; also known as: blow a gasket

I didn't know he'd blow a fuse when he saw the telephone bill.

blow a line (*verb phrase*) Entertainment: to make a mistake reading the lines of a script

I have to be careful not to blow this line because it's so crucial to the scene.

blow away (*verb phrase*) Teen & College: to amaze
My dad was blown away when he heard me speaking German to those tourists.

blow hot and cold (*verb phrase*) General: to have fluctuating feelings or opinions about something
I'm really blowing hot and cold on the paint color we've chosen for the house.

blow in (*verb phrase*) General: to arrive quickly or unexpectedly
I'm just blowing in to the city to do a bit of shopping.

blow it (*verb phrase*) General: to fail
Daniel's friends frequently advised him not to blow it with Kathy, who they all felt was a good match for him.

blow off (*verb phrase*) Teen & College: to skip
I blew off my lunch date because I had to study.

blow off one's doors (*verb phrase*) Cartalk: to surpass a challenger or competitor definitively
With a 40 percent share of the market for the third quarter, Acme blew the doors off of Ace.

blow off steam (*verb phrase*) General: to vent anger or irritation
The pressure got so bad at work that I just had to blow off some steam.

blow one's cover (*verb phrase*) General: to reveal one's identity
Zach called me "Mom" and blew my cover at the store.

blow one's mind (*verb phrase*) General: to astonish, amaze, or stun
After seeing him on television so many years, it really blew my mind to meet the famous boxer.

blow the lid off something (*verb phrase*) General: to expose something
That reporter blew the lid off the school board scandal.

blow the whistle on someone (*verb phrase*) General: to expose illegalities or improprieties
After watching him sell a phony antique to a collector, Sally blew the whistle on Marcus' merchandise fraud.

blow town (*verb phrase*) General: to leave or escape in a rush
When the twins heard the police were looking for them, they blew town immediately.

blow up (*verb phrase*) Street: to improve, get better and stronger
With high-protein meals and long hours in the gym, Barney's upper body really blew up.

blow wide open (*verb phrase*) General: to expose a secret
The case was blown wide open when the detective found a telephone message from the agent in the murder victim's apartment.

blue (*adj.*) Computerspeak:

IBM computer, from the nickname for IBM called Big Blue
I'd like to take advantage of the bargains on other brands, but frankly I've always favored a blue system.

blue-bloods (*noun*) Social: aristocratic elite
I heard that Evan's folks are some blue-bloods from Boston.

blue blower (*noun phrase*) Medical: person with advanced lung disease
"I don't think the blue blower in #309 is going to check out this time," one orderly noted to another.

blue book (*noun phrase*) Cartalk: value of a used car, from the name of a guide that standardizes prices for used cars
Listen to what the seller has to say about the price, but you'd finally better go by the blue book.

blue chip (*adj. phrase*) Wall Street: common stock in an established corporation, stock that can be depended on to generate solid profits and dividends
The reliable performance of blue chip stocks is reflected in the high purchase price per share.

blue collar (*adj. phrase*) General, Business: working class, nonmanagerial and nonprofessional
The candidate liked to boast that he was from a regular, blue collar background who would look out for the common folks.

bluehair (*noun*) Teen & College: elderly person
I've been mowing lawns for the bluehairs on my block all summer. It's a good deal—one tips big and the other one makes me a glass of iced tea when I'm done.

blue pipe (*noun phrase*) Medical: vein, as opposed to red pipe, which is an artery
I'm having trouble finding a decent blue pipe for the I.V.

blues, the (*noun*) General: depression; a low dispirited feeling
I've had the blues since Pierre left for France.

blue top (*noun phrase*) Military: a press release, from the blue bordered releases issued by the Department of Defense
Did you get the blue top on the new Pentagon appointments?

blue-water boating (*noun phrase*) Seafarer: boating that takes place on the open sea rather than close to shore
My dad likes to go blue-water boating, but I prefer exploring the edges of the coast.

blunt (*verb*) Entertainment: to compete with a television show on another network by running a similar show at the same time, so as to diminish the ratings of the rival show
The network was able to blunt their rival's success in that slot with a new tabloid program of their own.

blurb (*noun*) Advertising, Word Biz: personal endorsement used to promote a product

The blurb on the back of the book was effusive but convincing.

board (*verb*) Teen & College: to skateboard

I was boarding to the library when I saw Julie riding her bike down Elm Street.

boarder (*noun*) Teen & College: skateboarder; *see also:* thrasher

The boarders all showed up at the beach at the same time, like some kind of motorcycle gang.

bo dereks (*noun phrase*) Wall Street: bonds due to mature in the year 2010; based on the actor's role in the movie 10.

The dividends are being deferred into bo dereks for tax purposes.

boardhead (*noun*) Surferspeak: avid surfer

Ginny's going out with some boardhead she met over the summer.

bobbybrown (*verb*) Street: to go off on one's own; refers to the singer Bobby Brown, who left a famous group to become a solo performing artist

Wyatt left the Dregs and bobbybrowned on a new record.

bod (*noun*) General: physique

That one's got a nice bod.

body womp (*verb phrase*) Surferspeak: to ride waves on one's stomach rather than using a surfboard; to bodysurf

Sometimes I just feel like body womping instead of taking my board out.

bof (*noun*) Entertainment: record album featuring the "best of" a performer's repertoire

When the super group released a bof for the 40th anniversary of their first album it became an instant bestseller.

boffo (*noun*) Entertainment: big box office success; *see also:* gorilla

The space adventure was the boffo hit of the summer.

bogon (*noun*) Computerspeak: individual who is considered phony and says phony things

The two programmers privately thought of their two-faced supervisor as a total bogon.

bogosity (*noun*) Computerspeak, College: the extent to which something is considered phony, or bogus

Miranda couldn't believe the bogosity of Mike's excuse for being late.

bogsatt (*acronym*) Military: Bunch of Guys Sitting Around the Table, an informal description of a decision-making style

The new procedures were quickly determined by bogsatt, not through the formal hearings, reports, and recommendations that usually were employed.

bogulate (*verb*) Surferspeak: to surf without skill
I've been bogulating all day.

bogus (*adj.*) Computerspeak, Surferspeak, Teen, College: phony, no good
The students rolled their eyes as the guest speaker told bogus stories of trekking in Tibet.

boiler room (*noun phrase*) Business, Law Enforcement: room in which slippery salespeople use the telephone to sell securities (or other products, services, or commodities) that are hugely overpriced or overrepresented in value or potential for profit
The consumer protection people exposed a boiler room operation that had been selling nonexistent cruise packages to unsuspecting customers.

boilerplate (*noun*) Real Estate, Law: the standard language in a contract or other official document
The landlord used a boilerplate lease for all the tenants in her buildings.

Boll Weevils (*proper noun*) Government & Politics: mildly derogatory term used by mainstream Democrats to describe conservative Southern Democrats
The Democratic majority knew they couldn't count on the Boll Weevils to vote with them on defense cuts so they had to look to liberal Republicans for supports.

bolo (*verb*) Crime & Law: short for "be on the lookout for;" term used primarily by police
"Bolo a teen in a red sweatshirt and blue jeans near First and Elm," the police radio announced.

bolt (*verb*) Food, Bars: to leave a restaurant or bar without paying the bill
"I had a feeling that clown was going to bolt," the waiter said disgustedly.

bomb 1. (*verb*) Computerspeak, Teen, College: to fail miserably or malfunction; *see also:* crash
The student sat with his head in his hands, distraught over bombing his Chem final.
2. (*noun*) Sports (Football): very long pass
The quarterback threw a bomb to the free man he saw near the end zone.
3. (*adj.*) Street: best
Veronica is convinced she's the bomb on the fencing team.

bomb thrower (*noun phrase*) Government & Politics: individual unwilling to compromise on an issue, or who disturbs the lawmaking process with unrelenting vocal opposition; the political equivalent of a spoilsport
Known as a bomb thrower, the minority whip always took a position as an obstacle to compromise on key legislation.

bona fide (*adj.*) Foreign (Latin): real, authentic, legitimate
I'm a bona fide dentist now and I'm starting a new practice in September.

bone (*adj.*) Street: sorry and useless; *see also:* lame
I'm not taking that bone job at the mall.

bone factory (*noun phrase*) Medical: hospital
I've been working at the bone factory for six months now.

bone out (*verb phrase*) Teen & College: to give up or quit
Don't bone out on me now.

bones (*noun*) Teen & College: dollars
I've got a couple of bones for gas.

bone to pick (*noun phrase*) General: dispute
I have a bone to pick with you over this dry cleaning bill.

bone up (*verb phrase*) General: refresh one's memory
I better bone up on everyone's name before the family reunion.

Bonus! (*expression*) Teen & College: Excellent!
You got tickets to see the Stones? Bonus!

bon vivant (*noun*) Foreign (French): one who richly and fully enjoys life
I love to be with Richard because he's such a bon vivant.

boogerhead (*noun*) Teen & College: fond term for one's buddy

What's up, boogerhead?

book 1. (*verb*) Sports: to run extremely fast
I was really booking on that play!

2. (*noun*) Sports: the statistics and general lowdown on a player or a team
So what's the book on that new pitcher?

3. (*noun*) Crime & Law: life sentence in prison; *see also:* all day and night
The murderer got the book for the heinous crime.

boom (*noun*) Teen & College: stereo system
I nagged for a full year and finally got a new boom for Christmas.

boomer (*noun*) Seafarer: nuclear submarine
For several years Marcia had been an engineer on the boomer project at the sub base.

boomer baby (*noun phrase*) Press: person who is the child of a baby boomer
In order to get their boomer babies into the popular nursery school, the baby boomers had to sign a three-year waiting list.

boonies, the (*noun*) General: a remote, inaccessible place; short for boondocks; also known as: the sticks
This party is way out in the boonies; we'll never find it.

boost (*verb*) Street: to steal or shoplift

Randy got caught boosting a bag of chips at the convenience store.

boot 1. (*noun*) Wall Street: cash incentive added to a stock acquisition to make the deal more appealing
Without the boot, it's unlikely Smithers would have gone for the deal.

2. (*noun*) Seafarer: a new naval recruit just out of boot camp
The officer encouraged the boots to avoid the off-limits establishments in town.

3. (*verb*) Computerspeak: to start
I've booted up the system so we're ready to go.

4. (*verb*) Teen & College: to vomit; also known as: barf, blow lunch, boag, decorate one's shoes, drive the porcelain bus, earl, heave, honk, hurl, ralph, reverse gears, shout at one's shoes, spew, toss, yak, yawn in technicolor, and zuke.
Janice drank too much at the frat party and booted all night.

bootstrap (*noun*) Computerspeak: accessory computer program that aids the user in starting up the computer system
If you got yourself a bootstrap, you'd save yourself five minutes every morning.

booty (*adj.*) Street, Rap: weak, unassertive
Let's give the sub a hard time. He's booty.

booze cruise (*noun phrase*) Bars: short boat trip where drinks are served; a floating cocktail party
So many people showed up for the Homecoming Weekend booze cruise that dozens were turned away.

bore to tears (*verb phrase*) General: to be so dull as to bring one to the point of exasperation
I was bored to tears watching those home movies again.

borking (*noun*) Government & Politics: close scrutiny to which cabinet and Supreme Court nominees are now subjected, including investigations into personal lifestyles and political and private philosophies; from the difficult and controversial Senate hearings on Judge Robert Bork's nomination to the Supreme Court
That committee is going to give the candidate a good borking before even considering confirmation.

born yesterday (*adj. phrase*) General: inexperienced
Don't act like you were born yesterday. You've done this before.

bottleneck (*noun*) Traffic: traffic congestion caused by one or more lanes being closed
There was a terrible bottleneck at the entrance to the bridge.

bottomless pit (*noun phrase*) General: person with a seemingly endless appetite
Every kid in this family has a

bottomless pit for a stomach.

bottom line (*noun phrase*)
General: final determination
*So what's the bottom line? Am I
hired or what?*

bottoms-up research (*noun
phrase*) Business: market research that entails the detailed
study of anything that might
affect the market value of a
product (customer reaction,
competition analysis, etc.)
*We'll be doing bottoms-up re-
search before we launch the new
computer enhancement product.*

bounce (*verb*) General: to
forcefully remove someone
*The rowdy group got bounced
from the beach dance for being
rude to the other guests.*

bounceback (*noun*) Medical:
person who returns to the hospital again and again because he
or she can't shake the ailment,
or because a new ailment has
developed
*"Would you take a look at my
bounceback with pneumonia?"
the physician asked a colleague.*

bouncer (*noun*) Bars: big,
beefy person who works in a bar
breaking up fights, usually by
"bouncing" troublemakers right
out of the bar
*Big Louie was a bouncer at
Bonnie Belle's for twelve years
until he joined the FBI.*

bourgeois (*adj.*) Foreign
(French): middle class
I'm tired of you and all your

bourgeois possessions.

bowhead (*noun*) Teen &
College: perky, cutesy girl; from
the likelihood that she has a
cheerful bow in her hair
*It was funny to see Wayne, who
was a dreg and a headbanger,
going out with a bowhead like
Lisa.*

box 1. (*noun*) Computerspeak:
computer
*The hacker's mother complained
that she never did anything on
weekends but play with her box.*
2. (*verb*) Medical: to die
*The coma case from Friday night
finally boxed this morning.*

box tonsils (*verb phrase*)
Teen & College: to kiss deeply
and passionately; *see also:* suck
face
*Evan's mother caught him box-
ing tonsils with Wendy in their
garage.*

bracelets (*noun*) Crime &
Law: handcuffs
*The suspected arsonist showed
little emotion as the police office
frisked her and put the bracelets
on.*

brain-dead (*adj.*) Teen &
College: doltish
*You must be brain-dead if you
can't figure out what she meant.*

brain drain (*noun phrase*)
General: cause for extreme mental exhaustion
*That seminar was a real brain
drain.*

brainiac (*noun*) Teen &

College: smart, studious person

The kids agreed that Violet was pretty cool, even if she was a brainiac.

brainstorm (*verb*) General: collective effort among a group to come up with a new idea or find a solution to a particular problem

The design department will have to brainstorm to find a more European look for its product packaging.

branwagon (*noun*) Food: health food movement

I think this no-fat, low-fat stuff is just a lot of branwagon baloney.

brass, the (*noun*) General: those in the highest positions of authority; also known as: top brass

We got word from the brass that no new accounts should be signed until the budget is re-organized.

brass ring (*noun*) Wall Street: partnership in a Wall Street firm

After landing his third huge account in six months, Johnson finally got the brass ring.

bread and butter (*noun phrase*) General: source of one's basic requirements

The summer tourist business was the boutique's bread and butter.

break (*noun*) Entertainment: the point at which a film breaks even and begins to make a profit for the distributor

Weekend after weekend of lines around the block brought the movie's break by the end of the summer.

break barracks (*verb phrase*) Military: to leave the premises with authorization

If we get caught breaking barracks, we're dead meat.

break it down (*verb*) Street: turn down the volume of the live music or stereo

Hey, could you break it down up there? I'm trying to get some sleep.

break one's neck (*verb phrase*) General: to try one's hardest

I'll break my neck to pick you up at the airport on time.

break out (*verb phrase*) Teen & College, Street: to leave

What time are you breaking out for the party?

break-out book (*noun phrase*) Word Biz: publishers' term for an author's first extremely successful book, in terms of the number of copies sold

June Stephens is a terrific writer, but she just hasn't had a break-out book yet.

break the ice (*verb phrase*) General: to initiate conversation

Let me break the ice and introduce myself.

breeze into a room (*verb phrase*) General: to enter a room nonchalantly

She breezed into the party three hours late.

brewhound (*noun*) Teen & College: one who is constantly drinking or getting drunk
I was such a brewhound last semester that I got two incompletes.

brewsky (*noun*) Bars: beer; also known as: chilly, suds, and swill
I'll have a brewsky, and make it an extra cold one.

BRI (*noun phrase*) Medical: initialism for Building Related Illness, referring to any medical problem whose cause is attributed to indoor environmental conditions
Dan's nagging cough was determined to be a BRI.

brick 1. (*verb*) Teen & College: to be frightened; shortened from the phrase shitting bricks
I sure was bricking before that midterm, but I think I did okay.
2. (*verb*) Teen & College: to fail
I bricked that basic economics course last semester.
3. (*adj.*) Street: cold or hard
Look, if you think I'm brick for walking out, let me tell you what she said to me.

brightwork (*noun*) Seafarers: brass in need of a good polishing
The brightwork on the cadet's uniform took a full hour to clean.

brilliant pebbles (*noun phrase*) Military: multitude of small satellites in space that could combine their power and capabilities to identify and destroy enemy missiles

The brilliant pebbles didn't actually exist, but many saw the system as the defense program of the future.

brillohead (*noun*) Teen & College: person with coarse, curly hair; from Brillo soapy scrub pads
That brillohead in my study group is giving me yesterday's notes.

bring down the house (*verb phrase*) General: to cause enthusiastic response
I don't think the President's new tax proposal will bring down the house.

bring home the bacon (*verb phrase*) General: to provide support for one's family
I know I've been working overtime a lot lately, but I've got to bring home the bacon.

bring in the big guns (*verb phrase*) General: to call on one's strongest allies for assistance
If that account doesn't pay its bill by Monday, I'm going to bring in the big guns and call my lawyer.

bring to light (*verb phrase*) General: to expose
It's time to bring to light his activities during the war.

bring up the rear (*verb phrase*) General: to be last
I'll be bringing up the rear when I finally turn in this project.

broadcast fax (*noun phrase*) Technology: facsimile sent simultaneously to multiple recipients

The press agent decided to send out the release as a broadcast fax.

broadside (*verb*) Traffic: to hit the side of another car with the front of one's own car

It's amazing that Lea wasn't hurt when that van broadsided her on Main Street yesterday.

broad strokes (*noun phrase*) Business, Government: generalization or summary of all that might be said on a matter in great detail

Don't give me fine points, just describe the new loan program in broad strokes.

broke (*adj.*) General: all out of money

I can't go out this weekend because I'm broke.

broken arrow (*noun phrase*) Military: accident involving nuclear weapons

There were confused reports about the broken arrow, which left several dead and scores wounded.

broke to the curb (*adj. phrase*) Street: extremely ugly; *see also:* buckled and crushed

Geez, that guy in the movie was broke to the curb, eh?

broom (*noun*) Crime & Law: police officer who is the station house gofer and janitor

Until Jim's probationary term ended, he was stuck being the precinct broom.

brown bag (*verb phrase*) Food: to carry one's homemade lunch in a paper bag

I'm running low on cash this month so I'll have to brown bag it to work for a while.

brownie (*noun*) Crime & Law: traffic police officer

Sheila moaned when she saw the brownie placing a ticket on her car.

brownnose (*verb*) Teen & College: to curry favor with flattery or attention; *see also:* kiss up

You've been brownnosing that professor all semester.

bruiser (*noun*) General: big, muscular, physically intimidating person

Who is that bruiser near the door?

brush up on (*verb phrase*) General: to refresh one's memory or skills

I'd like to brush up on my French before going to Paris in April.

brush-off (*noun*) General: a snub

I can't believe Mel gave me the brush-off when I tried to invite him to my party.

buck (*noun*) Entertainment: $100,000

After making it big, the actor began demanding as much as 40 bucks a film.

bucked (*adj.*) Street: naked

Emily got bucked and jumped into the pool during the party.

bucket of nugs (*noun phrase*) Surferspeak: plenty of waves

There's a bucket of nugs out there today.

buckled (*adj.*) Street: ugly; *see also:* broke to the curb *and* crushed

Mikey's dog is so buckled he scares other dogs.

buckle down (*verb phrase*) General: to focus on something completely

I've got to buckle down and study for my final exams.

buck private (*noun phrase*) Military: regular Army soldier, private rank

Did you hear? Some buck private won the drawing for a weekend in Las Vegas!

buff 1. (*noun*) Cartalk: superb-looking car

A Camaro is nice but a Porsche is truly buff.

2. (*adj.*) Teen & College: muscular, well-built

Why does Trevor suddenly seem so buff?

buffalo (*verb*) General: to trick

That kid buffaloed me into giving him money for bus fare home.

buff up (*verb phrase*) Medical: to prepare a patient to be released from the hospital

Buff up Riley in #309, will you? His wife's coming for him today.

bug 1. (*noun*) Computerspeak: a software error or flaw; to eliminate the error or flaw is to debug

The software package touted the program as bug-free.

2. (*noun*) Crime & Law: elec-tronic listening device used to eavesdrop secretly on conversations or telephone calls in order to gather evidence

The attorney found a bug under her desk, but she wasn't sure whether it was the FBI, her ex-husband, or the IRS who put it there.

3. (*noun*) Crime & Law: criminal who totally lacks compassion or a sense of the human impact of his or her actions

The detectives knew the serial killer they were tracking was a bug who would never show re-morse for his actions.

bug-eyed (*adj.*) General: very surprised

My mom was bug-eyed when she saw the new outfit I got with my own money.

bug juice 1. (*noun phrase*) Kids: a generic term for any sort of fruit-flavored beverage served at sleep-away camp

When it was hot, Warren downed pitchers of bug juice like they were water.

2. (*noun*) Medical: antibiotics

Let's get this patient fixed up with some bug juice to knock out that infection.

bugging (*adj.*) Teen & College: upset

Felicia was bugging over her bi-ology grade.

build castles in the air (*verb phrase*) General: to dream for the impossible

You're building castles in the air if you think you can win that match.

bulk up (*verb phrase*) Sports: to increase muscle mass on one's body by lifting weights and exercising strenuously
Tory had really bulked up since she started working out with a personal trainer.

bull (*noun*) Crime & Law: prison guard
When the bulls changed shifts at ten o'clock, they didn't expect the night would turn into a riot.

bullcrit (*noun*) Social: criticism of a book, film, art, etc., which is not based on personal experience, but rather on critical reviews or word of mouth.
Thomas was the king of bullcrit; he never read a book but he always managed to appear like he had.

bulldoze (*verb*) General: to force something
I had to bulldoze that bill through committee to bring it to a vote before the legislative session ended.

bullet (*noun*) Drug World: a single helping of cocaine, i.e., a line or snort; *see also:* blast
The undercover cop had to shoot a blast in front of the dealers or risk losing his cover.

bullet bait (*noun phrase*) General: disparaging term for a common soldier
Stuck in trenches, the buck privates felt like bullet bait, especially since all the officers were safe at headquarters.

bulletproof (*adj.*) Computer-speak: descriptive term for a computer program thought to be safe from possible harm from beginners or hackers
The CIA hoped their new computer program would be bulletproof.

bullheaded (*adj.*) General: stubborn
Don't be so bullheaded! Try to see it my way for once.

bull session (*noun phrase*) General: lengthy, informal conversation
We had a bull session last night about the committee's plans for the future.

bum (*verb*) Teen & College: to be disappointed; also known as: bum out
I'm really bummed you can't come to my party.

bummer (*noun*) Teen & College: unfortunate situation, disappoint
So you can't go to the dance after all? What a bummer!

bump'n (*adj.*) Teen & College: excellent
That outfit is bump'n! Can I borrow it Friday night?

bumper-to-bumper (*adj. phrase*) Traffic: heavy, slow-moving traffic
Traffic was bumper-to-bumper for three miles before the toll plaza.

bum rap (*noun phrase*)
General: unfair punishment
Denise felt she got a bum rap when she was the only one punished for painting the fence with graffiti.

bum-rush (*verb*) Teen & College: to enter or depart with a great deal of fanfare
The guys bum-rushed the party, but no one was impressed.

bundle (*noun*) General: plenty of money
We made a bundle painting houses over the summer.

bundling (*noun*) Government & Politics: way political action committees (PACs) get around contribution limits by giving elected officials a bundle of small contributions rather than one large contribution
Many election reformers argue that bundling is unethical and violates the spirit of campaign fundraising restrictions.

bunged up (*adj. phrase*) Teen & College: tangled or scrunched up in an uncomfortable way
My underwear is bunged up and my pants are too tight to fix it.

bunk (*adj.*) Teen & College: bad, uncool
Dad, I appreciate the thought, but that shirt you bought me is sort of bunk.

buns (*noun*) General: buttocks
My buns are killing me from horseback riding all afternoon.

buppie (*acronym*) Press: Black Upwardly-mobile Urban Professional
The old brownstones were being bought and renovated by the buppies who grew up in the neighborhood.

burly (*adj.*) Surferspeak: very cold
It's too burly to surf today.

burn 1. (*verb*) Sports: to score against or defeat
I burned Winston in the sprints yesterday, but he'll get me on the hurdles today.

2. (*verb*) Drug World: to cheat someone by selling phony or heavily diluted drugs; *see also:* cut and stomp on
Donny got burned on that ounce he bought.

Burn! (*expression*) Teen & College: Aha! I have embarrassed you!
You're not invited to Sandra's party? Burn!

burn a copy (*verb phrase*) Military, Office Talk: to make a photocopy
Burn me a copy of those plans, Sergeant, and make it quick.

burner (*noun*) Street: a firearm
That guy's got a burner in his jacket. Let's get out of here.

burn on (*verb phrase*) Teen & College: to insult
Why are you always burning on me?

burn one's bridges (*verb phrase*) General: to take an action that cannot be reversed, to sever connections

Sue burned her bridges when she sold her home and moved to Italy.

burn out (*verb phrase*) General: to tire of an activity or thing because of constant exposure to it

After a year of struggling against the bureaucracy, many of the activists burned out and quit attending organizing meetings.

burnout 1. (*noun*) Drug World: one who has smoked so much marijuana either in one sitting or over time so as to be debilitated, truly dopey, from the experience *"What a bunch of burnouts," the kids said of their classmates, who were huddled behind the gymnasium smoking again.*

2. (*noun*) Teen & College: loser *Charlene's such a burnout. Who would have imagined it?*

burn rubber 1. (*verb phrase*) Cartalk: to accelerate dramatically to the point of making a car's tire's smoke and squeal *When the bank robbers spotted the police, their getaway driver burned rubber.*

2. (*verb phrase*) General: to make a quick exit

Josh is going to have to burn rubber to get home before his curfew.

burnt (*adj.*) Teen & College: exhausted or drained

I was so burnt after that exam I went to my room and took a nap.

burn the midnight oil (*verb phrase*) General: stay up late

My sister burned the midnight oil finishing the suit she was making.

burro (*noun*) Drug World: person who carries drugs into the country on his or her body; *see also:* mule

For a while after college, Jeff traveled back and forth to South America as a burro for his dealer.

burst (*verb*) Computerspeak: to separate pages of computer paper along the perforated lines *Printing the document took five minutes. Bursting it took fifteen.*

burst at the seams (*verb phrase*) General: too full

This elevator is going to burst at the seams.

bus (*noun*) Computerspeak: electronic elements of a computer that enable data to move from one place to another *The technician found a flaw in the bus, but once it was repaired he had no trouble installing the system.*

bus head (*noun phrase*) Teen & College: bedraggled mess, as one might look after a long bus trip

She showed up for that interview looking like a real bus head.

bushing (*verb*) Cartalk: raising the price of a car after the buyer has agreed to buy it for a lower price

Before all the papers are signed,

some salespeople will try bushing on a handshake.

bush-league (*adj.*) General: inferior, amateurish
The judge complained that the defense attorney's tactics were bush-league.

business, the (*noun*) Entertainment: television, to those who work in the field
I've been in the business for thirty years, so trust me.

bust 1. (*verb*) Teen & College: to harass or needle someone
I saw you helping your mother at the grocery store—you're going to get busted.

2. (*adj.*) Street: dirty and disheveled
You look busted today.

3. (*verb*) Crime & Law, Drug World: to arrest, usually on drug charges; *see also:* bite
June got off probation last month for possession, but she got busted on Thursday for selling the stuff.

bust a few (*verb phrase*) Surferspeak: to surf a few waves
What do you say we go bust a few before the storm comes in?

bust a move (*verb phrase*) Teen & College, Street: to dance
Did you know Jeffrey could bust a move like that?

bust a rhyme (*verb phrase*) Street: to rap
Did you know Cheryl's brother could bust a rhyme?

busted (*adj.*) General: out of money and luck
After two failed ventures in the frozen yogurt business, Sheila was busted.

bust fresh (*verb*) Street: to dress stylishly
Marco's busting fresh today.

bust it (*verb phrase*) Street: listen; as a command
Bust it, you go wait in the back and I'll sneak around the front.

bust one's hump (*verb phrase*) General: to try one's hardest
I've been busting my hump for two years to save enough to buy a car.

bust something (*verb phrase*) Street: to listen to something
Bust this new song. It's the bomb.

butt 1. (*noun*) Street: a weak, unassertive person; *see also:* weenie, wimp, and wuss
That butt let a fifth grader beat him up.

2. (*adv.*) Teen & College: extremely
That train I'm taking leaves butt early.

butt in (*verb phrase*) General: to interrupt or interfere
I wish you wouldn't butt in on our conversations like that.

butt out (*verb phrase*) General: to tend to one's own concerns
You just don't know how to butt out, do you?

butt ugly (adj. phrase) General: extremely unattractive

Jennifer's new dog is butt ugly.

butter (*noun*) Surferspeak: women or girls

The butter on this beach is better later in the afternoons.

button one's lip (*verb phrase*) General: to stop speaking, to keep a confidence

I've always felt comfortable talking to Judy because she knows how to button her lip.

buttons (*noun*) Teen & College: the television remote control device

Give me the buttons, will you? This show is beat.

buy the farm (*verb phrase*) General: to die

As the ice cream truck rattled down the residential block at an alarming speed, Susie feared that her unsuspecting poodle was going to buy the farm.

buzz (*noun*) General: telephone call; also known as ring

Give me a buzz when you find out what time the movie starts.

buzz crusher (*noun phrase*) Teen & College: one who spoils the fun of others

We were just fooling around on the wrestling mats when Coach came in an yelled at us. What a buzz crusher!

buzzed (*adj.*) College, Drug World: high on alcohol or drugs; *see also:* lit up

I was so buzzed on Friday night, I don't know how I got home.

by leaps and bounds (*prep.*

phrase) General: with rapid progress

Samantha's French was improving by leaps and bounds.

by the skin of one's teeth (*prep. phrase*) General: just barely

I passed Trig this term by the skin of my teeth.

byte (*noun*) Computerspeak: standard unit of computer information, exactly eight bits

Vance didn't know if he gotten a bargain until he determined the system's byte capacity.

C

cafeteria plan (*noun phrase*) Business: benefit plan that offers the employee the opportunity to select from a variety of options

One of the perks of making junior partner was getting in on the cafeteria plan.

cake (*noun*) Street: woman or girl

Those cakes at your house Thursday night, were they your sister's friends?

cakewalk (*noun*) Teen & College: an easy job; *see also:* piece of cake

What a cakewalk that report was!

call foul (*verb phrase*) General: to assert that someone is behaving unethically or illegally

Anita decided to call foul when she saw that some illegal bids were being submitted on the job.

call it a day (*verb phrase*)

General: to quit; also known as call it quits

We both know this plan isn't working, so let's just call it a day.

call one's bluff (*verb phrase*) General: to insist that someone prove what he or she is saying is true

I called his bluff and told him to show me his bank statements.

call on the carpet (*verb phrase*) General: to reprimand

Vera was often called on the carpet for being late.

call the shots (*verb phrase*) General: to be in charge

You're calling the shots, so what do you want us to do?

camper (*noun*) Medical: patient in an oxygen tent

The camper at the end of the hall has already rung twice for assistance.

can 1. (*noun*) Crime & Law: prison; *see also:* joint

Wanda spent two years in the can while her accomplice went free.

2. (*noun*) General: lavoratory, toilet; also known as jane, john

Give me ten minutes, I gotta use the can.

3. (*noun*) Seafarers: a destroyer ship

Anything's better than an 18-month tour on a can in the Pacific.

Can I kick it? Yes, you can. (*expression*) Street: Am I good? Yes, you are; a rap-inspired call and response that expresses

good feelings about an accomplishment

After scoring the game-winning basket, LaReese called, "Can I kick it?" and her teammates responded, "Yes, you can."

can of worms (*noun phrase*) General: complicated, problematic situation

Just when I think I've got this project licked, someone comes along and opens a whole new can of worms.

cancer (*noun*) Cartalk: rust or corrosion

Josie went to Sears hoping to find a cure for her Buick's cancer.

candy-assed (*adj.*) General: weak and unassertive

What kind of candy-assed answer was that?

cap (*verb*) Teen & College: to insult

Melanie capped Doris in front of all her teammates.

captain of the head (*noun phrase*) Seafarers: sailor responsible for cleaning the lavoratory

Just for returning an hour late from shore leave, Magda was assigned captain of the head for a week.

car clout (*noun phrase*) Crime & Law: car break-in

The mall's parking lot had suffered from a rash of car clouts.

card up one's sleeve (*noun phrase*) General: last trick or alternative that might resolve a situation to one's satisfaction

The incumbent was afraid her challenger might have a card up her sleeve for the week before the election.

carpool (*verb*) Traffic: to share a ride somewhere with others on a regular basis

I carpool to work to save a bit of money on transportation.

carry (*verb*) Crime & Law: to be armed with a gun; short for carry the difference; also known as: pack, pack heat, and be heeled

When Ivan announced that he was carrying that night, everyone in the car gasped.

carry a torch (*verb phrase*) General: to maintain unwavering love or devotion long after being rejected

Twenty years after their breakup, Millie still carried a torch for John.

carry baggage (*verb phrase*) General: to bring past emotional pain or problems into a new situation or relationship

I had a good time on our first date but I'm afraid Chris might be carrying a lot of baggage.

carry the ball (*verb phrase*) Sports, General: to take responsibility for a crucial aspect of an action

The junior executives were glad to know their superiors thought they could carry the ball in difficult negotiations.

carry the day (*verb phrase*) General: to win or be completely successful

The candidate's thoughtful responses in the debate helped her carry the day.

cart before the horse (*noun phrase*) General: things in the wrong order

Milton put the cart before the horse when he bought a wedding suit before proposing to Debbie.

carte blanche (*noun phrase*) Foreign (French): complete freedom

You have carte blanche to develop this program in whatever way you see fit.

cartwheels (*noun*) Drug World: amphetamines

Jack's friend was so high on cartwheels he couldn't stop talking.

carve (*verb*) Surferspeak: to surf well

The waves were so great today, I was carving.

carved in stone (*adj. phrase*) General: permanent, not subject to change

I wouldn't say our plans are carved in stone, but we're fairly sure we're going to Hawaii next month.

cas (pronounced "kazh") (*adj.*) Teen & College: casual

Don't dress up too much because this party is totally cas.

casework (*noun*) Government & Politics: work done by an elected official and his or her staff directly on behalf of constituents

The Senator's office devoted significant energy to constituent case work, such as requests to fill highway potholes or install traffic signals.

cash cow (*noun*) Business: business endeavor that generates tangible cash surplus, not just profits purported in projections or financial reports

In its first year of operation, the television shopping channel proved to be a real cash cow for the network.

cashed (*adj.*) Teen & College: used up, ran out of

That shampoo is cashed. Can you get me some more?

cash in one's chips (*verb phrase*) General: to expire or give up

After a bear ransacked our tent and we lost all our campfuel, I was ready to cash in my chips and head back to civilization.

casper (*noun*) Surferspeak: person with no suntan

Those caspers who just came on the beach are white as snow.

cat around (*verb phrase*) General: to go out looking for romantic or physical encounters

Bella was catting around with her girlfriends one night when she met the man who became her husband.

cat call (*noun phrase*) General: whistle or hoot indicating

attraction or admiration

Gwyneth was tired of the cat calls she had to endure every morning on her way to the office.

catch-22 (*noun*) General: paradoxical situation; from Joseph Heller's novel, *Catch-22*

I'm in a real catch-22 here: I want that promotion but I'll have to transfer if I get it.

catch a buzz (*verb phrase*) College, Drug World: to get high on drugs or alcohol

Bill caught a buzz after one martini.

catch fire (*verb phrase*) General: to become enthusiastic or excited

The audience finally caught fire when the star started singing his greatest hits.

catch flack (*verb phrase*) Teen & College: to receive criticism

I'm going to catch flack from my father if I don't get my hair cut before going home.

catch one (*verb*) Teen & College: to become intoxicated from drinking beer

After our last exam Friday night, we just caught one at O'Toole's and went home.

catch one's breath (*verb phrase*) General: to rest after great exertion

After working overseas for a year, Jody felt the need for a couple weeks off to catch her breath.

catch one's eye (*verb phrase*)

General: to attract one's attention

That purple jacket really caught my eye.

catch redhanded (*verb phrase*) General: to discover someone in the middle of an illegal or forbidden act

The youths were caught redhanded spray-painting their names on the gymnasium door.

catch some Zs (*verb phrase*) Teen & College: to sleep

I'm going to catch some Zs before we get ready for the play tonight.

catch the drift (*verb phrase*) General: to understand the essence of something

Did you catch the drift of that lecture this afternoon?

Catch you on the flip flop (*expression*) Teen & College: see you later.

Hey, Dave, I'll catch you on the flip flop when I return.

cats and dogs (*noun phrase*) Wall Street: stocks whose value has not been proven

The broker saved the cats and dogs for his more risk-taking accounts.

catslide (*noun*) Real Estate: Southern term for a house that is known as a "salt box" elsewhere in the country

The young couple saved five years for the downpayment on their first home, a catslide on the edge of town.

catwalk (*noun*) Fashion: fashion show runway for models

As the models moved along the catwalk the audience clapped appreciatively.

caught with a hand in the cookie jar (*expression*) General: to be caught in the act of something

Jan claimed nobody was tampering with accounts, but I caught her with her hand in the cookie jar.

caught with one's pants down (*verb phrase*) General: to be unprepared

I'm sorry I don't have your report yet. You really caught me with my pants down.

C & C (*noun phrase*) Medical: initialism for Corns and Calluses, referring to an easy patient in the parlance of podiatrists

I have just two C & Cs on my schedule today so I'm going golfing this afternoon.

CE (*acronym*) Sci-fi: Close Encounter with an unidentified flying object (UFO) or its extra-terrestrial occupants

The authorities tried to keep Joe's haunting account of a CE quiet, for fear of public hysteria.

C & T Ward (*noun phrase*) Medical: Cabbages and Turnips Ward, where comatose patients are assigned; *see also:* vegetable garden

The orderly didn't mind his shift on the C & T Ward because

none of the patients complained.

cellar (*noun*) Sports: last place
The Redbirds were in the cellar at the start of the season and never budged.

cement (*noun*) Sports (Skiing): wet, dense snow
None of the contestants looked forward to skiing in cement.

cerebrally challenged (*adj. phrase*) PC: with slow or limited learning capabilities
The progressive school had a special program for the cerebrally challenged.

chainsmoke (*verb*) General: to smoke cigarettes one right after the other
Gert chainsmoked two packs a day for so many years that her doctor had become seriously worried about her health.

chair, the (*noun*) Crime & Law: Short for the electric chair, which is used for criminal executions
Death row inmates make every appeal possible to avoid ending up in the chair.

chalk talk (*noun phrase*) Sports: coach's strategy session in which a chalk board is used to diagram plays
The coach practically fired the two players on the spot when they giggled during his chalk talk.

change horses midstream (*verb phrase*) General: to change plans or leaders in the middle of an activity

The company wants to hire a new law firm to handle the trial, but they're worried about changing horses midstream.

change one's tune (*verb phrase*) General: to change one's position or behavior
She's really changed her tune since she started volunteering at the homeless shelter.

channel-surf (*verb phrase*) Entertainment: to flip television channels aimlessly using the remote control
Whitney channel-surfed for fifteen minutes or so but finally turned off the set in disgust.

chapter and verse (*noun phrase*) General: total, honest truth
So that's how it happened, chapter and verse.

chaser (*noun*) Bars: a mild drink (usually beer) which quickly follows a hard drink (usually straight liquor)
I'll have a shot of tequila and a beer chaser.

chase the dragon (*verb phrase*) Drug World: to smoke a potent mixture of heroine and cocaine
We were shocked to find squeaky clean Sean all dregged out, chasing the dragon.

chasing butterflies (*verb phrase*) General: in a mentally diminished state
"If I don't start spending time with some adults, I'll be chasing

butterflies soon," the kindergarten teacher moaned.

cheap seats (*noun phrase*) Sports: the inexpensive seats which are far away from the action on the court or field

There was a big fight in the cheap seats during the seventh inning.

cheat sheet (*noun phrase*) Computerspeak: the template which aids a user in identifying the codes or commands necessary to operate a certain program

Cara had trouble getting used to the new word processing program and had to use the cheat sheet for months.

cheap shot (*noun phrase*) Sports: a nasty, unethical act

That elbow Jenson gave me was a cheap shot! Why doesn't anyone ever call a foul on this guy?

check 1. (*verb*) Sports (Hockey): to become an obstacle to an opponent by using the body or hockey stick; these methods are body checks and stick checks, respectively

Lefeu checked Walton so aggressively throughout the game that a fight broke out between them in the final period.

2. (*verb*) Teen & College: to pull down another person's pants as a prank; *see also:* shorts

While Riley was standing there talking to Luanne, I crept up behind him and checked him.

Check it! (*expression*) Teen & College, Street: Get away from me! Get lost!

Hey, you better check it before I have to get mean.

Check it out! (*expression*) Teen & College: Look at this!

What a bargain! Check it out!

check out (*verb phrase*) Surferspeak: look at

Check out those waves! I'm going home to get my board.

check the plumbing (*verb phrase*) General: to visit the bathroom

Nadine will be right back; she's just checking the plumbing.

cheesecake (*noun*) General: a photograph of a woman which reveals plenty of skin; beefcake is a similar type of photograph of a man

Lorelei had just one cheesecake shot in her portfolio.

cheesehead (*noun*) Teen & College: jerk

Billy was such a cheesehead no one could stand to sit next to him in class.

cheese it (*verb phrase*) General: to move quickly, to hurry

You better cheese it or you'll be late for your curfew.

cheese off (*verb phrase*) Teen & College: to borrow from others regularly

He's always cheesing money off the guys in his dorm.

cheeser (*noun*) Teen & College: someone who is always

borrowing from others; *see also:* mooch

The guy's a cheeser and never returns a favor.

cheesy (*adj.*) Teen & College: cheap, phony

That movie was just a cheesy imitation of the "Freddy" films.

cherry (*adj.*) Teen & College: premium, very cool

That Mustang is so cherry, I'm going to ask my parents if I can borrow from my savings to buy it.

cherry pick (*verb*) Sports (Basketball): to hover near one's own basket while plays are being made at the other end of the court waiting for a breakaway or long pass

Because Mara patiently cherry picked, she was able to grab the long lob and score the winning point.

chew on (*verb phrase*) Teen & College: to nag

My mother's always chewing on me to read more books.

chew out (*verb phrase*) General: to scold and berate

The lifeguard chewed out those kids for playing rough in the pool.

chickenshit (*adj.*) General: petty and nasty

Ratting on me like that was a real chickenshit thing to do.

chicken feed (*noun phrase*) General: a paltry amount; usually referring to money

I don't care about that commission; it's chicken feed.

chill 1. (*verb*) Teen & College: to calm down, relax; short for chill out; *see also:* kick back

I think I'll just chill in the backyard this afternoon.

2. (*verb*) Crime & Law: to kill; *see also:* off, waste, and whack

The kids couldn't stop talking about the rumor that someone in their class had chilled the convenience-store clerk.

chill hard (*verb phrase*) Teen & College, Street: to relax and socialize with others

We were just chilling hard at the Burger Cave when Diana's brother drove up.

chilly (*adj.*) Teen & College: very hip

He's pretty chilly, always telling us the new music to listen to.

Chinese wall (*noun phrase*) Wall Street: effort to prevent traders from operating on inside information to which they may be privy; a Chinese wall letter is a trader's written pledge not to trade in securities to which he or she may have inside information

The firm's partners insisted on the use of an impenetrable Chinese wall to protect the integrity of their longstanding client.

chip (*noun*) Computerspeak: tiny integrated computer circuit; generally made of silicon

Bart had to return the system to the manufacturer because its

chip appeared to have been damaged in transit.

chiphead (*noun*) Computer-speak, Teen: computer fanatic

The high school lunchroom was evenly divided up along chipheads, metalheads, jocks, and the rest.

chipper (*noun*) Drug World: a heavy weekend drug user

I wouldn't call Paul a junkie, but he is a pretty serious chipper.

chisel in (*verb phrase*) General: to intrude to the point of crowding others out

That new rep has been chiseling in on my sales territory.

choice (*adj.*) Teen & College: prime, very appealing

That dress is choice but I don't know if my parents will let me wear it.

choke (*verb*) Teen & College: to fail unexpectedly

I can't believe I choked during the oral exam today.

choke point (*noun phrase*) Real Estate: point at which mortgage interest rates become a deterrent for buyers

Interest rates had been hovering at the choke point for almost two years.

chop, the (*noun*) Sports (Baseball): short for the *Tomahawk Chop*, the gesture of solidarity adopted by Atlanta Braves fan, much to the dismay of many Native Americans, who find it offensive

The sea of fans doing the chop gave encouragement to the team.

chop shop (*noun phrase*) Cartalk, Law Enforcement: place where stolen cars are cut up into parts to be sold off separately

The state police discovered the car thieves' chop shop less than a mile from the interstate.

choppers (*noun*) General: teeth

I'm going to the dentist this afternoon for a chopper check-up.

chow (*noun*) General: food

This is the best chow!

chowderhead (*noun*) General: dolt

You left your backpack in the diner? What a chowderhead!

chow down (*verb*) Teen & College: to eat hungrily

We chowed down on the barbecue last night

Christmas tree bill (*noun phrase*) Government & Politics: a bill that carries a variety of unrelated bits of legislation, allowing expenditures to be slipped through Congress

The congresswoman was elated to see that funding for the bridge repair in her district made it through the House on the Christmas tree bill.

chug (*verb*) Teen & College: to drink quickly and thirstily

We chugged a whole bottle of

wine before we went back to the room.

chugalug (*verb*) Bars: to down a drink in its entirety without taking a breath; to swallow completely

Vinnie chugalugged a pint of beer without a blink.

churn (*verb*) Wall Street: to urge a client to buy and sell securities simply for the purpose of generating broker's commissions

Stevens was having a sudden cash flow problem, and for the first time he resorted to churning his clients.

Cinderella liberty (*noun phrase*) Seafarers: shore leave pass that expires at midnight

Having just gotten engaged, the ensign planned to make the most of his Cinderella liberty.

circular file (*noun phrase*) Office Talk: wastebasket

Go ahead and put that memo into the circular file.

clam up (*verb phrase*) General: to become quiet suddenly out of fear of exposure

The detective couldn't do much when his prime witness suddenly clammed up.

clean (*adj.*) Drug World: free from the effects of drug use and dependency

Listen, I've been clean for six months, so I hope you'll give me another chance at my job.

clean bill (*noun phrase*) Government & Politics: bill that has been revised in committee, then move through the voting process as a new bill

After so much work on revisions, the committee members held their breaths when the clean bill was finally voted on.

clean bill of health (*noun phrase*) General: report that certifies a person to be healthy, or, figuratively, free of fault

The accounting department received a clean bill of health after the month-long investigation.

clean deal (*noun phrase*) Cartalk: car sale that doesn't hinge on a trade-in

The salesfolks love selling cars to teenagers because so many of them walk in to make clean deals.

clean peeler (*noun phrase*) Surferspeak: wave that is perfect for surfing

Die-hard surfers spend their lives praying for clean peelers.

clean slate (*noun phrase*) General: record of good behavior or a record that does not reflect past misdeeds

Let's begin this semester with a clean slate, shall we?

clean someone's clock (*verb phrase*) General: to beat or beat up

After Tony stole Diane's idea for a political cartoon, she felt a strong urge to clean his clock.

clean up (*verb phrase*) General: to make lots of money

I know we're going to clean up on this raffle at the bazaar.

clean up one's act (*verb phrase*) General: to discontinue improper behavior, dress, demeanor, etc.

Patty cleaned up her act after she attended the inspirational seminar.

clear shot (*noun*) Traffic: unobstructed opening in traffic

The driver was relieved to find a clear shot on the freeway after crossing the bridge out of the city.

clear the air (*verb phrase*) General: to eliminate any confusion or resentment

We needed to clear the air after our argument last night.

clear title (*noun phrase*) Real Estate: ownership not encumbered by liens or other such prohibitive attachments

The sale went through unusually quickly, probably because the seller had clear title.

click 1. (*verb*) General: to have a naturally smooth relationship

Mel and I clicked the moment we met.

2. (*noun*) Military: kilometer

The base is about twenty clicks from the city.

cliffdweller (*noun*) General: person who lives in a city highrise

I grew up on a farm, but I've been a cliffdweller for twenty years.

cliffhanger (*noun*) Entertainment: television program or film featuring a suspenseful and unresolved ending

The cliffhanger left me wondering all summer whether my favorite character would live or die.

climb the wall (*verb phrase*) General: to have an overly emotional reaction

My mother will climb the wall when I tell her I'm going to the prom with Zeke.

clip 1. (*noun*) Entertainment: short bit of sample footage used in the promotion of a film

The actor looked really embarrassed when the talk-show host showed a clip from his earliest movie.

2. (*noun*) Traffic: speed

Traffic was moving along at a nice clip until a pileup on the freeway slowed everything down.

3. (*noun*) General: per each; also known as: a pop, a throw, and a whack

Those special toy-action figures sell for over $5 a clip.

clip artist (*noun phrase*) Crime & Law: swindler; also known as: con artist

The tourists left the booth without a cent after their encounter with a clip artist.

clip joint (*noun phrase*) General: business where people are regularly overcharged or cheated

I'm not shopping at this clip joint anymore!

clip one's wings (*verb phrase*) General: to restrict one's behavior

Jarred got his wings clipped when he came home an hour after his curfew.

cloak-and-dagger (*adj.*) General: relating to espionage

That cloak-and-dagger story was exciting but unfortunately not very realistic.

cloakroom (*noun*) Government & Politics: large anteroom off each of the main chambers in Congress where legislators and staffers conduct informal meetings

The senator could often be seen in the cloakroom with an assistant signing correspondence between floor debates.

clock (*verb*) Street: to watch

That clerk has been clocking me since I walked into the store.

clone 1. (*noun*) Computerspeak: cheaper version of a big brand-name computer or computer software

The computer salesperson advised the customer to consider a clone if she wanted to save money.

2. (*verb*) Computerspeak: to copy

The hacker cloned the program hoping to make some money reselling it.

3. (*noun*) Teen, College: an imitator

The rest of the wrestlers had become clones of the team captain.

close doors (*verb phrase*) Business: to go out of business; *see also:* go belly up and went toes

The sign read "75 percent Off Everything. We're closing our doors forever!"

close ranks (*verb phrase*) General: to set aside differences and come together for a common purpose

The family closed ranks to help Toby overcome his addiction.

close the books (*verb phrase*) to bring to a conclusion

I'm glad to hear we've closed the book on those nasty rumors.

clothesline (*verb*) Sports (Football): to grab an opposing player by the neck; this is an illegal maneuver

Mighty Mack was injured when he was clotheslined in the last minutes of the game.

cloud (*noun*) Real Estate: lien or other such prohibitive attachment precluding a smooth transfer of the title of a property

The roofing company had filed a cloud against the homeowners over an unpaid bill.

clown 1. (*noun*) General: stupid or rude person

This clown ahead of me on the freeway cut me off.

2. (*noun*) Travel: mildly derogatory term used by travel agents to describe customers who change their plans and reservations frequently

I wish that clown I've been working with would make up his mind about where he wants to go and when!

clubhouse lawyer (*noun phrase*) General: one who is obnoxiously opinionated on all matters regarding the rules and regulations of an organization
Chris tried to avoid the known clubhouse lawyers on the golf courses. They could really ruin a relaxing afternoon game.

clueless (*adj.*) Teen, College: without any sense of what is really happening
"My parents are totally clueless," the teenager bragged to friends.

Clydesdale (*proper noun*) Teen & College: attractive guy, derived from handsome horse breed
Now that Joe is a senior and he's got a decent weekend job, he's walking around like he's some kind of Clydesdale.

coast to coast (*noun phrase*) Sports (Basketball): from one end of the court to the other, referring to a player who manages to grab a rebound and take the ball to the other end of the court to score
Quentin was really hot last night, taking the ball coast to coast four different times.

coast is clear (*expression*) General: no danger is in sight
Let's cross the street now that the coast is clear.

coasty (*noun*) Seafarers: member of the Coast Guard
The coasties boarded the unmarked boat with great caution.

cob (*adj.*) Teen & College: stupid, dense
That teacher is cob if he thinks we're going to get this assignment done by Wednesday.

cock-and-bull story (*noun phrase*) General: incredible, usually untrue story
When I asked her for her homework, she gave me some cock-and-bull story about her dog eating it.

Code 1 (*noun phrase*) Military: term used in reference to the President, with the number 1 reflecting the highest possible rank; Codes 2 through 6 break down the levels of rank and are also used in messages to refer to various officials
Let the troops assemble for inspection. We have Code 1 approaching in Air Force One.

Code Blue (*noun*) Medical: alert that all possible measures should be taken to save an extremely ill or injured patient
The crash victim is having a seizure. This is a Code Blue!

code word (*adj. phrase*) Military: ultra-super top secret
That report is code word, for your eyes only.

coequal (*noun*) Government: equal or peer; typical contrived redundancy used by government bureaucrats

The congresswoman hated giving the two aides different raises since they were widely considered to be coequals.

coffee cooler (*noun phrase*) General: person who either can't or won't focus on his or her work

The assistant is a regular coffee cooler and rarely gets anything accomplished.

cold (*adj.*) Street: attractive

Tasha's looking cold with that new do.

cold call (*noun phrase*) Business, Wall Street, Salespeople: telephone call or personal visit made without an appointment or introduction, to induce a stranger to make a purchase

With his agreeable manner, Barney had better luck making cold calls than anyone else in his office.

cold dark matter (*noun phrase*) Science: subatomic particles that some scientists claim make up 90 percent of matter of the universe

The scientist spent most of his career trying to prove the existence of cold dark matter.

cold fish (*noun phrase*) General: aloof person

What a cold fish she turned out to be! And she seems so friendly on television.

cold, hard cash (*noun phrase*)

General: real currency

He needed cold, hard cash to complete the renovations.

cold snap (*noun phrase*) General: short period of cold weather in the midst of generally warm weather

The herbs in my garden didn't live through that last cold snap.

cold steel and sunshine (*noun phrase*) Medical: dentist's term for a dental situation cured only by a radical tooth extraction; also known as CSS

This patient's decay is too advanced for fillings. Book an appointment for cold steel and sunshine.

collar (*noun*) Crime & Law: arrest; *see also:* bag and pinched

The two rookies were praised for making the collar on the long-sought counterfeiters.

collateral damage (*noun phrase*) Military: harm that comes to civilians from a nuclear strike

We hope to avoid collateral damage by striking at industrial targets.

come apart at the seams (*verb phrase*) General: to lose control or composure completely

Victoria came apart at the seams after her mother died.

come clean (*verb phrase*) General: to be completely honest with someone, especially in hopes of having a second chance

The bank officer decided to

come clean about her role in the loan scandal.

come-down (*noun*) General: a lowering of status

It was a big come-down for Joe to buy an economy car after driving a Cadillac all those years.

come down hard on (*verb phrase*) General: to reprimand, criticize, or punish severely

Don't you think you came down too hard on Jimmy for scratching your car?

come down to earth (*verb phrase*) General: to be realistic, return to ordinary, real life

Ginger found it difficult to come down to earth after her idyllic island vacation.

come full circle (*verb phrase*) General: to reverse one's opinion and then return to one's original position

I've come full circle on those new sedans; I think they're great.

come hell or high water (*expression*) General: no matter what happens

I'll be at your wedding, come hell or high water.

come-on (*noun*) General: appeal for cooperation that is often indirect and usually sexual

Josie laughed at the street merchant's blatant come-on.

come on like gangbusters (*verb phrase*) General: to launch into a situation with great energy and enthusiasm

The new health club came on like gangbusters, with expensive advertising as well as good locations.

come on strong (*verb phrase*) General: to make an aggressive appeal

Do you think I came on too strong when I asked for a raise?

come on the heels of (*verb phrase*) General: to follow closely

My illness came on the heels of a year-long tour of the jungles of South America.

come out of left field (*verb phrase*) General: to turn up unexpectedly

Well, that comment came out of left field!

come out of the closet (verb phrase) General: to make public one's private inclinations; usually refers to revealing one's sexual preferences

When the council member came out of the closet, he received great support from his core constituency.

come to (*verb phrase*) General: to regain consciousness

Byron didn't come to until the medics waved smelling salts under his nose.

come to blows (verb phrase) General: to reach a point of fighting physically or verbally

Those two men came to blows over the empty seat on the bus.

come to grips with (*verb*

phrase) General: to struggle with, to the point of resolution

I've got to come to grips with this news about my father.

come to one's senses (*verb phrase*) General: to think clearly and sensibly

I wish Jenna would come to her senses and break up with Donny.

come unglued (*verb phrase*) General: to fall apart; often refers to one's emotional state

The contract negotiations came unglued when their attorney accused us of lying about our financial condition.

comfort zone (*noun phrase*) Business: living and working conditions to which one is accustomed to and satisfied with

In order to make any progress in this shrinking market, we've got to be willing to work outside of our comfort zone.

communitarian (*noun*) PC: one who believes that the state of the community has suffered over time as the rights of individuals have been enhanced, and that only when the focus returns to the community will quality of life improve

As a communitarian, Delores believed that allowing kids to verbally abuse each other would ultimately harm the school's climate.

community (*noun*) Government, Politics: group of people with a common interest or heritage, who are not linked geographically; for example, the gay community or the Latino community

The author had hoped his message would reach the community of scholars interested in his field.

commuter mug (*noun phrase*) Traffic: specially designed plastic coffee cup with a tight lid and small opening for sipping, used by commuters without fear of spilling

Armed with her briefcase and commuter mug, Chantal ran to catch her train.

comp (*noun*) Entertainment: complimentary ticket

I love to go to concerts with my friend, the music critic, because he always gets comps.

compare notes (*verb phrase*) General: to exchange thoughts and opinions

I'd like to compare notes on that new art exhibit.

compassionate fare (*noun phrase*) Travel: discounted fare occasionally offered by airlines or railroads to allow for family emergencies, such as grave illness or death; also known as: bereavement fare

When his sister died, Marcus was given a compassionate fare by the airline so he could go home for the funeral.

con artist (*noun phrase*) General: one who is adept at lies, deceit, and swindles

That salesperson seems like a con artist—all smooth talk and sly smiles.

conk out (*verb phrase*) General: to collapse from exhaustion
After the last guest left, we conked out on the couch.

connoisseur (*noun*) Foreign (French): devoted expert
I've become a bit of a wine connoisseur over the years.

consume (*verb*) Teen & College: to drink alcohol
I'm ready to consume tonight.

content testing (*noun phrase*) Entertainment: testing of audience reaction to a film before it is officially released, in case changes are necessary to enhance the film's commercial potential
The film's ending was completely changed as a result of the content testing done on several sample audiences.

contingent work force (*noun phrase*) Business: those who work part-time, free-lance, or on a temporary basis
The contingent work force was swelling even as regular full-time jobs were disappearing in industry.

conversation piece (*noun phrase*) General: something that stimulates interest and discussion
Ted's crazy new haircut was the conversation piece of the party.

cook one's goose (*verb phrase*) General: to cause one insurmountable difficulties
If I get another speeding ticket, it'll cook my goose.

cook something up (*verb phrase*) General: to plan or scheme
Let's cook something up for Friday, like a cocktail party at my house?

cook the numbers (*verb phrase*) Government & Politics: to manipulate statistics to support one's argument
Isn't there any way we can cook these numbers so that the economy doesn't look so bad?

cooker (*noun*) Drug World: implement in which drug is heated before being injected
The agents found and confiscated three cookers when they raided the apartment.

cool (*adj.*) Teen & College: great, hip, okay; a longstanding term that is probably no longer slang
Don't worry about paying me back. Everything's cool.

cool one's heels (*verb phrase*) General: to wait
I cooled my heels in the waiting room for forty-five minutes before the doctor examined me.

cool pose (*noun phrase*) Street: bold posture affected to convey confidence or toughness
The three guys stood on the corner in cool poses to intimidate possible challengers.

cooler (*noun*) General: jail; *see also:* hole, klink, pokey, and slammer
Maybe a week in the cooler will straighten you out.

cop 1. (*noun*) Crime & Law: a longstanding term for a police officer, used by criminals and law enforcement officers alike
Stan was pleased to find out that LaToya had become a cop.

2. (*verb*) Drug World: to buy drugs
Lester was copping a dime bag in the park when he got busted.

cop a plea (*verb phrase*) Crime & Law: to plead guilty or "nolo contendre" with an agreement limiting the severity of the sentencing
The attorney advised her client to cop a plea as his chances of winning in court were slim at best.

copious (*adj.*) Teen & College: a lot of
That girl's got copious hair.

copreneur (*noun*) Business: couple who operates a business together as partners
The Madsens were copreneurs with a successful combination dry cleaning-video business.

core dump (*verb phrase*) Computerspeak: to clear out a computer's memory
We've got to core dump before we install the new operating system.

corner like it's on rails (*verb phrase*) Cartalk: to handle tricky maneuvers well
Randy's sports car corners like it's on rails.

corporate (*adj.*) Teen & College: professional in appearance
You look so corporate today. Do you have a job interview?

cost (*verb*) Teen & College: to be expensive
Those jeans must have cost.

cost an arm and a leg (*verb phrase*) General: to be very expensive
That coat looks great on you, but it must have cost an arm and a leg.

couch case (*noun phrase*) General: mentally or emotionally disturbed person who requires psychiatric treatment
She feared the stress was turning him into a couch case.

couch commander (*noun phrase*) Teen & College: person who wields the television remote control
I'm the couch commander so we're watching the ballgame.

couch doctor (*noun phrase*) General: general term for physicians in the mental health field
If I don't have a vacation soon, I'm going to end up visiting a couch doctor.

couch potato (*noun phrase*) Press: one whose primary form of entertainment (or activity of any kind) is watching television;

hence, unathletic and out of shape

Oh, we never go out anymore. We're just a couple of couch potatoes.

cough up (*verb phrase*) General: to give with some resistance

After grave misgivings, I finally coughed up some money to help Karen with her problem.

count one's chickens before they hatch (*verb phrase*) General: to act on something in anticipation, rather than on actual conditions; usually used in the negative

I think I'll be offered the job, but I don't want to count my chickens before they hatch.

counterprogramming (*noun*) Entertainment: to compete with a television show on another network by running a program that will attract an entirely different audience

Running the award-winning drama against the country music special was a brilliant bit of counterprogramming.

count to ten (*verb phrase*) General: to take time to get one's anger under control

I better count to ten before I say something I might regret.

court-in (*noun*) Street: initiation ceremony for new female gang members, usually consisting of a beating or other rite of passage

Marie was officially nicknamed "LaQueen" at her court-in.

cover-up (*noun*) General: plan for hiding the truth to avoid scandal or prosecution

The newspaper reported a massive cover-up of the high casualties and property damage caused by the military invasion.

cowboy (*noun*) General: someone who behaves recklessly in order to attract attention (*see also* **hotdogger**)

Kevin's such a cowboy on his Harley.

cozy (*adj.*) Teen & College: dull

That ride looks cozy. Let's skip it.

crack 1.(*noun*) Drug World: highly addictive, smokable form of cocaine

Marcus couldn't believe what crack had done to his former classmate

2.(*verb*) Teen & College: to be hilarious

You were cracking in class today.

cracker (*noun*) Computerspeak: individual who is skilled at gaining unauthorized access to a computer

It was difficult for the authorities to identify the cracker who was wreaking havoc on the university's computer system.

crackerjack (*noun*) Travel: business trip that adds many miles to the traveler's frequent flyer account

The crackerjack Perkins took in May earned him a free trip to Brazil in the fall.

crackhead (*noun*) Drug World: individual addicted to crack

The neighborhood kids knew who all the crackheads were within a twenty-block radius.

crack house (*noun phrase*) Drug World: place where crack is bought and smoked

The block association was furious to discover that the empty basement apartment at the corner had become a crack house.

crack on someone (*verb phrase*) Street: to criticize someone

I wish my aunt would quit cracking on me about my grades.

crack up 1. (*verb phrase*) General: to have an emotional breakdown

How could I know my parents would crack up when I told her I was enlisting?

2. (*verb phrase*) General: to laugh hard

We cracked up when the three of them walked into class dressed like characters from the book.

crack the books (*verb phrase*) Teen & College: to study

I've got to crack the books tonight or I'll be way behind.

crack the whip (*verb phrase*) General: to push hard in order to achieve cooperation or performance

I'm going to have to crack the

whip to get you kids to clean your rooms.

cram (*verb*) General: to study or memorize a lot of material in a short period of time

I'll just cram for my driver's test on my way over to the exam.

cramp one's style (*verb phrase*) General: to restrict one's freedom

Going out with just one guy really cramps my style.

crank 1. (*verb*) Real Estate, Banking: to refinance

The interest rates dropped to an unprecedented low, and homeowners were cranking their mortgages in droves.

2. (*verb*) Teen & College: to perform quickly and efficiently

I cranked mowing that lawn today.

cranking (*adj.*) Teen & College: excellent, especially referring to music

That party was cranking and everyone was dancing.

crash 1. (*verb*) Computerspeak: to fail or malfunction

The system crashed just as the year-end statements were being generated.

2. (*verb*) Teen, College: to spend the night

Can I crash here tonight? My roommate's got a guest.

crash and burn (*verb phrase*) General: to fail in a spectacular fashion

After years of irrational be-

havior no one was surprised to see the famous singer crash and burn.

crash the gate (*verb phrase*) General: to enter or attend an event without paying for a ticket or receiving an invitation; also known as: crash

I'd like to crash that party but I'm afraid my ex-girlfriend will be there.

crash TV (*noun phrase*) Entertainment: physical sports action programs that tend to be fleshy and violent, such as "The American Gladiators"

Marta wouldn't let the kids watch the crash TV that filled the air waves every Saturday afternoon.

crawl (*verb*) Sports (Football): to continue advancing with a football even after one is tackled

Davis tried to crawl with the ball for another yard on that play.

crawling with (*verb phrase*) General: crowded with

This block is crawling with cops.

cream of the crop (*noun phrase*) General: the finest, the best choice; *see also:* creme de la creme

The principal appointed the cream of the crop to the student legislature.

cream puff (*noun phrase*) Car-talk: used car in prime condition

The cream puff on the lot had five years, 6,000 miles, and had been stored every winter!

creative accounting (*noun phrase*) General: manipulation of bookkeeping to one's advantage

It took the Internal Revenue Service years to make a case against the company for what they called creative accounting.

creep (*verb*) Street: to cheat on one's mate

If you ever creep on me, we'll be history!

creepers (*noun*) Teen & College: clunky, thick-soled shoes; *see also:* clodhoppers

Teresa got the coolest creepers to wear to the concert.

creeps, the (*noun*) General: a fearful feeling; also known as: the willies

Those two guys hanging around the pay phone are giving me the creeps.

creme de la creme (*noun phrase*) Foreign (French): best of the best; literally: cream of the cream

Only the creme de la creme were chosen for the exclusive diplomatic training program.

crest (*verb*) Street: to smile; referring to the Crest brand of toothpaste

Monroe couldn't help cresting at the new counselor at camp.

cretin maggot (*noun phrase*) Teen & College: loathsome person

Who is that cretin maggot that spray-painted Bobby's car?

crew (*noun*) Teen & College: group of friends

*During the summer my crew just likes to **hang** on the weekends.*

crib (*noun*) Teen & College, Street: one's home

Let's go back to my crib and watch some videos.

crit (*adj.*) Teen & College: cool

That new CD by the Destroyers is totally crit.

crock (*noun*) Medical: patient who complains incessantly

Dr. Diamond hoped the crock in room III would recuperate quickly.

cross one's fingers (*verb phrase*) General: to wish for good luck

Let's cross our fingers that Daddy's plane is on time.

cross one's heart (*verb phrase*) General: to promise that one is telling the truth

Cross my heart, I didn't touch your diary.

cross the wire (*verb phrase*) General: to finish a contest

Acme crossed the wire just behind Toyco in volume of sales.

crossover artist (*noun phrase*) Entertainment: performer, usually a musician, who is able to appeal to more than one audience

Angelique was the ultimate crossover artist, equally popular among her core country fans,

mainstream music lovers, as well as filmgoers.

crowd swim (*verb phrase*) Teen & College: to make one's way through a large group of people

I had to crowd swim for ten minutes just to get back to my table.

cruelty-free (*adj.*) PC: describing a product that has never in its developing relied on animal testing or the harsh treatment of animals; term used primarily by animal-rights activists

Norma decided to buy the organic makeup labeled "cruelty-free" because she believed in the rights of animals.

crufty (*adj.*) Computerspeak: poorly built

Sheila wasn't about to shell out her savings for such a cheap, crufty clone.

cruising for a bruising (*verb phrase*) General: headed for a conflict

Billy is cruising for a bruising if he thinks he can pass geometry without studying.

crunch time (*noun phrase*) Sports (Basketball): period in a game when a team must exert maximum effort to come from behind or protect its lead

The team's captain always played with complete calm and control during a game's crunch time.

crunchy (*adj.*) Teen & College:

natural-looking, earthy; also known as: crunchy granola
That's girl's nice but a little too crunchy for me.

crush'n (*adj.*) Teen & College: good-looking, especially referring to material items
That outfit is crush'n!

crushed (*adj.*) Teen & College, Street: ugly; *see also:* broke to the curb and buckled
That plaid jacket your father wears is way crushed.

cry wolf (*verb phrase*) General: to express false alarm
I think the school board is crying wolf over those budget cuts.

cubed out (*verb phrase*) Military: completely full
This transport is cubed out; you'll have to wait for the next one.

cultural genocide (*noun phrase*) PC: belief that minority groups are oppressed by society's systematic efforts to quash their individuality and cultural identity
The controversial professor advocated bilingual education to stem the cultural genocide he claimed was being perpetuated on second-generation children.

cultural jammer (*noun phrase*) Art: artist who uses the familiar icons of mass media to protest or satirize the mass media
The critics called the rapper a cultural jammer because she used a well-known cigarette jingle to make a feminist point.

culture vulture (*noun phrase*) General: one preoccupied with things cultural
I don't want to be a culture vulture like my mother. All she ever does is go to galleries, museums and concerts.

cumshaw (*noun*) Seafarers: legal goods obtained through illegal or unethical means
The load of cigarettes were cumshaw from a property swap the materials officer had arranged.

cup of tea (*noun phrase*) General: preference
Jogging isn't my cup of tea, but I love biking.

curl one's hair (*verb phrase*) General: to horrify
This news is going to curl your hair.

curtains (*noun*) General: disaster, failure
Failing that entrance exam meant curtains for Sean's hopes of becoming a doctor.

cuspy (*adj.*) Computerspeak: excellent
"This is a cuspy game," the youth exclaimed.

cut (*verb*) Drug World: to mix a nonnarcotic substance with the real thing in order to stretch the quantity, unbeknownst to the buyer; *see also:* burn and stomp on
The dealer didn't know he was being watched when he cut the blow.

2. (*adj.*) Health & Fitness: characterized by distinct muscular delineations

Bodybuilders work hard to get cut before competition.

cut and dried (*adj. phrase*) General: easy to predict

Most people think the senator will win reelection, but I don't think it's that cut and dried.

cut corners (*verb phrase*) General: to do something the short, inexpensive, or easy way

We'll have to cut corners for the rest of this vacation because we're way over budget.

cut down to size (*verb phrase*) General: to bring down an inflated view of oneself

The professor's comments on my paper really cut me down to size.

cut it (*verb phrase*) General: to meet expectations, to succeed

I'm not sure I can cut it as a salesperson.

cut on (*verb phrase*) Teen & College: to insult

Those kids in my phys ed class were cutting on me so bad last week I just bailed it this morning.

cut one's losses (*verb phrase*) General: to accept one's misfortune and proceed from there

Before we lose any more money at the blackjack table, let's cut our losses and go home.

cut one's throat (*verb phrase*) General: to ruin one's chances for success

The candidate cut his own throat when he accepted that illegal contribution.

cut out for something (*verb phrase*) General: to be a natural at something

Of the whole camp, Leora was best cut out for the lead role.

cut-rate (*adj.*) General: lower priced

These cut-rate paper towels aren't the best, but they'll be fine for the picnic.

cut the mustard (*verb phrase*) General: to meet expectations

I'm not sure I'm cutting the mustard in my new job.

cut to the chase (*verb phrase*) Entertainment: to skip the boring parts of a story and go right to the exciting part, derived from film editing

So cut to the chase. Did you ask her out or what?

cut up (*verb phrase*) Teen & College: to joke around and behave mischievously

The two kids cutting up in the back of the room were finally sent to the principal's office.

cybercrud (*noun*) Computerspeak: computer hype

Compuco's announcement of the "System of the Future" sounded like cybercrud to those familiar with its features.

cyberculture (*noun*) Sci-fi: futurist's vision of a fully automated society

It's shocking that the writer's

fantastic depictions of cyberculture are now beginning to seem possible.

cybermetrician (*noun*) Sci-fi: in a science fiction setting, the person with the most sophisticated understanding of, and relationship with, computers

Juan was the ship's cybermetrician, but even he often had trouble making sense of the computer's garbled responses.

cyberphobe (*noun*) Computerspeak: person with a fear of computers

With a little bit of humor and a few simple instructions, the trainer could cure any cyberphobe that crossed his path.

cyberpunk (*noun*) Sci-fi: contemporary strain of science fiction that reflects a hard, mean vision of the future where technology is highly sophisticated, but society is a menacing mix of crime, drugs, and cybernetics; the "Robocop" movies are a good, if mild, example of the genre

In his leathers and studs, Whit looked like a refugee from a cyberpunk flick as he staggered up the driveway.

cyborg (*noun*) Sci-fi: human being implanted with electronic elements

Television's "Six Million Dollar Man" may have been the first popularly known cyborg.

cybot (*noun*) Sci-fi: robot with cybernetic abilities, that is, the ability to reason, conclude, make decisions, etc.

The teens joked that boring Mrs. Johnson was really a cybot posing as their history teacher.

CYA (Cover Your Ass) (*expression*) Government: to protect oneself from blame in the event that something goes wrong

As soon as she anticipates a potential crisis, Lizette always prepares a quick CYA memo for the file.

D

d. (*adj.*) Teen & College: no good

That story we had to read last night was d., don't you think?

D & D (*proper noun*) Fantasy: initialism for the popular role-playing game, Dungeons & Dragons

"We spent the entire weekend in D & D," the two teens bragged to friends.

dag (*verb*) Teen & College: to slow down

Tina dagged as she passed the parking lot, hoping to find friend Brittany.

dailies (*noun*) Entertainment: rough tape of a day's film production work

The star wasn't happy with the dailies he viewed that evening and demanded that the scenes be reshot.

damage control (*noun phrase*)

Government & Politics, Public Relations: keeping harm to a minimum

We better do some damage control before the press gets a hold of the Senator's report.

damages (*noun*) Bars, Food: final bill at a bar or restaurant

"So, what are the damages?" the host asked ruefully as he observed the bar littered with empty glasses.

dance hall (*noun phrase*) Crime & Law: room in a prison where executions take place

The inmates of death row silently watched as their cellmate walked past them on the way to the dance hall.

dangle a carrot in front of (*verb phrase*) General: to tempt someone with something they will never be able to have

My boss always dangles a carrot in front of me, talking about a promotion, but I know she's not being straight.

dark (*adj.*) Entertainment: closed, referring to a theater

I think I'll go to the dentist on Monday when the theater's dark.

dark horse (*noun phrase*) General: most unlikely candidate to win

Stevens knew she was the dark horse to win the contract, but she campaigned for it vigorously.

dawn raid (*noun phrase*) Wall Street: quick purchase of substantial quantities of a company's stock before the market realizes that something is afoot

Mr. Big ordered a dawn raid on Acme; by noon, the market had noticed and everyone was scrambling to get at the remains.

day in court (*noun phrase*) General: an opportunity to explain

I know you're angry, but I think I deserve my day in court.

day one (*noun phrase*) General: the beginning

The manager had had suspicions about his thieving clerk from day one.

DDT (*proper noun*) Computerspeak: debugging program, named for the well-known insecticide

What this system needs is a big dose of DDT.

dead ahead (*adv. phrase*) General: directly in front

There's the library, dead ahead.

dead-cat bounce (*noun phrase*) Wall Street: brief and temporary upturn in the market that falsely indicates a surge or recovery

It was clear to the analysts that the market was experiencing a dead-cat bounce and would soon enough nose-dive.

dead center (*noun phrase*) General: precisely in the middle

The conference room was located at the dead center of the office.

Dead dancing (*noun phrase*)
Teen & College: uninhibited, free-flowing, individually expressive dancing that originated at Grateful Dead concerts
Marta was Dead dancing in her room when she looked up to see her little brother snapping her picture.

dead duck (*noun phrase*)
General: bound to be in trouble or harmed
If I don't get my car off these railroad tracks, I'll be a dead duck.

deadhead 1. (*noun*) Drug World: heavy marijuana user
Jackie had become known as something of a deadhead, and she was having trouble getting a job.
2. (*proper noun*) Teen & College: a fan of the Grateful Dead, a legendary rock band
Maureen has been a Deadhead since she was twelve when she discovered her mom's old records.

dead horse (*noun phrase*)
Seafarers: debt, to a member of the Navy
That's one dead horse I won't be able to take care of until after payday.

deadly (*adj.*) Teen & College: very attractive
Those shoes are deadly with that skirt.

dead meat (*noun phrase*)
General: one who is doomed
I knew I was dead meat when I saw that message from the boss.

deadpan (*verb*) Entertainment: to reflect no response on one's face
Tom deadpans so brilliantly that you never know whether or not he is joking.

dead presidents (*noun phrase*) Crime & Law: cash, American paper currency
"That'll cost you some dead presidents," the informer told the detectives.

dead ringer (*noun phrase*)
General: exact look-alike
Did anyone ever tell you you're a dead ringer for the President?

dead serious (*adj. phrase*)
General: extremely serious
I'm dead serious, there's a huge bug crawling on your shoulder.

dead stop (*noun phrase*)
Traffic: a complete stop
The multi-car accident caused traffic to come to a dead stop for about two hours.

deadtime (*noun*) Ecology: time it takes something to biodegrade completely
It was true that the new disposable diapers were biodegradable, but the deadtime was a significant number of years.

dead to the world (*adj. phrase*) General: deeply asleep
I was dead to the world when you called last night.

dead wood (*noun phrase*)
General: unnecessary or useless people or things

There's plenty of dead wood in this company.

dealing (*adj.*) Surferspeak: excellent, referring to surfing conditions where there is one great wave after another; from the image of cards being dealt one after the other

Those waves are dealing today. I'm going home to get my board.

Dear Colleague letter (*noun phrase*) Government & Politics: written entreaty from one member of Congress to another asking for support on an issue or a bill

The majority leader's carefully worded "Dear Colleague" letter put subtle pressure on junior members to vote party-line on the bill.

death (*adj.*) Teen & College: extremely appealing; *see also:* to die for

Those jeans are death on you.

deathbelt (*noun*) Crime & Law: states of Alabama, Arkansas, Mississippi, and Texas, where more convicted criminals are executed than anywhere else in the union

Ray was convicted of murder in the deathbelt and was sure to face the electric chair.

death knell (*noun phrase*) General: signal that warns of pending doom

The defeat of a related bill in the Senate was a death knell for the President's tax package.

death trap (*noun phrase*) Cartalk: rusted, beat-up car that probably has bad brakes and other dangerous flaws

Bob loved his 19-year-old jalopy, but everyone agreed it was a death trap.

debrief (*verb*) Military, Air & Space: to gather information from someone, usually after an extraordinary event in which the person has been involved

The former hostages were debriefed for several days at the military hospital before being released to their families' care.

debug (*verb*) Computerspeak: to eliminate a software error or flaw

The expert worked all night debugging the new program.

decent (*adj.*) Teen & College: excellent

That book was decent. I'll probably read it again.

decoy (*noun*) Surferspeak: nonsurfer

This place is too crowded with decoys. Let's get out of here.

deep background (*noun*) Government, Politics, News: government official's term for special inside information shared with a reporter on condition that the source is never revealed. (*See also:* backgrounder, and leaks, which are often called "deep background" by the leaker.)

The campaign manager offered a choice tidbit to the reporter, slyly describing the news as deep background.

deep cuts (*noun phrase*) Government & Politics: severe reductions

The President is calling for deep cuts in the military budget.

deep doo-doo (*noun phrase*) General: serious trouble, derived from a child's term for fecal matter

I'm in deep doo-doo if I don't finish this report by Monday.

deep fry (*noun phrase*) Medical: cobalt treatment used to arrest the spread of cancer

She's a little weak for the deep fry, so we'll use only chemo until she gets her strength back.

deep-six (*verb*) General: to abort

I'd like to deep-six these elaborate wedding plans and elope instead.

deep space (*noun phrase*) Air & Space: beyond Pluto

The intergalactic exploratory satellite was sent into deep space.

deep water (*noun phrase*) General: serious difficulty

I'll be in deep water if I don't get these bills paid.

def (*adj.*) Teen & College, Street: excellent

"That new guy is def," Bonnie noted admiringly.

deffest (*adj.*) Teen & College: the best

That is the deffest mountain bike I've ever seen.

deliver the goods (*verb phrase*) General: to perform as expected

After signing a contract worth many millions of dollars, that baseball player better deliver the goods.

demagogue (*verb*) Government & Politics: to take a vocal, high-profile position on an issue only to enhance one's public image

A certain congressman was becoming something of a joke in the cloakroom for blatantly demagoguing on so many issues.

desk jockey (*noun phrase*) Office Talk: ordinary office employee

Hey, I'm just a desk jockey. I don't make the decisions around here.

destabilize (*verb*) Government, Military: to upset or overthrow

To disrupt the dictator's regime, the agents began by destabilizing the country's economy.

detox (*noun*) Drug World: attempt to discontinue the use of drugs and/or to get drugs out of one's system; short for detoxification

The tabloids reported on one celebrity after another who had announced they were in detox.

Detroit (*adj.*) Cartalk: American, American-made

Joe's Car Mart featured three Mazdas, a VW, a Subaru, and eight Detroits.

deuce (*noun*) Food: a table for two

"Give the walk-ins the deuce near the kitchen," the manager whispered to the maitre d'.

deuce-five (*noun*) Crime & Law: a .25 caliber handgun

The victim was shot with a deuce-five, three bullets to the heart.

developing nations (*noun phrase*) Government, Politically Correct: formerly known as underdeveloped nations, this is a carefully nonjudgmental term used to describe countries that are in a primitive technological or stagnant economic condition

More than $4 Million has been budgeted for soap and penicillin to be sent to certin developing nations.

dexter (*noun*) Teen & College: studious, bookish person; short for poindexter; *see also:* digithead, floppy disk, mensan, and pointhead

Only a dexter is going to spend spring break writing this history paper.

dial in on someone (*verb phrase*) Surferspeak: to speak with someone

I was just dialing in on my buddy here when some guy ran into my board.

diddle (*verb*) General: to putter or work without serious purpose

I diddled at my desk for a while, then just gave up and went home.

die 1.(*verb*) Entertainment: to fail miserably at a performance

When their microphones lost power, the band just died onstage.

2.(*verb*) Teen & College: to have a difficult time

I was dying on that last question of the exam.

die laughing (*verb phrase*) General: to laugh hysterically

After Pauline finished the story, I thought I'd die laughing.

die on the vine (*verb phrase*) General: to fail before something comes to fruition

The mayor's reform proposal died on the vine.

differently abled (*adj. phrase*) PC: handicapped

This program was designed to serve the differently abled.

digithead (*noun*) Teen & College: studious, bookish person; one who spends a lot of time working on a computer

As the digithead of the group, Kim could always be found in the computer lab.

digits (*noun*) Teen & College: telephone number

What are the digits for that pizza shop?

dime a dozen (*adj. phrase*) General: easy to acquire and of little value

Those "antique" pendants are a dime a dozen down on Main Street.

dime bag (*noun phrase*) Drug

World: ten dollars' worth of a drug

Times had changed and Deke now thought twice about risking his life for a dime bag.

dimple (*noun*) Cartalk: dent; *see also:* ding

Al was enraged when he returned to his car in the crowded parking lot and found a fresh dimple in the door.

ding (*noun*) Cartalk, Surferspeak: dent; *see also:* dimple

Bob the Wavemaster hated to see the dings a rough surf delivered to his best board.

dink (*acronym*) Press: Dual Income, No Kids; referring to a childless couple, where both parties work

The new travel guide serious was blatantly geared for dinks, who like to spend money on vacations.

dip 1. (*verb*) Street: to run fast

When we saw Monty's mother coming down the street, we started dipping.

2. (*verb*) Teen & College: to eavesdrop

I was dipping on Jean and Gary's fight and you won't believe what she called him.

dipstick (*noun*) Teen & College: jerk

Jenny and her brother acted like such dipsticks at the party nobody offered to give them a ride home.

dirt (*noun*) General: gossip

What's the dirt on the new trainer at the gym?

dirty pool (*noun phrase*) General: dishonest or deceitful behavior

I refuse to copy that document for you—I won't get involved in dirty pool.

dis (*verb*) Teen & College, Street: to show disrespect or insult; sometimes spelled diss

We totally dissed Sheila and left her party early.

disadvantaged (*adj.*) Government, Politically Correct: poor, a euphemism; *see also:* economically challenged

The aid package is geared primarily to the especially disadvantaged.

dish out (*verb phrase*) General: to give something in large quantities

That new boy on the block really knows how to dish out compliments.

dish the dirt (*verb phrase*) General: to spread rumors

Jocko's been dishing the dirt about me to all my friends.

District, the (*noun*) Government: Washington, D.C., or the District of Columbia, as referred to by those who live and work in and around the city

Bernice had to get out of the District on weekends, just to escape the incessant political noise.

dismo (*noun*) Surferspeak: mildly derogatory term for an avid nonsurfing fan of surfing

This party is crawling with dismos.

dive (*noun*) Food & Drink: a low-quality restaurant or bar
I wouldn't eat in this dive if you paid me.

D.L. side (*noun phrase*) Street: Down Low, or secretly
I told Derrick what Lisa said on the D.L. side.

D.M. (*proper noun*) Fantasy: initialism for Dungeon Master, the character in a session of Dungeons & Dragons who maps out the adventure course the other players must follow
In their ongoing game of D & D, Vince and Violet took turns as D.M.

do (*noun*) Teen & College: short for hairdo
What an awful do! You better get a hat.

do-able (*adv.*) Government: possible to achieve; *see also:* viable
The idealistic legislator believed that with spending restraints and careful cutting, a lean budget was do-able.

do a double take (*verb phrase*) General: to take a second look out of surprise
I did a double take when Jerry came out of the salon with that new hairstyle.

do a drop-by (verb phrase) Government & Politics: to make a brief appearance
I'll do a drop-by at that fund-raiser and then go to the reception for the senator.

do a number on (*verb phrase*) General: to damage; also known as: do a job on
Geez, Keith really did a number on your skateboard.

dockominium (*noun*) Real Estate: marina where the buyers of slips form an association similar to a condominium community
After the children moved away, Marge and Charlie sold their house and bought into a dockominium.

docs (*noun*) Computerspeak: computer's instruction manual; short for documentation
The technician was frustrated to learn that the docs had been discarded with the computer's packaging.

docudrama (*noun*) Entertainment: fictionalized treatment or reenactment of a real incident
Marilee was totally taken in by the Elvis docudramas, even though she knew they weren't altogether accurate.

doctor shop (*verb phrase*) Drug World: to obtain drugs with a legal prescription from a doctor
Marty certainly knew where to doctor shop; she'd amassed quite a stash without ever breaking the law.

dode (*noun*) Teen & College: an idiot

Only a dode would come up with a comment like that!

does windows (*verb phrase*) Sports (Basketball): is able to dunk the ball
You've got to see that ninth grader do windows like a pro.

dog 1. (*verb*) Teen & College: to insult, harass
Don't dog me about that assignment, Ms. Spencer. I promise I'll have it by Friday.

2. (*noun*) Business: enterprise that is more costly to operate than is justified by the income it produces
The brothers decided to close "Cap'n Jack's"; the restaurant they opened together turned out to be a dog.

dog-and-pony-show (*noun phrase*) Business, Government, Military: presentation that relies on visual support such as graphs, charts, handouts, etc., to develop support for a program or issue
The erstwhile candidate from Texas brought his dog-and-pony show to the public via television.

dog-eared (*adj.*) General: ragged and shabby
My mom's book on child care was dog-eared from years of raising five children.

dog-eat-dog (*adj.*) General: aggressively competitive
I don't know if I'm cut out for working on Wall Street—it's such a dog-eat-dog business.

dog it (*verb phrase*) Sports: to play lazily or below one's full potential
I don't know what's wrong with me today; I can't seem to quit dogging it.

dogleg (*noun*) Sports (Golf): distinct turn on a fairway
Tootie always had trouble with the dogleg near the seventh hole.

dogs (*noun*) Air & Space: mildly derogatory term used by airline personnel to describe commercial airline passengers
The dogs on the flight between Spokane and Des Moines really complained about the food.

dog tired (*adj. phrase*) General: exhausted
I was dog tired after working a double shift.

do in (*verb phrase*) General: to destroy
My competitors have been trying to do me in for the last thirty years.

doing donuts (*verb phrase*) Cartalk: driving a car around in tight circle on a snowy or sandy parking lot, just for fun
When arrested for reckless driving, the four youths claimed they were just "doin' donuts" and didn't mean any harm.

dolled out (*adj. phrase*) Teen & College: well dressed
She's all dolled out for dinner tonight.

dollsheets (*noun*) Fashion:

sketches of designs given to potential buyers

The department store buyer considered the season's dollsheets carefully before making an order.

dolo (*adv.*) Street: on one's own

I'm going to the movies dolo, but I'll meet Martin afterwards.

dolphin safe (*noun phrase*) PC: not dangerous to dolphins, referring to tuna caught in nets that do no harm dolphins

I only eat dolphin-safe tuna and free-range chicken.

dolphin think (*noun phrase*) Business: approach in business that stresses cleverly outmaneuvering larger competitors

We used a little dolphin think and edged Toyco out of the top spot in bike sales this year.

domestic partnership (*noun phrase*) Government & Politics: relationship that is in all ways except legally like an actual marriage; i.e. the partners cohabitate and share household responsibilities and expenses, etc., often describes the relationships of homosexual couples

Tom complained that his company would not recognize their domestic partnership and allow his mate to participate in his health benefits.

dommo (*verb*) Surferspeak: to surf extraordinarily well, to dominate the waves

You can always count on Bean-

head to dommo on when the waves are good.

done for (*adj. phrase*) General: ruined, defeated

When my mother sees my report card, I'm done for.

donuts (*noun*) Cartalk: tires

The slick sales rep tried to gloss over the fact that the used car sported the baldest donuts on the lot.

do one out of (*verb phrase*) General: to take away from one or cause one to lose through trickery

I think my step-father managed to do me out of my inheritance.

do oneself (*verb phrase*) Teen & College: to embarrass oneself

You really did yourself this afternoon at the game when you spilled soda on the mascot.

do one's thing (*verb phrase*) General: to do as one pleases

Why don't you do your thing for a while and then we'll meet at the cafe for lunch?

do-or-die (*adj.*) General: extremely determined

The sales force had a real do-or-die attitude and broke all records for the period.

dope 1. (*verb*) Street: to lie or deceive

You were doping me about where you were last night.

2. (*adj.*) Teen & College, Street: excellent

That suit is dope. It must have cost a fortune.

dope on a rope (*adj. phrase*)
Teen & College: terrific
Hey, that new Action Pak comic is dope on a rope.

dope sheet (*noun phrase*)
General: pertinent statistics on someone or something; *also known as:* book, dope, and stats
What's the dope sheet on this horse? Is it a good bet?

dork (*noun*) Teen & College: unpopular, awkward person; *see also:* dweeb, fred, geek, goob, goof, nerd, squid, and swivel neck
Jenny couldn't believe her best friend would go out with such a dork.

dose (*noun*) Drug World: LSD; *see also:* tab
The dose he took last night gave him the weirdest hallucinations.

do the honors (*verb phrase*)
General: to act as host or hostess
Would you do the honors and carve the Thanksgiving turkey?

do the trick (*verb phrase*)
General: to be the solution
I think a stitch or two on your hem will do the trick.

double bagger (*noun phrase*)
Teen & College: one who is so unattractive or who has done something so embarrassing that he or she needs two bags over his or her head to hide instead of only one
That double bagger not only forgot the lyrics of the school anthem, but also cracked on the high note.

double-cross (*verb*) General: to deceive
Benny double-crossed me when he sold my history notes to some other kids in class.

double-dipping (*verb phrase*)
Government: collecting compensation from the government as well as a private institution
Grandpa can afford a new car every other year because he's double-dipping on social security and his union distress fund.

doublespeak (*noun*) General: purposefully convoluted, manipulative, and often redundant language, usually applied to government and similar bureaucracies; from George Orwell's novel, 1984
Even uneducated people could see through the government's doublespeak on the health-care program.

double-talk (*noun*) General: something interpreted in more than one way or that makes no sense
Her speech was just a lot of double-talk and the audience knew it.

double whammy (*noun phrase*) General: two devastating or disrupting events in a row
I crashed my car and lost my job in the same day. What a double whammy!

dough (*noun*) General: money; also known as: cabbage, coin, green, jack, lettuce, simoleons, and skins

No, I can't go to the movies tonight, I'm trying to save dough.

dove (*noun*) Government & Politics: elected official who opposes military efforts of any kind, and who generally argues for reduction in military spending

Afraid of being tagged as doves by a pro-war public, the legislators voted reluctantly in favor of the invasion.

down (*adj.*) Computerspeak: descriptive term for a computer system that is out of order

The store manager was afraid to announce to the long line of impatient customers that the system was down.

down a few (*verb phrase*) Bars: to have a couple of drinks

Let's go down a few after work today.

down for the count (*adj.*) Sports (Boxing): laid out in the ring while the referee counts to ten, signifying a knock-out and thus defeat; generally, refers to being almost out of luck and money

I saw a former co-worker at the coffee shop who really seemed down for the count this time.

down in the dumps (*adj.*) General: depressed; also known as: down in the mouth

I've been down in the dumps ever since I was fired.

downsize (*verb*) Business, Human Resources, Government:

euphemism for laying off employees

The department was downsized as a cost-cutting measure.

downstroke (*noun*) Real Estate: initial cash required to finance an investment

The terms of the deal were good but the downstroke was somewhat prohibitive.

down the drain (*adj. phrase*) General: wasted

All our plans to organize a beach clean-up went down the drain when the town committee took over the project.

down-to-earth (*adj. phrase*) General: very basic, uncomplicated, unpretentious

As wealthy as the Smiths were, they had a very down-to-earth lifestyle.

downtown (*noun*) Sports (Basketball): deep, referring to a pass or shot

Martin's unlikely three-pointer came from downtown and won the game.

down to the wire (*adj. phrase*) General: nearing a deadline

I'm really down to the wire on this report and may not finish in time.

down with (*prep. phrase*) Street: a part of

I'm down with that group from Hillside Avenue.

Do you follow me? (*expression*) General: Do you understand what I am saying?

Stay out of my office—do you follow me?

Do you see skid marks on my forehead? (*expression*)
Teen & College: Do I seem stupid to you?
I told you I wouldn't tell your brother. Do you see skid marks on my forehead?

dozmo (*noun*) Sci-fi: science fiction fan who is annoying to outsiders and fellow fans
Gene is just a dozmo and no one can stand sitting next to him in the lunchroom at school.

drag (*noun*) General: boring person or experience
If I had known this trip was going to be such a drag, I would have stayed home!

drag one's heels (*verb phrase*) General: to act reluctantly
My supervisor dragged her heels on firing those new fellows who were disrupting our shift.

dragging (*adj.*) Teen & College: tired or lethargic
I watched the late movie last night and I'm really dragging this morning.

dramedy (*noun*) Entertainment: dramatic comedy television program
*"M*A*S*H" was one of the first, best dramedies on television.*

draw a blank (*verb phrase*) General: to forget suddenly
I'm sorry I can't remember your name. I'm just drawing a blank.

draw blood (*verb phrase*)
General: to hurt or anger someone
Look, I didn't mean to draw blood when I gave you that constructive criticism.

dregged out (*adj. phrase*) College: condition where one's appearance is in grubby disarray
After staying up all night to cram for that final, Yvonne looked really dregged out.

dressed to the nines (*verb phrase*) General: very well dressed
Marcus was dressed to the nines for his birthday dinner.

Dr. Feelgood (*proper noun*)
Medical, Drug World: physician who prescribes drugs indiscriminately
Francesca just called her Dr. Feelgood when she was running low on little yellow pills.

drip (*noun*) General: boring, unappealing person
Our tour guide was such a drip we dropped out of the group and spent the rest of the day on our own.

drive a hard bargain (*verb phrase*) General: to press for an agreement or arrangement that is more advantageous to oneself than to another
You drive a hard bargain, but I love this car so I guess I'll take it.

drive-by (*noun*) Crime & Law: crime committed from a moving vehicle, usually a shooting

The police were hunting the gang who had masterminded the drive-by that night.

drive someone up the wall (*verb phrase*) General: to bother someone excessively

You're driving me up the wall with all the ridiculous requests.

drive time (*noun phrase*) Entertainment: radio programming that occurs while listeners are commuting to work in their cars

The controversial radio hosts had become the King of Drive Time, as all the trade magazines proclaimed.

driving in reverse (*expression*) General: in a diminished mental state

Joey's been driving in reverse these days ever since his wife left him.

drobe (*noun*) Sci-fi: science fiction fan who wears costumes to conventions

The drobes at sci-fi conventions always get media attention for their wild outfits.

drooling (*noun*) Entertainment: spontaneous filler conversation between radio or television personalities to kill dead time between segments

Cora Jean was admired by all for the sassy drooling she pulled off with her cohost on their morning talk show.

drop a dime (*verb phrase*) Crime & Law: to call an investigating police officer with a tip or piece of information on a crime

"Be sure to drop a dime if you hear anything on the robbery," the detective told his undercover agent.

drop a line (*verb phrase*) General: to write a letter

Will you drop me a line when you get settled in your new home?

drop-dead gorgeous (*adj. phrase*) General: strikingly beautiful

Carlie's new dress was drop-dead gorgeous.

drop some iron (*verb phrase*) Teen & College: to spend some money

Virgil really dropped some iron to fix up his car.

drop the ball (*verb phrase*) General: to make a crucial mistake

I dropped the ball in those contract negotiations when I didn't sign on time.

drown one's sorrows (*verb phrase*) General: to address one's problems by drinking

Before he sobered up, George used to drown his sorrows at O'Tooles.

drug war (*noun phrase*) Government & Politics: federal government's efforts to fight drug smuggling, production, and sales

Some argue that the government should stop fighting the

drug war and start supporting drug treatment.

drum up (*verb phrase*) General: to make a continued and concerted effort

I've been drumming up support for the new library for months.

dry run (*noun phrase*) Air & Space: rehearsal for a take-off or a launch

The actual launch is scheduled for Wednesday; Tuesday is only a dry run.

duck 1.(*noun*) Street: unattractive female

I hope there aren't a bunch of ducks at that party.

2. (*noun*) Government & Politics: nuisance, such as a relentlessly activist constituent or a pesky lobbyist

The animal-rights activist who had been so helpful to the congresswoman in her campaign became a duck to her staff after six months in office.

duck squeezer (*noun phrase*) General: mildly derogatory term for an environmentalist; *see also:* tree hugger

Marcie started hanging around with the duck squeezers during college.

dude (*noun*) Surferspeak, Teen & College: person; term used as a form of address; formerly known as "guy" or "man," applies to both sexes

Hey, dude, what's been happening?

dudical (*noun*) Teen & College: unconventional person; a combined form of radical dude

He's a smart guy, but an oddball, a real dudical.

duke breath (*noun phrase*) Teen & College: stinky breath

Millie's going out with some guy with military hair and duke breath.

dump 1.(*verb*) Teen & College: to break up a romantic relationship

Rosanna dumped Myers the minute she met Demi.

2.(*verb*) Business: to sell an oversupply of goods in a foreign country at a very low price

Toyco managed to dump a million of the action figures in Eastern Europe.

3.(*verb*) Medical: to send a patient to another medical facility because he or she is undesirable or can't pay

The emergency facility was cited by the investigating authorities for dumping an uninsured pregnant woman who was about to deliver.

dump on (*verb phrase*) General: to criticize

Why are you always dumping on me?

dust (*verb*) Teen & College: to humiliate

Lily really dusted George when she didn't show up for their date.

dust bunny (*noun phrase*)

Drug World: a person visibly under the influence of PCP
Angelica was acting like a dust bunny when Milt walked into the arcade looking for her.

dusty *(adj.)* Teen & College: cranky or unpleasant
What are you so dusty about? I was just a few minutes late.

dweeb *(noun)* Teen & College: an unpopular, awkward person; *see also:* dork, fred, geek, goob, goof, nerd, squid, and swivel-neck
Benny decided to stand up and fight when the gang called his brother a dweeb.

dwindles, the *(noun)* Medical: general effects of old age
Mr. Spofford's records didn't reflect any major illness, just the collective symptoms of the dwindles.

dysfunctional *(adj.)* Psychology: not working properly, full of neurotic behavior
When everyone in the group began talking about their dysfunctional families, Steve felt out of place believing that he had a happy childhood.

E

eager beaver *(noun phrase)* General: earnest, ambitious person
The new associate is a bit too much of an eager beaver, always trying to network at every party.

eagle eyes *(noun phrase)* General: alert person
My grandmother is an eagle eyes for foul balls at the stadium.

earful *(noun)* General: plenty of verbal input; usually in a scolding tone
Zeke got an earful from his neighbors for painting his house bright green.

earl *(verb)* Street: to vomit; also known as: barf, blow lunch, boag boot, decorate one's shoes, drive the porcelain bus, heave, honk, hurl, ralph, reverse gears, shout at one's shoes, spew, toss, yak, yawn in technicolor, and zuke
I guess I have the flu because I've been earling all day.

earmarks *(noun)* General: indicators
That kid's behavior has all the earmarks of a troubled home.

earn one's wings *(verb phrase)* General: to become qualified for something through hard work and experience
Jennifer felt like she had earned her wings when she was promoted to a full-time staff position.

earnest money *(noun phrase)* Real Estate: cash payments which lock parties into the sale of a property
After the earnest money had changed hands, the seller began to feel more confident about the deal.

easy as pie *(adj. phrase)* General: simple

Winning this game is going to be easy as pie.

easy *(adv.)* Seafarers: in a cautious manner

You better dock easy. The water seems low.

eat chain *(verb phrase)* Teen & College: get lost, drop dead; short for eat a chain saw

When Deborah told the guy who was bugging her to eat chain, he finally left the party.

eat crow *(verb phrase)* General: to admit that one is mistaken

I really had to eat crow when my estimates turned out to be wrong.

eat dirt *(verb phrase)* General: to accept someone's criticism or insult without response

I had to eat dirt from that customer just because he knows my father.

eat it *(verb phrase)* General: to suffer the consequences

You lent money to that crook and now you're going to have to eat it.

eat one's heart out *(verb phrase)* General: to be jealous of something someone else has

I got the last pair of those boots at the Shoe Shack, so eat your heart out.

eat one's words *(verb phrase)* General: to admit one has said something that is untrue

I'll make you eat your words for calling me lazy.

eat someone out of house and home *(verb phrase)*

General: to eat excessively and constantly

My parents complain that I'm eating them out of house and home.

eat someone's dust *(verb phrase)* General: to be thoroughly defeated

I can't wait to make this announcement at the meeting— my rivals are going to eat my dust!

eat the ball *(verb phrase)* Sports (Football): to hold onto the ball and allow oneself to be tackled rather than throw it

I can't believe Leo ate the ball when I was wide open for a pass!

eat the cookie *(verb phrase)* Surferspeak: to be treated roughly by a wave; *see also:* get biffed, get creamed, get lunched, get pounded, get prosecuted, take gas, and toad

I really ate the cookie on that one!

eco-office *(noun)* Ecology: environmentally safe office, free of indoor pollutants and other physically hazardous elements

Molly swore that working in an eco-office had helped cure her chronic headaches.

economically challenged *(phrase)* PC: poor

There were several passages in the Vice President's speech that suggested he was sensitive to the plight of the economically challenged.

ecotourism *(noun)* Ecology: nature and ecology-oriented travel

The ecotourism industry is beginning to surge, thanks to promotion among the big conservation groups.

eddie *(noun)* Teen & College: unattractive male

There were only eddies at that party last night. What a bummer.

edge city *(noun phrase)* Real Estate: thriving residential and commercial area that develops on the outskirts of town in response to increased population or commerce, as well as to the decrease in livability of downtown areas

Monica preferred living in Weston, an edge city offering her a wealth of housing options as well as convenient shopping and transportation.

edgy car *(noun phrase)* Cartalk: car that needs body work or other concentrated renovation; an automotive fixer-upper

The station wagon was driven hard by two teenage boys for three years and now is an edgy car.

egg *(verb)* Teen & College: to pelt a car, house, etc., with raw eggs

Neighborhood delinquents egged our house three nights in a row.

egg on *(verb phrase)* General: to urge to action

I egged her on until she asked the new guy for a date.

egghead *(noun)* General: smart, studious person; an intellectual; *see also:* dexter, digithead, floppy disk, mensan, and pointhead

Jason ignores the kids who call him an egghead for reading during lunch.

ego massage *(noun phrase)* General: flattering reassurance

After losing to her opponent in the primaries, Anastasia felt the last thing she needed was an ego massage from well-meaning but overly optimistic supporters.

ego pricing *(verb phrase)* Real Estate: when a seller places too high a price on a property, based on her or his own assumption of value

Against their broker's advice, the couple had insisted on ego pricing the property in order to recoup their losses.

ejecta *(noun)* Military: debris from a missile explosion

The ejecta caused as much damage in the immediately surrounding areas as the direct hit of the missile itself.

elbow in *(verb phrase)* General: to force oneself into a situation where one is not invited; also known as: horn in

At the wedding banquet, the little boy elbowed his way in to get to the dessert table first.

elbow room *(noun phrase)*
General: space to maneuver
If you want dinner, give me some elbow room in this kitchen.

electronic cadaver *(noun phrase)* Medical: a computer program/system that simulates the experience of dissecting a cadaver
Students practice their technique on electronic cadavers before graduating to the real thing.

electronic town hall *(noun phrase)* Technology: the use of televised public meetings to discuss political issues through debate, thereby providing a forum to gauge constituent response
The candidate welcomed the chance to participate in an electronic town hall meeting on defense spending.

elegant *(adj.)* Computerspeak: smooth, uncomplicated, referring to a successful programming solution; opposite of kludge
The programmer admired the elegant work of her partner.

elevator music *(noun phrase)* Entertainment: popular songs reproduced in a light, breezy style as background music
The pop star was horrified to hear her hit song on the radio played as elevator music.

elevator surfing *(noun phrase)* Street: dangerous sport of jumping from the top of one elevator shaft to another

Mario's little brother was badly injured while he was elevator surfing.

empty calories *(noun phrase)* Food: food usually high in calories but with negligible nutritional value
After losing forty pounds on a nutritious diet, Rhaj couldn't help pointing out the empty calories on everyone else's plate.

empty-nesters *(noun)* Real Estate: individuals whose housing requirements have changed because their children have grown and left home
The agent showed the empty-nesters several modest condominiums that suited their new life-style perfectly.

equalizer *(noun)* Crime & Law: gun; *see also:* heat, piece and rod
The hoodlum felt safe with the equalizer in his pocket.

end result *(noun phrase)* Government, Business: result
"We know the cause, but what's the end result?" the Senate aide asked earnestly.

environmental racism *(noun phrase)* PC: exposure of minorities or Third World citizens to environmentally dangerous elements
The activists argued that the plastics company commits environmental racism by allowing its toxic waste to be stored so close to certain residential areas.

ersatz *(noun)* Foreign (German): imitation
This is ersatz coffee, isn't it?

escalate *(verb)* Military: to intensify military efforts
The relief effort escalated into a skirmish with local rebel forces.

ETI *(acronym)* Sci-fi: Extra-Terrestrial Intelligence
Sal was a big believer in ETI and waited patiently for secret government evidence to be released.

event *(noun)* Military: nuclear incident
The military technicians worked to avoid an event at all costs.

even up the score *(verb phrase)* General: to make the advantages equal
I think nabbing that new account will even up the score with our competitors.

excess baggage *(noun phrase)* General: someone or something considered to be in the way and unnecessary
Your cousin will just be excess baggage at dinner.

executive session *(noun phrase)* Government & Politics: meeting of legislators and/or officials from which the public and press are barred
The committee met in executive session to discuss congressional pay raises.

exotics *(noun)* Cartalk: cars that are out of the ordinary, custom-made, or foreign made
After buying a rare, custom-built brougham, Jane confessed to a weakness for exotics.

extra *(noun)* Entertainment: performer who appears on screen but who has no lines
Jeff was delighted to be an extra in the crowd scene of that new action picture.

eyes *(noun)* Street: sunglasses
Where are my eyes? I can't see a thing in this glare.

F

faced *(verb)* Teen & College: to have lost face
Brandon was faced when the guys on his team refused to invite him to the post-season party.

face the music *(verb phrase)* General: to accept the consequences or punishment for one's actions
I guess I should face the music and tell my parents about the accident.

face time *(noun phrase)* Computerspeak: the time one engages in actual face-to-face communication with someone, as opposed to electronic conversation
I never had any face time with Jane so I didn't even know what she looked like.

face up to *(verb phrase)* General: to accept something unpleasant or difficult
I just can't face up to the fact that Sammy is gone.

fail (*verb*) Teen & College: do not understand; short for fail to comprehend
I don't know what Janet is so angry about. I fail.

fair game (*noun phrase*) General: likely target
Ever since you broke up with Juanita, you're fair game at parties.

fair-weather friend (*noun phrase*) General: friend who can only be relied upon when times are good
When Dan's dad was indicted last year, he saw how many fair-weather friends he really had.

fake-bake (*noun*) Teen & College: tanning salon or a tan acquired at a tanning salon
I'm getting a fake-bake before I go on vacation.

fall flat (*verb phrase*) General: to fail
The jokes in my speech fell flat.

fall for (*verb phrase*) General: to become fond of
I'm really falling for this guy I'm dating.

fall from grace (*verb phrase*) General: to lose approval
Seth fell from grace at home when his parents caught him skipping school.

fall in (*verb phrase*) Street: to arrive
When did you fall in at the block party?

fall off the wagon (*verb phrase*) General: to go back to drinking alcohol or taking drugs after a period of abstinence
Monty fell of the wagon this weekend at that fraternity party.

fall on deaf ears (*verb phrase*) General: to be said to one who isn't paying attention
If you criticize her work, it'll just fall on deaf ears.

fall short (*verb phrase*) General: to not meet expectations
I'm afraid I'm falling short on the campaign contributions.

fallback position (*noun phrase*) Government: alternative course to be taken in case the first course fails
Your plan is certainly feasible, but we better have a fallback position, just in case.

falling-out (*noun*) General: argument
We had a falling-out over who would pay for dinner.

fallout (*noun*) General: unpleasant aftereffects
What's the fallout from the fight at the town council meeting last night?

False! (*expression*) Teen & College: That's impossible!
Robbie drank two whole liters of Coke? False!

fan (*verb*) Teen & College: to skip; *see also:* **flag**
I decided to fan the last lecture of the seminar.

fandom (*noun*) Sci-fi: the **community** of science fiction fans
Arthur Clarke may be one of the

all-time heroes of fandom.

fanger *(noun)* Medical: oral surgeon

The dentist advised his patient to see a fanger about removing the wisdom teeth.

fan it *(verb phrase)* Teen & College: never mind, forget it

I think we should fan it on the movie and just go over to Margo's house.

fannish *(adj.)* Sci-fi: exclusively of interest to science fiction fans

"You can't understand because it's a fannish thing," Lisa tried to explain to her puzzled date.

farm-out *(verb phrase)* General: to delegate or send away work to be done

I'd like to farm-out this proposal to a free-lancer.

fascinoma *(noun)* Medical: unusual and interesting illness, from the perspective of the physician

The resident was fixated on the new patient's fascinoma.

fashion criminal *(noun phrase)* Teen & College: one who unsuccessfully attempts to assert a certain fashion style

She's got all that leather on but it's not working. She's a total fashion criminal.

fashion police *(noun phrase)* Teen & College: imaginary squad responsible for patrolling the population and apprehending fashion criminals or others with unfashionable clothing

Look at that outfit! Somebody call the fashion police!

fashion victim *(noun phrase)* Teen & College: one who has attempted to achieve a certain trendy look but has unwittingly failed

Those bell bottoms make Lila look like a fashion victim.

fast buck *(noun phrase)* General: quickly earned money

I think we can make a fast buck selling this wood we chopped.

fat *(adj.)* Teen & College: good

I got a fat B on my history exam.

fat chance *(noun phrase)* General: little or no possibility; *see also:* slim chance

There's a fat chance I'll be chosen for the debate team.

fat tooth *(noun phrase)* Food & Drink: tendency to be drawn to foods with a high fat content

Margie's doctor told her that her fat tooth had caused the gallstones plaguing her most of her adult life.

favorite *(noun)* Sports: team, player, or contestant who seems, based on past performance, to be most likely to win

Montgomery had long been the favorite to win the spelling bee, so everyone was shocked when Sheila blew his doors off in the last round.

favorite son *(noun phrase)* Government & Politics: candidate supported by his or her home state for President

The senator was the favorite son from Texas but he couldn't count on any other support in the Southwest.

Fear! *(expression)* Teen & College: That's scary.

You have three finals in one day? Fear!

feather in one's cap *(noun phrase)* General: honor or an accomplishment

Winning that contract for her company was a real feather in Rochelle's cap.

feather one's nest *(verb phrase)* General: to tend to one's own interests

Although Amy says she wants to help our store succeed, I think she's really out to feather her nest.

feedback *(noun)* Government: response

After proposing the sweeping tax changes, the President relied on pollsters to gather the public's feedback.

feep *(noun)* Computerspeak: beeping noise made when a computer is turned on

The feeps coming from George's computer told him everything was okay.

feet on the ground *(noun phrase)* General: a sensible attitude

Despite all the tragedies that have happened, Annie really has her feet on the ground.

fender belly *(noun phrase)* Seafarers: round, robust sailor,

often in the Navy for life

Potter's a good guy, a real fender belly from the old days.

fender bender *(noun phrase)* Traffic: minor traffic accident with little damage

It was just a fender bender, but I was angry about it for weeks.

-fest *(suffix)* Teen & College: abundance

Christmas is now a real baby-fest since all of my brothers and sisters have kids.

fierce *(adj.)* Teen & College: intense, terrific

Patrick looks so fierce in his new suit.

fifty-fifty *(adv.)* General: equal chances

It's fifty-fifty whether Misra will get that promotion or not.

fight tooth and nail *(verb phrase)* General: to fight or argue aggressively

We fought tooth and nail over the changes in the script.

filet (pronounced fee-lay) *(noun)* Teen & College: attractive female

Who was that filet driving around with Marcus this afternoon?

fill one's shoes *(verb phrase)* General: to be a proper replacement for someone

Pat was afraid he wouldn't be able to fill his boss's shoes while she was on vacation.

fill the bill *(verb phrase)* General: to be just what is required

This new screw seems to fill the bill for fixing the broken washing machine.

filthy *(adj.)* Teen & College, Street: cool
What a filthy car!

fin *(noun)* General: five-dollar bill
Can you lend me a fin until Friday?

final-final *(noun)* Bars: the last drink of the evening, usually after a long night of overindulgence
Let's go to the hotel bar for a final-final.

fine *(adj.)* Teen & College: extremely attractive
That waiter is one fine specimen.

fine-tooth comb *(noun phrase)* General: careful attention
I went over those figures with a fine-tooth comb to be sure there were no errors.

finesse *(noun)* Foreign (French): diplomatic skill
Aunt Inge has a lot of finesse and always manages to clear up these family squabbles.

fine-tune *(verb phrase)* General: to polish and made precise
I'd like to fine-tune this report before we turn it in.

fingerpoint *(verb)* General: to focus blame for a situation on others, rather than on oneself
After the protest demonstrations turned violent, city officials were quick to engage in furious fingerpointing.

finger wave *(noun phrase)* Medical: rectal examination
The patient winced at the thought of the finger wave that the doctor had planned for the morning.

fired up *(verb phrase)* Teen & College: enthusiastic, excited
Josie was all fired up about her latest art project.

fire up *(verb phrase)* Teen & College: to become excited
I want to get everyone fired up for the festival this weekend.

fire on *(verb phrase)* Teen & College: to pound or punch
The coach was horrified to see half his team fire on the opposing team's goalie.

first strike *(noun phrase)* Military: surprise nuclear attack
Surveillance technology uncovered the country's attempts to develop first strike capabilities.

fish *(noun)* Seafarers: torpedo
We're carrying some mighty powerful fish on this mission, so let's not make any mistakes.

fish for *(verb phrase)* General: to hint or angle for
You've been fishing for compliments about your outfit all night.

fishing without bait *(expression)* General: in a diminished mental state
The new music teacher must be fishing without bait if she thinks we're going to perform the other school's anthem.

fish or cut bait *(verb phrase)* General: make a decision;

decide to pursue an activity or quit

You're going to have to fish or cut bait here because I've got to get the car back before noon.

fish out of water *(noun phrase)* General: person who is awkward and out of place

Stella's like a fish out of water at these fancy receptions her mother makes her attend.

fit like a glove *(verb phrase)* General: to fit perfectly

This new hat fits like a glove.

five-O *(noun)* Street: police

the five-O showed up at the school auditorium to give a talk about gangs.

fix *(noun)* Drug World: injection of drugs

The final fix Moe took sent him over the edge.

fixed pie *(noun phrase)* Science: theory that surviving in the future requires acknowledging that the earth's resources are finite

"Hey, this is a fixed pie situation on this earth, so for every one of those disposable cartons you throw away, a new one doesn't grow back on a tree!" the angry protester yelled at passersby.

fix someone's wagon *(verb phrase)* General: create a difficult situation for someone

If Scott doesn't stop borrowing my clothes, I'm going to fix his wagon.

fizzbo *(noun)* Real Estate: disparaging term used by realtors for homes that are "For Sale By Owner"

Every time the broker drove by the fizzbo on Lawndale Avenue he cursed because he knew he could get a better price for the property.

fizzle *(verb)* General: to die out; also known as: fizzle out

Support for the candidate in the Southern states fizzled as the election drew near.

flag 1. *(verb)* Teen & College: to skip; *see also:* fan

Marnie got detention for flagging three classes this week.

2. *(verb)* Teen & College: to fail

I'm going to have to work my butt off to not flag this class.

flack *(noun)* Advertising, Public Relations: one who promotes or publicizes a person, product, or event

The partners hired a flack to get their pictures in the paper.

flail *(verb)* Surferspeak: to behave awkwardly and without confidence while surfing

I get embarrassed watching T.J. flail when the surf's crowded with beards.

flake 1. *(verb)* Street: to back down from an argument

I can't believe you flaked like that!

2. *(verb)* Teen & College: to forget or lose track of

I flaked my driver's license exam even though I'd studied for a month.

flame *(verb)* Teen & College: to become extremely angry
I was flaming when I got a D on my history paper.

flap one's gums *(verb phrase)* General: to talk a lot without saying anything memorable
I avoid relatives who flap their gums at family gatherings.

flare up *(verb phrase)* General: to begin again suddenly
Hostilities between the two countries flared up after the most recent incident at the border.

flash and trash *(noun phrase)* Entertainment: derogatory term for special segments on violent or sexy subjects featured on television news to attract viewers during ratings periods
The local anchor worried that the flash and trash turning up on her show every Friday would hurt her reputation.

flat tire *(noun phrase)* Kids: prank that calls for stepping on the back of someone's shoe so that it comes off, forcing the wearer to stumble
As the chorus was marching out onto the platform Carla gave Mark a flat tire.

flat top *(noun phrase)* Seafarers: aircraft carrier; *see also:* bird farm
After a long spell on the flight deck of a flat top you want nothing but a little peace and quiet.

flatline *(verb)* Medical: to die; *see also:* box and tube

The patient is flatlining—get out the resuscitation equipment!

flavor *(noun)* General: variety
Which flavor movie do you want to watch—action or romance?

flavor of the week *(noun phrase)* General: what's most current and popular
Monty sure seems to be the flavor of the week at the office lately.

flesh *(noun)* PC: meat; term used by animal rights activists
After reading several books on vegetarianism, Tasha decided to give up flesh.

flesh and blood *(noun phrase)* General: relative
I love that guy like he's my own flesh and blood.

flip *(verb)* Teen & College: to be shocked; also known as **flip out**
My mother flipped when she saw my new haircut.

flip off *(verb phrase)* General: to make an obscene gesture with the middle finger; also known as: flip someone the bird
I asked Jelly for a ride home and he just flipped me off.

flipped *(verb)* Crime & Law: to become a witness for the government in aid of the prosecution of a co-defendant or another party; *see also:* rolled over
Sunny lost her chance of beating the charges when her partner flipped halfway through the trial.

flip side *(noun phrase)* General: opposite perspective on a matter

Because Rebecca can always argue the flip side of any issue, it's hard to know what her real opinion is.

flop *(noun)* Entertainment: failure

What a flop that new Broadway play was.

floor 1. *(noun)* Government & Politics: main chambers of the House or Senate

The senator worked the floor to determine the level of support for her proposed amendment to the bill.

2. *(noun)* Wall Street: area where stocks and bonds are traded; *see also:*

The CEO enjoyed visiting the Exchange to watch the action on the floor.

floppy disk *(noun phrase)* Teen & College: studious, bookish person; *see also:* dexter, digit-head, mensan and pointhead

He might be a floppy disk during the day, but you should see him dance.

flop sweat *(noun phrase)* Entertainment: anxiety suffered by producers and investors when they fear their film or play may fail

The investors' flop sweat was justified when the play closed after just seven performances.

fluff and fold *(verb phrase)* Food: to give a restaurant patron or patrons special VIP treatment

The owner instructed the maitre d' to fluff and fold the party at table #22.

fluids and electrolytes *(noun phrase)* Medical: cocktails

Let's meet across the street at seven o'clock for some fluids and electrolytes.

fly *(adj.)* Street: cool, very appealing

My new haircut looks fly, to be sure.

fly boy/girl *(noun phrase)* Teen & College: attractive male or female

There were some serious fly boys at that party.

fly gear *(noun phrase)* Street: great clothes

That's some fly gear she's wearing today!

fly off the handle *(verb phrase)* General: to become angry or disturbed

When Glen quit the track team his dad flew off the handle.

foam at the mouth *(verb phrase)* General: to be extremely angry, like a rabid animal

My dad was foaming at the mouth when he saw the dent in the car.

FOB *(noun phrase)* **1.** General: friend of Bill; developed at Alcoholics Anonymous, referring to Bill Wilson, the founder of A.A., as a code to identify other members.

I'd like you to meet Chet. He's an FOB, too.

2. Government & Politics: initialism for Friend of Bill, referring to claims many have made of being friends with President Bill Clinton

Being a genuine FOB gave the environmentalist plenty of access to the White House and other Washington power circles.

fold *(verb)* Teen & College: to become too exhausted

I just folded before the end of the movie.

folkie *(noun)* Entertainment: folk musician or folk music fan

The benefit concert was performed by an eclectic mix of folkies and rockers.

follow in one's footsteps *(verb phrase)* General: to follow someone's example

My grandmother hoped I'd follow in her footsteps and become a scientist.

follow suit *(verb phrase)* General: to do as someone else has done

Once a few kids started dancing, everyone else followed suit.

food for thought *(noun phrase)* General: something to ponder

Janine marrying John.

Now that's food for thought!

foodie *(noun)* Food: food professional or a serious food aficionado

The restaurant reviewer was a long-time foodie, who had started out as a pastry chef in San Francisco.

foof *(noun)* Teen & College: superficial person

He's just a foof so don't count on him to understand the problem.

footprint *(noun)* Military: area affected by a nuclear hit

The footprint left by the missile had an amazing radius.

foot the bill *(verb phrase)* General: to pay for

I didn't realize I was going to have to foot the bill for this research project.

for all one's worth *(prep. phrase)* General: with all one's effort

Deirdre tried to start the car for all her worth.

for all the world *(prep. phrase)* General: at any price; usually used in the negative

I wouldn't hire that guy for all the world.

for a song *(prep. phrase)* General: at a minimal cost

I got this jacket for a song at Daley's Department Store.

force one's hand *(verb phrase)* General: to make someone do something

Wanda had no intention of telling her parents about her grades, but her guidance counselor forced her hand.

for dear life *(prep. phrase)* General: as though fearful for one's life

Zelda held on to the rope for dear life.

forever and a day *(noun phrase)* General: always, endlessly

Mary Ann waited forever and a day to hear if she'd been accepted at the university.

forex *(noun)* Wall Street: foreign currency trading market
I noticed that the dollar is way down on the forex so it will be expensive to travel in Europe next week.

forget it 1. *(expression)* General: no, under no circumstances
Forget it—you're not wearing my sweater.

2. *(expression)* General: don't worry, it's no problem; also known as: forget about it
Forget it. I didn't mind helping you with the dishes.

for keeps *(prep. phrase)* General: forever
I hope we'll stay together for keeps this time.

for love or money *(prep. phrase)* General: at any price; usually used in the negative
I wouldn't sell my car for love or money.

forte *(noun)* Foreign (Italian): specialty
Languages aren't my forte but I do have a great interest in foreign music.

Fort Fumble *(proper noun)* Military: Pentagon
Don't expect Fort Fumble to come up with an alternative plan for handling the conflict in the Middle East.

for the birds *(prep. phrase)* General: foolish

These new company rules are for the birds.

for the life of one *(prep. phrase)* General: no matter what one does
I can't figure this puzzle out for the life of me.

fossil *(noun)* Teen & College: college student who has stayed well beyond his or her four years
Jonathan is the fossil from our class. I don't think he'll ever graduate.

four-oh *(noun)* College, Seafarers: excellence or perfection; from the highest possible academic grade point average, or from the highest possible score on a Naval fitness exam
John's just a pointheaded four-oh who spent so much time studying that he forgot to make friends.

fourth medium *(noun phrase)* Military: space, the fourth arena where war might be waged; the first three are land, sea, and, air
I hate to think of the day when our military efforts are conducted in the fourth medium.

freak *(noun)* Street: sexy, attractive person
What a freak that new student assistant is!

fred *(noun)* Teen & College: awkward or unpopular male; from the main character of television's "The Flintstones"; *see also:* dork, dweeb, geek, goob, goof, nerd, squid, and swivel-neck

I don't want that fred as my lab partner!

free-for-all *(noun)* General: chaotic situation

The sale at Delaney's was a total free-for-all.

freebie *(noun)* General: something given away at no cost

The theater was giving away freebies for the next performance.

freebase *(verb)* Drug World: to smoke pure cocaine

The gang used to hide in a burnt-out factory all day and freebase.

free-range *(adj.)* Food: descriptive term applied to fowl raised outside of a traditional coop

The animal-rights activist would only eat free-range chicken as a protest against the cruelty chickens suffer when raised in a coop.

free trip *(noun phrase)* Sports (Baseball): walk

Plato got a free trip, stole second and third, and then got thrown out in a play at home.

frequent flyer *(noun phrase)* Travel: air traveler who participates in the airlines' promotional programs, which offer free flights after a certain number of miles have been flown on the airline

As a frequent flyer, Dawson had earned a free trip to Europe for his family.

fresh *(adj.)* Teen & College: very good, very appealing

That new CD is fresh. Could you turn it up?

fresh dip *(noun phrase)* Teen & College, Street: casual clothing

I'm just going to wear fresh dip to the party at Dean's house.

freshman *(noun)* Government & Politics: newly elected, first-term member of either house of Congress

Even as a freshman, the congresswoman introduced controversial anti-discrimination legislation.

friction costs *(noun phrase)* Wall Street: expenses associated with the buying and selling of securities

The friction costs on the deal were modest, including only a fair commission, a deferrable tax, and a minimal surcharge.

frog *(noun)* Travel: New York-to-London flight; refers to the idea of a frog hopping over a patch of water

I'll take the four o'clock frog so I can make the morning meeting.

frogman *(noun)* Seafarers: fully trained diver; frogman in training is known as a tadpole

The team of frogmen moved silently through the water to investigate the unmarked boat anchored not far from shore.

from hell *(prep. phrase)* Teen & College: of the worst kind

My brother got carsick and it was the road trip from hell.

from the horse's mouth *(prep. phrase)* General: straight from the source

I got it from the horse's mouth that Keith's getting married.

front *(verb)* Street: to be coy, to act like one is not interested when one is

Stop fronting, Jerry. Just admit you like Roberta.

front-end money *(noun phrase)* Entertainment: money that is made even before a film is released

Because the film was being handled by an independent distributor, the investors were likely to see a little front-end money before the film's opening date.

front foot *(noun phrase)* Real Estate: property line that abuts a street, sidewalk, or other public byway

The prospective buyers' only complaint was that the front foot of the property was too close to the house.

front money *(noun phrase)* Real Estate: downpayment

The couple finally found the perfect house and prayed they'd be able to come up with the front money.

frontload *(verb)* Bars: to drink a lot of liquor before attending an event at which liquor will not be served

Kimberly went to the hotel bar to frontload before her niece's piano recital.

front runner *(noun phrase)* General: party most likely to win a contest

No candidate wants to be an early front runner because that spot is an easy target for criticism.

frosted 1. *(adj.)* Teen & College, Street: to be cold and unfeeling

Mariah's mom always seems frosted when I say hello to her.

2. *(adj.)* Teen & College: intoxicated

When I got to the party last night, those two were already frosted.

FTL *(acronym)* Sci-fi: Faster Than Light; referring to space travel

If we don't get out of here FTL, we're going to be late for the movie.

fudge it *(verb phrase)* General: to improvise, fake something

I forgot my notes so I'll just have to fudge it on my lecture.

full blast *(adv. phrase)* General: without restraint

I'm exhausted—we ran full blast all the way home.

full-court press *(noun phrase)* Sports (Basketball): concentrated, coordinated effort, from defensive strategy that requires players to apply a general defensive pressure; alternative to player to player, which calls for each defensive player to follow a specific offensive player

I'm sure if we apply a full-court press, we can get Mom and Dad to take us to the Grand Canyon.

full house *(noun phrase)* Entertainment: a performance space where every seat is filled

We've got a full house tonight, so let's get it right, okay?

full of acid *(adj. phrase)* Teen & College: on steroids

That guy is really buff, but he's probably full of acid.

full of piss and vinegar *(adj. phrase)* General: lively and energetic; also known as: full of ginger

When the students came in from recess they were so full of piss and vinegar the student teacher had to calm them down before trying to explain fractions.

full of steam *(adj. phrase)* General: enthusiastic and energetic

The whole class was full of steam about the photography project.

full-on *(adj.)* Teen & College: absolute

What a full-on jerk that guy is!

fully on *(adv. phrase)* Teen & College: excellent

The graduation party Kendra's parents threw was fully on.

fun and games *(noun phrase)* General: easy, enjoyable task

Babysitting for those Miller twins is no fun and games.

fund *(verb)* Government: to finance, pay for

The program is expensive, but the tax increase should fund it.

fundies *(noun)* Government & Politics: fundamentalist Christians

The fundies staged a nationwide protest of the President's position on prayer in public schools.

funk *(adj.)* Teen & College: not cool at all

That funk senior keeps hanging around our study hall trying to hook up with a sophomore.

furniture *(noun)* Sports (Tennis): tennis racket's frame; from the days when all rackets had wood frames

The temperamental star damaged the furniture when he threw his racket across the court.

fuss *(adj.)* Street: angry

I'm not fuss, I'm just tired.

fuzz *(verb)* Government: to be purposely unclear or indirect

The Labor Department spokesperson fuzzed on the real unemployment figures in order to protect the administration.

G

G *(noun)* Street: one's best friend; from grand, a term for one thousand dollars (as in 50 grand, or 50 Gs)

Hey, G, what's up?

gaffer *(noun)* Entertainment: chief electrician on a film set

By his fourth film, Wendell had become the gaffer and supervised a staff of ten.

gafiate *(verb)* General: to relax on a vacation
I'm going to be doing some serious gafiating next week so don't even think of calling me.

gagger *(noun)* Teen & College: disgusting person or situation
The whole conversation was a gagger.

gag rule *(noun)* Government & Politics: enforced restriction of debate or discussion of an issue; most recently and specifically associated with prohibitions against discussing abortion with patients at federally funded health clinics
Feminists and medical professionals were outraged at the Administration's gag rule on abortion, as they felt it violated a patient's right to know all possible medical options.

galley yarn *(noun phrase)* Seafarers: rumor
Travis isn't getting married. That's just a galley yarn.

gamer *(noun)* Fantasy: person avidly involved in role-playing games
Josh has become such a gamer he quit track because it was interfering with his schedule.

gangsta *(noun)* Teen & College: member of a gang
That kid dresses like a gangsta but I think he just wants to look cool.

gank *(verb)* Teen & College: to flirt

That new guy was ganking all over Marcie and her sister at the beach.

garbage 1. *(noun)* Computer speak: unnecessary data that tends to accumulate over time in a computer system
The intern never deleted the stray data, so by the end of the summer the computer was filled with garbage.
2. *(noun)* Food: restaurant term for usable leftovers
Today's garbage is a pasta dish containing yesterday's unused grilled chicken and vegetable entrees.

garbage down *(verb phrase)* General: to devour hungrily and sloppily
The dogs garbaged down their dinner and then lingered in the kitchen hoping for more.

garbage fees *(noun phrase)* Real Estate: expensive fees charged by lenders at the closing of the sale of a property
The country folks were appalled at the exorbitant garbage fees charged by the bank when they bought an apartment in the city.

garbage time *(noun phrase)* Sports: time left on the clock when the score is so lopsided that both teams put in back-up squads because the outcome of the game is indisputably clear
I'd rather not play at all than be put in for five minutes of garbage time at the end of the game.

garmento *(noun)* Fashion: person who works in the fashion industry; originally referred to those who work pushing racks of clothing up and down Seventh Avenue in New York
Several garmentos gathered at the restaurant to read the season's reviews in the newspaper.

garp *(verb)* Word Biz: to become an author's first bestseller or break-out book; from John Irving's *The World According to Garp*, which became his first huge success, making its first editions suddenly quite valuable
I'm not sure Lee's new novel will garp, but it's getting very nice reviews.

gasser *(noun)* Medical: anesthesiologist
After fifteen hours of labor, Jill was delighted to see the gasser arrive, despite her natural birth training.

gate   1. *(noun)* College, Street, Drug World: home; *see also:* crib
Come back to my gate and we'll do a little partying.
2. *(noun)* Entertainment: gross income generated by ticket sales to an event
What was the gate from the concert last night?

-gate *(suffix)* Government & Politics: scandal; derived from Watergate, most well known of the scandals; applicable to anything that smacks of impropriety
The angry PTA parents picketed the town hall with signs that read "This is School Budget-gate and We Won't Stand for It!"

gavel-to-gavel *(noun phrase)* Government & Politics: period from opening to adjournment of a session of Congress
Freshmen in Congress didn't dare leave the Capitol from gavel-to-gavel, for fear of seeming irresponsible.

gazump *(verb)* Real Estate: to raise the price on a property after an informal deal has been made, although no contract has been signed
Just when Jack thought he'd found an apartment he liked, the seller gazumped him and the deal fell through.

gazunder *(verb)* Real Estate: to bargain down the price on a property after a deal has been struck
The buyer gazundered before the closing, but the seller capitulated because the market was so bad.

gearhead *(noun)* Computerspeak: computer programmer
Mario couldn't wait to finish his course, get a job, and enter the ranks of the gearheads he so admired.

geek 1. *(noun)* Teen & College: unpopular, awkward person; *see also:* dork, dweeb, fred, goob, goof, nerd, squid and swivelneck
Teresa may have looked like a

geek last year, but you should see her now.

2. *(noun)* Drug World: crack addict

"When did you turn into such a geek?" the youths asked their friend disgustedly.

gel *(verb)* Surferspeak: to calm down

*You better gel, **dude**, before you get yourself into real trouble.*

gender illusionist (noun phrase) PC: transvestite

Wally liked to think of himself as a part-time gender illusionist.

Generation X *(noun phrase)* Press: term applied to those born after 1965, who have proven to be an indefinable block in many socio-economic sectors

The product was cleverly marketed to Generation X, who had plenty of disposable income but no distinct trends as consumers.

generously cut *(adj. phrase)* PC: loose and nonbinding, describing clothing made for large people

Lilly's dress was generously cut and flattered her coloring beautifully.

Georgia credit card (also Okie credit card, Tijuana credit card) *(noun phrase)* Cartalk, Law Enforcement: siphon used to steal gasoline from another car's tank

The rough-looking kids were apprehended in a parking lot with a three-foot length of hose, no doubt a Georgia credit card.

geronimos *(noun)* Drug World: barbituates

Larry couldn't sleep, but he knew enough not to mix geronimos with hard liquor.

get a body *(verb phrase)* Crime & Law: to kill someone

The gang vowed to get a body from the rival gang across town.

get a clue *(verb phrase)* Teen & College: to become aware

*I wish Monique would get a clue about Bobby because I can't stand to see him **scamming** other girls.*

get a fix on *(verb phrase)* General: to make a reasoned judgment about

I need to know Jack a bit better to get a real fix on him.

get a foot in the door *(verb phrase)* General: to get a first opportunity to succeed

With luck I'll be able to get my foot in the door at that law firm.

get a job *(expression)* Teen & College: do somthing useful and quit acting like a loser

Look at you, Pat. You've got nothing going on. Get a job!

get a life *(expression)* Teen & College: find something interesting or meaningful to do with yourself

You're so obsessed with celebrities. Get a life.

get all bent out of shape *(verb phrase)* General: to become annoyed

Dad, don't get all bent out of shape. I'll clean my room tonight.

get all that out of your mouth (*expression*) Street: stop lying

Get all that out of your mouth, and tell me you're in love.

get a load of (*verb phrase*) General: to take a look at

Get a load of that pair with the purple hair at the end of the bar.

get a move on (*verb phrase*) General: to hurry

Let's get a move on or we'll miss the bus.

get a rush (*verb phrase*) Teen & College: to become energized, excited, or intoxicated; also known as: get a headrush

I really got a rush from that rollercoaster ride!

get away with murder (*verb phrase*) General: to not get caught or punished for doing something illegal, unethical, or outrageous

Lynn complained that her parents always let her little brother get away with murder.

get a word in edgewise (*verb phrase*) General: to find a chance to speak when someone else is speaking excessively

Barbara was so excited to tell us about her trip I could hardly get a word in edgewise.

get axed (*verb phrase*) Surferspeak: to be thrown by a wave

I was worried when I couldn't see Elaine for a minute after she got axed.

get back on one's feet (*verb phrase*) General: to return to normal after an illness or serious problem

It was good to see Joelle back on her feet after going through bankruptcy.

get back to one's roots (*verb phrase*) General: to return to or rediscover one's heritage, racially, ancestrally, or emotionally; refers to Alex Haley's novel, *Roots*

Disillusioned with America, Abdul planned a trip to Egypt to get back to his roots.

get big air (*verb phrase*) Surferspeak: to be thrown high into the air by a wave, but not off the board

I'm still waiting for the day I get really big air on a wave.

get benched (*verb phrase*) Sports: to be removed from play due to injury, strategic considerations, or disciplinary measure

Vince was benched for three games for challenging the coach during a game.

get biffed (*verb phrase*) Surferspeak: to be tossed around by a wave while surfing; *see also:* eat the cookie, get creamed, get lunched, get pounded, get prosecuted, take gas, and toad

Dave got a concussion when he got biffed by a big one this afternoon.

get busy (*verb phrase*) Crime

& Law: street criminal's term for robbing someone

Here comes a pocketbook, let's get busy.

get canned (*verb phrase*) General: to be fired from one's job; *see also:* get sacked

I sure hope I don't get canned for being late three mornings in a row.

get cold feet (*verb phrase*) General: to lose one's nerve at the last moment

Maurice got cold feet before he went into business with his brother.

get cracking (*verb phrase*) General: to hurry

I better get cracking if I want to serve dinner at eight.

get creamed (*verb phrase*) Surferspeak: to be treated roughly by a wave while surfing; *see also:* eat the cookie, get biffed, get lunched, get pounded, get prosecuted, take gas, and toad

I'm not ready to get creamed, so I just ride the little ones.

get down to brass tacks (*verb phrase*) General: focus on essentials

Should we get down to brass tacks and discuss the layoffs now?

get hitched (*verb phrase*) General: to get married

Nicole and Mark are getting hitched this weekend.

get horizontal (*verb phrase*) Teen & College: to lie down

I crammed all last night for the trig final, so I've got to get horizontal before I keel over.

Get hot and get lucky! (*expression*) General: No way! You've got to be kidding!

Let you borrow my best suit for your date? Get hot and get lucky!

get it through one's head (*verb phrase*) General: to understand; also known as: get it through one's thick skull

Can't you get it through your head that our relationship is over?

get it together (*verb phrase*) General: to be in control of one's faculties

I need a few weeks off to get it together.

get lucky (*verb phrase*) General: to meet someone with whom one has a romantic or sexual encounter

The bar was full of people who all seemed looking to get lucky.

get lunched (*verb phrase*) Surferspeak: to be treated roughly by a wave while surfing; *see also:* eat the cookie, get biffed, get pounded, get prosecuted, take gas, and toad

If I get lunched one more time, I'm going to quit for the day.

get moded (*verb phrase*) Teen & College: to be humiliated

I got moded when I lost my car keys and had to ask my mother for a ride to the game.

get naked (*verb phrase*) Teen & College: to have fun
Let's get naked and go for a drive.

get off (*verb phrase*) Teen & College: to stop bothering or criticizing
Get off me, will you? I'm doing the best I can.

get off easy (*verb phrase*) General: to escape with little punishment or consequences
Bernie got off easy this time for forgetting his sales report, but next time he could get axed.

get off one's back (*verb phrase*) General: to stop nagging someone
The only way to get this journalist off our backs is to offer her an exclusive interview.

get off on the wrong foot (*verb phrase*) General: to establish a relationship with a bad start
I think we got off on the wrong foot at that tense meeting this morning.

get off the ground (*verb phrase*) General: to make a successful beginning
If we could just get this business off the ground, I'd be very relieved.

get off with your bad self (*verb phrase*) Teen & College: to be pleased with oneself
You got an A on that paper, so I guess you're getting off with your bad self.

get one's back up (*verb phrase*) General: to get riled
It really gets Debby's back up when cars speed down her street.

get one's feet wet (*verb phrase*) General: to do something for the first time, to become familiar with something
Ryan had never worked in a restaurant, so he spent his first week as a waiter just getting his feet wet.

get one's nose out of joint (*verb phrase*) General: to become offended
My mother got her nose out of joint at the wedding reception when my brother forgot to dance with her.

get one's panties in a bunch (*verb phrase*) General: to become upset and irrational; also known as: get one's shorts in a bunch
I know if I ask my supervisor for another day off he's going to get his panties in a bunch and say no.

get one's rear in gear (*verb phrase*) General: to hurry
Get your rear in gear and do those dishes.

get on the ball (*verb phrase*) General: to pay closer attention, to try harder
If you don't get on the ball soon, you're going to miss your chance to apply to medical school.

get on the stick (*verb phrase*) General: to start working hard

You better get on the stick and finish trimming those hedges.

get out of here (*expression*) Teen & College: You're lying! Quit lying!

Get out of here! You don't know anything about horses.

get out of my face (*expression*) Street: Get away from me.

Get out of my face or I'll call the cops right now.

get out of one's hair (*verb phrase*) General: to relieve the nuisance

I wish my little brother would get out of my hair today.

get paid (*verb phrase*) Crime & Law: street criminal's term for completing a successful robbery

"Me and the Turk just got paid," the youth bragged to friends.

get pounded (*verb phrase*) Surferspeak: to be tossed around by a wave while surfing; *see also:* eat the cookie, get biffed, get lunched, get prosecuted, take gas, and toad

*Did I look like a **barney** getting pounded by that wave out there?*

get prosecuted (verb) Surferspeak: to be handled roughly by a wave while surfing; see also: Eat the cookie, get biffed, get lunched, get pounded, take gas, and toad

"Oh, wow, my head is rattling. I just got prosecuted."

get real (*expression*) Teen & College: Be serious! Be realistic with yourself!

You know you can't borrow Karla's car. Get real!

get sacked (*verb phrase*) General: to be fired from one's job; *see also:* get canned

Uncle Ed got sacked in the big layoffs at the factory.

get small (*verb phrase*) Crime & Law: to disappear, especially if one is a suspect

Angela's brother better get small fast before he's picked up for the jewelry heist.

get someone's goat (*verb phrase*) General: to irritate someone

I think it really got Dinah's goat that Mallory won the composition contest.

get stiffed (*verb phrase*) Food, Bars: to be left without a tip by a restaurant or bar patron; term used by restaurant and bar servers

Bummer! That table stiffed me after ordering me around like a servant for three hours!

get the hook (*verb phrase*) Entertainment: to remove a performer from the stage when he or she is performing badly

Sonia was so off-key during the audition she got the hook.

get through to (*verb phrase*) General: to make someone understand

I hope I'm getting through to you on the new house rules.

get to first base (*verb phrase*) General: to succeed at the first stage of something; literally, to succeed in reaching first base as a batter

I've got to get to first base with Toyco before I can convince them to hire us.

get to the bottom of (*verb phrase*) General: to determine the real cause of

I'd like to get to the bottom of this budget-gate right now.

get to the heart of (*verb phrase*) General: to determine the most important element of

I'm hoping a therapist will help you get to the heart of your problems with your parents.

get the ax (*verb phrase*) General: to be fired

I'm afraid I'm going to get the ax when they begin those layoffs.

get the ball rolling (*verb phrase*) General: to begin

Let's get the ball rolling on the kitchen renovations.

get the goods on (*verb phrase*) General: to find proof of one's guilt

Wally's got the goods on Denise, who's been embezzling from the company.

get the lead out (*verb phrase*) General: to hurry

I wish you'd get the lead out so we're not late for school again

get the message (*verb phrase*) General: to understand fully; also known as get the picture

Do you get the message? I said, no more roughhousing at the pool.

get the show on the road (*verb phrase*) General: to begin

I'd like to get to Tulsa by night-fall, so let's get this show on the road.

get under one's skin (*verb phrase*) General: to upset

Don't let that attorney get under your skin when she's questioning you.

get what's coming to one (*verb phrase*) General: to receive what one deserves, good or bad

She cheated me out my chance at the lead, and now she's going to get what's coming to her.

get wind of (*verb phrase*) General: to hear about

I got wind of your promotion from our old college buddies.

get with it (*verb phrase*) General: to pay attention

You better get with it and start making some money.

get with the program (*verb phrase*) General: to make one-self aware

I wish she'd read the newspaper once in a while and get with the program.

ghost (*noun*) Teen & College: one who rarely makes an appearance

I guess I've been a ghost since I started working nights.

ghost of a chance (*noun phrase*) General: the least hint of

You don't have a ghost of a chance of winning that lottery.

ghost speech (*noun phrase*)

Government: legislator's speech that is not actually delivered, but simply inserted in the Congressional Record as if it had been
As they near the end of a long and difficult session most legislators are grateful when their colleagues give a ghost speech instead of the real thing.

gifted child (*noun phrase*) Education: child with special skills or talents, or with a great aptitude for learning; also known as: exceptional child
Alicia was placed in the gifted child program at the grammar school.

gilligan (*noun*) Surferspeak: idiot; *see also:* Barney
Who's that gilligan blocking your car in the parking lot?

ginzy trading (*noun*) Wall Street: unethical practice of quoting different prices to customers on the same buy and sell order
Jerry was dismissed from his position when the partners discovered he had been ginzy trading with long-time clients of the firm.

girly mon (*noun phrase*) Teen & College: weak, unassertive guy; from the Hans and Franz skits on "Saturday Night Live"
Don't be such a girly mon and go get me the sandwich I ordered.

give a hand (*verb phrase*) General: to assist
I'd be happy to give you a hand with those groceries.

give-and-take (*noun*) General: flexibility, sense of sharing
Let's use a little give-and-take here and I think we can come up with a solution.

give chase (*verb phrase*) General: to run after
The little boy gave chase to the butterfly, but soon it was gone.

give cuts (*verb phrase*) Teen & College: to allow someone to step ahead in line
I gave Janie cuts in the lunch line because she had to rush back to her office.

give five (*verb phrase*) General: to greet someone by hand; also known as: give some skin
Hey, give me five! I haven't seen you since last winter!

give ground (*verb phrase*) General: to retreat
I'm not going to give ground on this policy.

give one's eyetooth for (*verb phrase*) General: to be willing to give anything to have something
I'd give my eyetooth for curly hair like Susan's.

give one's right arm (*verb phrase*) General: to give something of great value
I'd give my right arm to have seen the Babe play baseball.

give skin (*verb phrase*) Street: to slap hands with someone, as a form of greeting or celebration
Give me some skin! That was a great shot!

give someone a piece of one's mind (*verb phrase*) General: to tell someone what one really thinks
Next time she snubs me in public like that, I'm going to give her a piece of my mind.

give someone the time of day (*verb phrase*) General: to care about someone enough to pay attention to them; usually used in the negative
Once the lawyer was promoted to partner, she refused to give the paralegals the time of day.

give someone a wedgie (*verb phrase*) Teen & College: to pull someone's underwear up in back so that it is uncomfortably wedged in between one's buttocks; a wedgie is also known as a Melvin
I was trying to have a nice conversation with Colleen when Darren came up behind me and gave me a wedgie. I was moded.

give someone the cold shoulder (*verb phrase*) General: to behave in an intentionally unfriendly way
I saw David at the beach and I gave him the cold shoulder.

give someone the once over (*verb phrase*) General: to look carefully at someone
Dennis gave the man at the door the once over before asking him to leave.

give someone the third degree (*verb phrase*) General: to question someone closely
Why are you giving me the third degree? I didn't do anything wrong!

give something a shot (*verb phrase*) General: to attempt something
I think I should give that new job at least a shot.

give the devil his due (*verb phrase*) General: to be fair to someone, even if he or she is bad or unlikable
He's mean, but to give the devil his due, he's a good teacher.

give the slip (*verb phrase*) General: to escape from
Mortimer gave the cops the slip when he hid in the alley behind the drugstore.

give up the digits (*verb phrase*) Teen & College, Street: to give out one's telephone number
Ron was upset that the young woman he had met at the party wouldn't give up the digits.

give up the ghost (*verb phrase*) General: to expire
Our car gave up the ghost about a mile from the Grand Canyon.

give up the ship (*verb phrase*) General: to surrender or give up; usually used in the negative
Our team is behind, but we won't give up the ship.

give wide berth to (*verb phrase*) General: to keep a safe distance from
The captain advised his guests

to give wide berth to the boat's churning motor.

gladhand (*verb*) General: to greet people superficially

The senator stopped in at the reception, gladhanded for few minutes, then left.

glass arm (*noun phrase*) Sports (Baseball): pitcher's arm that is highly prone to injury or strain

Against all expectations, the Redbirds' new pitcher turned out to have a glass arm.

glass ceiling (*noun phrase*) Press: perceived limits to the advancement of women and minorities in the public and private sector

Though women had made great strides in the film industry, there was no sense that the glass ceiling had been shattered in the upper echelons of power.

glass jaw (*noun phrase*) Sports (Boxing): boxer's tendency to succumb to a strong hit to the chin

The Bammer knew his opponent had a glass jaw, so he concentrated on connecting to the chin.

glitch (*noun*) Computerspeak: hardware error or flaw

The technician was relieved to see that a simple loose connection caused the glitch.

gloss over (*verb phrase*) General: to make things look easy or better

My parents are always glossing over the problems in our family.

glue foot (*noun phrase*) Surferspeak: surfer who is sure-footed on the surfboard

Joanna's a real glue foot out there.

G.M. (*proper noun*) Fantasy: initialism for Game Master, the person in a role-playing game who is responsible for coordinating the story, defining the game world for the players, and acting as an overall supervisor

Tom made a perfect G.M. because he had a lot of imagination and loved to be in control.

gnarlatious (*adj.*) Surferspeak: terrific

I've had one gnarlatious day of surfing after another this week.

gnarly 1. (*adj.*) Surferspeak: tough and dangerous, referring to a wave

I have this recurring nightmare that I lose two teeth wrestling with a gnarly wave.

2. (*adj.*) Teen & College: gruesome and disgusting

That slasher movie was so gnarly I couldn't even watch.

go (*verb*) Teen & College: to say

So then I go, "What do you want me to do about it?"

go against the grain (*verb phrase*) General: to cause trouble or dissension

The new tenant's loud and messy habits went against the grain of his quiet, orderly neighbors.

go ape *(verb phrase)* General: to become excited

You should have seen Dylan go ape when the Redbirds won the game.

goat *(noun)* Government & Politics: mildly derogatory term for constituents, usually used by legislators' staff members.

The Congressional intern was assigned the task of responding to goat's mail, and by the end of the summer she had developed a hard disdain for the insensitivity of the political process.

goat food *(noun phrase)* Government & Politics: action done by a legislator simply to look good in the eyes of the constituents

The senator's impassioned speech on human rights was pure goat food, and the press reported it as such.

go ballistic *(verb phrase)* Teen & College: to become extremely upset

My parents went ballistic when they heard my brother skipped school yesterday.

gobbing *(verb)* Entertainment: spitting at punk rock musicians as a sign of appreciation for their performance

The delirious fans were gobbing on the Dregheads at the end of the concert.

go belly up *(verb phrase)* Business: to go out of business;

see also: close doors, go south, and went toes

The 75-year-old department store finally went belly up after years of difficult business.

god *(noun)* Teen & College: attractive male

Suzette's going out with some god from the fraternity.

godly *(adj.)* Teen & College: cool, very appealing

That new guy seems godly. Have you met him yet?

go down in flames *(verb phrase)* General: to fail disastrously; *see also:* **go up in smoke**

The artist's career went down in flames after a third unsuccessful movie.

go every which way *(verb phrase)* General: to be askew, chaotic

When Darla stepped out of her convertible, her hair was flying every which way.

go eyeball to eyeball *(verb phrase)* General: to accept or initiate a challenge

I'll go eyeball to eyeball on the tennis court with you.

gofer *(noun)* General: low-level employee, whose responsibility is usually to run around and fetch things

When I was a teenager, I was a gofer on an archeological dig for a summer.

go flat *(verb phrase)* General: to stop increasing

After a brief surge at the beginning of the year, the soft drink's sales went flat.

go for broke *(verb phrase)* General: to risk everything

I've decided to go for broke and open a restaurant.

Go for it! *(expression)* General: Go ahead, take a risk, do it!

I think you should take that job. Go for it!

go-getter *(noun)* General: ambitious person

Seema, always a go-getter, made her first million dollars before she was thirty.

Go-go *(acronym)* Military: Government-Owned, Government-Operated facility

The space lab was pure go-go, and no private enterprises were involved in the top-secret research project.

go haywire *(verb phrase)* General: to become inoperative

My computer went haywire over the weekend, so I couldn't finish that project.

go hell for leather *(verb phrase)* General: to move very rapidly

You've been going hell for leather ever since you got that promotion.

go home in a box *(verb phrase)* General: to die

I'm no sissy, but I don't want to go home in a box.

going for one *(adj. phrase)* General: working in one's favor

You'll get that job; you've got a lot going for you.

goldbricker *(noun)* General: one who connives to avoid work

It irked Sally that her boss had no idea what a goldbricker Steve was.

golden *(adj.)* Teen & College: excellent, in prime condition

The doctor says as soon as I finish physical therapy on my knee I'll be golden.

golden ager *(noun phrase)* Press: senior citizen

When Mark's dad turned sixty, he qualified for many golden ager discounts.

golden coffin *(noun phrase)* Business: benefits package payable to an executive's heirs upon his or her death

Monroe insisted that his contract feature a golden coffin, which would take care of his wife's needs on his passing.

golden gater *(noun phrase)* Entertainment: truly awful, unredeemable script; referring to San Francisco's Golden Gate Bridge, where many have chosen to commit suicide

The studio executives first tried to salvage the golden gater, then decided they'd have to scrap it.

golden handcuffs *(noun phrase)* Business: compelling package of perks and benefits offered to executives to keep them locked into their jobs for a certain period of time

The top executives were the key to the company's value, so they were plied with golden hand-cuffs.

golden parachute *(noun phrase)* Business: compensation package offered to executives to entice them to stay on, even though they fear the company will be taken over by an outside party

The CEO accepted the generous golden parachute, though there was every indication that the company would not be able to thwart the takeover.

gold mine *(noun phrase)* General: profitable enterprise

Terry's frozen lemonade stand at the beach was a gold mine.

go naked *(verb phrase)* Wall Street: risky maneuver where one sells a stock one does not actually own or sells an option without owning the security to which it is linked

The broker must have been desperate or overconfident to jeopardize his best account by going naked on the Bestco stock.

go negative *(verb phrase)* Government & Politics: to take the adverse approach; from the emergence in the 1980s of strong negative advertising in political campaigns

Senator Dogood's handlers finally convinced him that it was time to go negative on his opponent or risk losing the election.

go–no-go *(noun phrase)* Air & Space: point beyond which there is no turning back when deciding whether or not to go ahead with a launch

The go–no-go depends on whether the blast shields are properly in place yet.

goob *(noun)* Teen & College: unpopular, awkward person; *see also:* dork, dweeb, fred, geek, goof, nerd, squid and swivel-neck

For the first three months in her new school, Terry felt like a total goob and a loser.

Good answer! *(expression)* Teen & College: Yes, that's right! Excellent!; from the television game show "Family Feud"

Did you say you could come over and help me with my math assignment? Good answer!

Good deal! *(expression)* Teen & College: That's great!

You got your package from home? Good deal!

good egg *(noun phrase)* General: agreeable, likeable sort of person

That new mail carrier really is a good egg.

goodfella *(noun)* Crime & Law: operative of the mob; see also: buttonman, goombah, soldier and wiseguy

The police observed a bunch of goodfellas smoking cigarettes in front of the cafe on Oak Street.

good guy 1. *(noun phrase)* General: honest, decent person in a situation; as opposed to the bad guy, who is the dishonest character (refers to both sexes); *see also:* white hat
The hospital accountant turned out to be the good guy in the scandal at the clinic.

2. *(noun phrase)* General: decent, friendly, likeable person; *see also:* regular guy
Joe is such a good guy; I wish he'd marry my sister.

good hands *(noun phrase)* Sports: natural ability to catch a ball and avoid dropping it
Littlefield was super-fast, had good hands, and a quick mind—a perfect player.

good hejab *(noun phrase)* Foreign (Arab): proper Islamic dress; *see also:* bad hejab
The elderly patriarch was proud to see all of his daughters and granddaughters wearing good hejab.

good to go *(adj. phrase)* Street: going well
My new classes are good to go, I'm glad to say.

gooey *(noun)* Teen & College: girlfriend
You can't even talk to Darryl anymore because he's all wrapped up in his gooey.

goof *(noun)* Teen & College: unpopular, awkward person; *see also:* dork, dweeb, fred, geek, goob, nerd, squid and swivelneck

Gerald felt like a goof after he screwed up his act in the school variety show.

go off half-cocked *(verb phrase)* General: to say or do something without preparing or thinking about it in advance
Devon went off half-cocked and bought a new Jeep.

go off the deep end *(verb phrase)* General: to have an emotional breakdown
I think Vinnie went off the deep end when Charlene left him.

goof off *(verb phrase)* General: to avoid one's responsibilities
You've been goofing off all afternoon and now there's no time to mow the lawn before dinner.

goo-goo *(noun)* Government & Politics: individual or group committed to Good Government and political reform; term used first in the early 1900s
The senator had become cynical over the years and had little patience left to cater to goo-goo groups.

goombah *(noun)* Crime & Law: operative of the mob; *see also:* button man, goodfella, soldier, and wiseguy
The feds picked up a couple of goombahs trying to slip out of the country with a suitcase of cash.

go on a _____ run *(verb phrase)* Teen & College: phrase used to describe a trip to pick up or buy something

I'm going out on a beer run. Need anything else?

goon squad *(noun phrase)* General: group enlisted to intimidate others

That team of lawyers Trilling hired is just a goon squad he's using to harass people who owe him money

goosy *(adj.)* General: nervous

I'm a little goosy about giving that speech tomorrow.

go out of one's way *(verb phrase)* General: to make a special effort

I don't want you to go out of your way to get me that book, but if it's no trouble, I'd appreciate it.

go out with a bang *(verb phrase)* General: to end something in an unforgettable way

I may be a low-key guy, but I'd like to go out with a bang.

go overboard *(verb phrase)* General: to be excessive

Please don't go overboard buying supplies for our camping trip.

go over someone's head *(verb phrase)* General: to attempt to accomplish something by bypassing one's immediate superior and appealing to a higher-placed individual; also known as: going around

I'm afraid I'll have to go over Johnny's head to get approval to hire a new assistant.

go over the wall *(verb phrase)* General: to escape

After three long weeks, the bored campers decided to go over the wall one Saturday night.

go public *(verb phrase)* General: to reveal openly; *see also:* **out**

We're not ready to go public with the study's findings because they're sure to be controversial.

gorilla *(noun)* Entertainment: huge hit; *see also:* **boffo**

The director had made two gorillas in a row and now had her choice of projects.

gork *(verb)* Medical: to anesthetize

When the patient was completely gorked, the orderlies moved the gurney to the operating room.

go sharking *(verb phrase)* Surferspeak: go surfing

We're going sharking after school, Mom.

go south *(verb phrase)* General: to go out of business, to fail; *see also:* close doors, go belly up, and went toes

No one could have predicted that the restaurant would go south so soon after opening.

go straight *(verb phrase)* General: to become an honest person

I promised my family I'd go straight when I got out of prison.

go the extra mile *(verb phrase)* General: to try as hard as possible

I promise I'll go the extra mile to make this partnership.

got it going on *(verb phrase)*
Street: looking good
Hey, you've got it going on tonight.

go toe-to-toe *(verb phrase)*
General: to challenge aggressively
I finally had to go toe-to-toe with Jim the other day.

go-to guy *(noun phrase)*
Sports: player upon whom a team can always rely to provide the extra spark or effort required to win a tough contest
Jann had proven to be the team's go-to guy that season, though he wasn't even a starter the year before.

go to bat for *(verb phrase)*
Sports (Baseball): to show support for someone; literally, to bat in place of someone else
I'd go to bat for you anytime. Just let me know what you need me to do.

go to one's head *(verb phrase)* General: to give one a distorted or inflated perception of oneself
All of those good reviews have gone to Bart Marlowe's head.

go to pieces *(verb phrase)*
General: to become anguished or emotionally unstable
When the value of the yen dropped sharply, the fledgling investor almost went to pieces.

go to pot *(verb phrase)* General: to degenerate
My garden went to pot when

I was on vacation.

go to the doctor *(verb phrase)*
Teen & College: to drink alcohol
I am so sick of studying I've got to go to the doctor tonight.

go to town 1. *(verb phrase)*
General: to do a great job
Those guys really went to town building that jungle gym in our back yard.
2. to enjoy oneself exceedingly, to celebrate
We really went to town last night after winning the game.

got to hand it to *(verb phrase)*
General: to give credit to
You've got to hand it to Denny for knowing his business so well.

gouge 1. *(verb)* Teen & College: to take something away from someone
How could you gouge Randy like that by going out with Moira?
2. *(verb)* General: to charge too much money for something
I think that office supply shop gouges on everything because it's the only one in town.

go under the knife *(verb phrase)* General: to have surgery
Listen, my father's about to go under the knife. Can we talk later?

go up in smoke *(verb phrase)*
General: to disappear; *see also:* go down in flames
Kristin's dreams of being a professional skater went up in smoke when her knee was injured in a car accident.

go upside one's face *(verb phrase)* Teen & College: to get into a physical altercation
I thought that woman on the train was going to go upside your face when you moved her coat to sit down.

go whole hog *(verb phrase)* General: to do something thoroughly
My mother wants to go whole hog and give us a big wedding.

go without saying *(verb phrase)* General: to be so obvious as to not need mentioning
It goes without saying that I think you're the best person for the job.

go with the flow *(verb phrase)* General: to be taken along with the natural chain of events
I'd like to go with the flow for a change, instead of trying to control everything in my life.

Grand Central Station *(proper noun)* General: very busy, crowded situation, refers to a train station in New York City
This kitchen is like Grand Central Station tonight.

grandstand *(verb)* General: to perform with special intent to garner positive audience reaction; also known as: play to the gallery
The candidate gave a speech that was the worst kind of grandstanding, all platitudes and populist catchphrases with no substance.

G.Q. *(adj.)* Teen & College: well dressed, sharp; from *Gentlemen's Quarterly* magazine
Todd looked real G.Q. for his senior pictures.

granny dumping *(noun phrase)* Government & Politics: purposeful disassociation of a family from their elderly relative as a way to force the government to pay the expenses of caring for that relative
The cost of caring for the elderly had skyrocketed due to the increased instances of granny dumping all over the country.

granny flat *(noun phrase)* Real Estate: renovation or addition to a residence, which is meant to house an elderly relative
Julie's great-aunt lived in a granny flat at the back of her house.

granola *(noun)* Teen & College: earthy and health-oriented, from granola, a popular health food; also known as: granola head and crunchy granola
This neighborhood is full of granolas with string bags who come to shop at the outdoor market.

grapes *(noun)* Medical: hemorrhoids
The doctor advised laser therapy for the patient with grapes.

grasp at straws *(verb phrase)* General: to make futile efforts
She was grasping at straws trying to come up with an excuse for her behavior.

grassroots *(adj.)* Government & Politics: local constituents, or common people, whose collective impressions form what is known as public opinion
The consultant advised her client to do some grassroots work to bolster the negative image caused by the check-bouncing scandal.

graunch *(noun)* Computer-speak: monumental error
Cora was horrified to discover the graunch that had rendered the day's work useless.

gravy train *(noun phrase)* General: position with excessively high compensation
Moe took this research associate's job that is a gravy train.

gravy *(noun)* General: benefits, monetary or otherwise, beyond what one expects
Once I meet my expenses this month, the rest is gravy.

gray area *(noun phrase)* General: matter that is unclear or uncertain
The long-term consequences of the new regulations were a gray area that legislators were not prepared to explore.

gray ghost *(noun phrase)* Government & Politics: legislator's top aide
The lobbyists joked that talking to the senator's gray ghost was better than talking to the aging senator himself, who could hardly hear anymore anyway.

gray market *(noun phrase)* Business: retail enterprise that is neither entirely legitimate nor illegal (black market)
Most electronics products are available at significant savings on the gray market.

gray matter *(noun phrase)* General: smarts, intelligence; refers to the gray tissues of the brain
Enough partying! I'm ready to develop my gray matter and get some A's.

graze *(verb)* Food: to eat several small portions or appetizers instead or a normal-sized entree
Ken often got annoyed when Claire grazed at a meal because she always ended up eating his food.

grease *(noun)* Wall Street: huge commission on the sale of a stock that was acquired by the broker or firm at a very cheap price, then sold to a customer
"There's nothing like some grease to make the hard deals go down a little easier," the broker bragged.

grease one's palm *(verb phrase)* General: to bribe someone
Why don't you grease the maitre d's palm so we can get a really nice table?

greasy spoon *(noun phrase)* General: inexpensive little restaurant; usually a diner
Let's get some lunch at that greasy spoon around the corner.

great guns (adv. phrase) General: extremely fast or vigorously

That new machine is operating great guns, turning out three thousand units an hour.

green (noun) General: money; also known as: cabbage, coin, dough, jack, lettuce, simoleons, and skins

That property must have cost you plenty of green.

greenback green (adj. phrase) Business, Ecology: describing those willing to spend money on environmental issues and environmentally sound products

The new line of paper products was slightly more expensive than its competitors, but was directly targeted at the greenback green consumer.

greenhorn (noun) General: inexperienced, unsophisticated person

Steve and Sonya felt like greenhorns among the political bigwigs and society people at the benefit.

greenie (noun) Government & Politics: environmentalist

The congresswoman's office was deluged with angry mail from greenies who protested her vote on the off-shore drilling bill.

greenlock (noun) Traffic: traffic congestion surrounding national parks and forests during the high tourist season

The kids couldn't wait to see "Old Faithful," but the car sat for an hour in greenlock outside of Yosemite.

green light (verb phrase) Entertainment: final studio executive approval that puts a film or television program on the track to production; also used as a general term for official approval

Only the studio's top executives had the power to green light a film that would cost so much to make.

greenmail (noun) Business: money paid by a company to thwart the efforts of those attempting a takeover

The small electronics company didn't have the resources to pay the greenmail that might hold the raider at bay.

green marketing (noun phrase) Business, Ecology: effort of corporations to convince the public that their products are environmentally sound and that they are ecologically committed on a global scale

Acme hired a special consultant to help the company shift into the green marketing arena.

green product (noun phrase) Business, Ecology: environmentally sound product

You have several choices, but perhaps you should consider the green product.

green monster (noun phrase) Surferspeak: huge wave

I got prosecuted by that green monster.

Green Room 1. *(proper noun)* Entertainment: place where performers or guests wait before going on stage—hardly ever green

The world champion baton twirler was thrilled to meet her favorite rock star in the Green Room of the Midnight Talk-a-lot Show.

2. *(noun)* Surferspeak: tube of a wave, as seen from the inside

The wave was so perfect I felt like I would stay in the green room forever.

green seal *(noun phrase)* Ecology: label on a product indicating that it is environmentally sound

I thought this stuff was biodegradable, but I don't see a green seal anywhere on the packaging.

green thumb *(noun phrase)* General: natural talent for gardening

My mother has a green thumb, but I couldn't grow weeds if I had to.

greenwashing *(verb phrase)* Media: company's extensive public relations efforts to convince consumers or investors that it is environmentally sensitive

Increased sales proved that Acme's costly greenwashing program was finally beginning to pay off.

gremlin *(noun)* Surferspeak: beginner surfer

What's with all the gremlins out today?

grifter *(noun phrase)* Crime & Law: one who makes a living off of money scams and swindles

J.T. wanted to become a blackjack dealer but ended up a grifter who worked the crowds at the casino.

grill *(noun)* Teen & College: face

Where'd you get that nasty scratch on your grill?

grind *(verb)* Surferspeak: to surf aggressively and well

I really think I was grinding today.

grindage *(noun)* Teen & College: food

Let's go to Timmy's and get some grindage.

grinder 1. *(noun)* Food: sandwich served on an Italian roll; also known as: hero, hoagie, sub, torpedo, and wedge

The kids were amazed when Molly set the humongous cold-cut grinder down on the table.

2. *(noun)* Seafarers: winch that controls the sails of a sailboat; also known as: a coffee grinder; person who operates this winch is also known as a grinder

The grinder was expected to have great stamina and coordination for the furious effort required during the race.

3. *(noun)* Surferspeak: large wave

I can't believe I missed that grinder!

grind to a halt *(verb phrase)*
General: to come to a slow,
complete stop
*All progress on the renovation
ground to a halt when the contractor stopped paying the suppliers.*

grip *(noun)* Entertainment:
technician on a film set
*Nora worked her way up from
gofer to key grip through hard
work and persistence.*

gritch *(verb)* Computerspeak:
to complain
*There was plenty of gritching in
the repair shop as the technicians
received their assignments.*

grok *(verb)* Computerspeak,
Sci-fi: to understand fully, especially in the cosmic sense;
from Robert Heinlein's science
fiction novel *Stranger in a
Strange Land*
*I finally grokked there was more
to life than pushing paper.*

grommet *(noun)* Surferspeak:
surfing beginner
*Tell that grommet to get out of
my way! I want this wave.*

gronk *(verb)* Computerspeak,
Office Talk: to clear a machine
that has jammed
*The assistant manager was the
only one who could gronk the
copy machine.*

gronked *(adj.)* Computerspeak:
not functioning
*I've been up all night and I'm
completely gronked.*

groovy *(adj.)* Teen & College:
out of date; usually used in

ironic reference to its original
meaning, which was hip or cool
*I'm sorry, but that teacher is too
groovy for me.*

gross player *(noun phrase)*
Entertainment: movie star so
bankable and successful that she
or he commands a percentage of
a film's gross income
*Bart Marlowe is one of only a
handful of Hollywood's gross
players working today.*

grounded *(adj.)* Teen &
College: confined at home as
punishment; *see also:* housed
*I got grounded for coming
home two hours late the other
night.*

ground zero *(noun phrase)*
Military: point at which a nuclear
weapon makes contact with its
target
*No one ever discussed what
would happen after ground zero,
only the steps leading up to it.*

groupie *(noun)* Entertainment:
obsessive fan who travels extensively to be near the object of
his or her obsession
*Chris was a Dreghead groupie
and traveled with the band for
almost a year.*

growzy *(adj.)* Computerspeak:
descriptive term for a computer
that is slow to respond to commands
*Etta cursed at the time wasted
by her growzy computer.*

grubbin' *(noun)* Teen &
College: delicious food

Julia's mom knows how to make some grubbin'.

grunge *(noun)* Entertainment, Fashion: cultural movement among young people touting spare, downscale clothing and alternative rock and roll

grunts *(noun)* Surferspeak: food
I've got to get some grunts before I keel over.

Gucci gulch *(noun phrase)* Government & Politics: mildly derogatory term for the lobbying community in Washington, D.C.
I'm sure you're making plenty of money down in Gucci gulch now that your party's back in power.

guerilla marketing *(noun phrase)* Business, Advertising: marketing tactic that calls for people to distribute samples of a product in order to determine consumer response on the spot.
The guerilla marketing of the new soft drink found a tendency of the consumer to be attracted more to the packaging than the flavor.

gumby *(noun)* Teen & College: doltish person
The substitute is a real gumby, and I don't think we'll have trouble getting out of class.

gun for *(verb phrase)* General: to try extremely hard to achieve
I'm working late again tonight because I'm gunning for a raise.

guns *(noun)* Teen & College: muscles
Hedda's gotten some serious

guns this season running cross country.

gun shy *(adj. phrase)* General: highly cautious, especially avoiding a situation one has had a bad experience with before
Gina became gun shy about driving at night after she wrecked her car coming home late from work.

guppie *(acronym)* Press: Gay Upwardly Mobile Professional
The new magazine was marketed toward guppies.

gut reaction *(noun phrase)* General: instinct
My gut reaction to your proposal is to say let's go for it.

gutter wear *(noun phrase)* Teen & College: hip, sloppy clothing; key to achieving the grunge look
Shelby's mom hated her spending money on gutter wear, which made her look like she shopped in a garbage can.

gweep *(noun)* Computerspeak: one who uses a computer; term used mostly by computer professionals or aficionados to describe people who only know enough about computers to get by at their jobs; *see also:* user
While Brenda explained the procedure for the third time, she had to silently remind herself she was dealing with gweeps.

gym rat *(noun phrase)* Teen & College: one who spends too much time in a gym

Naomi was so into gymnastics the kids were starting to call her a gym rat.

Gypsy Moth *(proper noun)* Government & Politics: liberal to moderate Republican, the Yankee equivalent of a Boll Weevil

The congresswoman was known as a pesky Gypsy Moth to her more conservative colleagues on the committee.

H

hack 1. (verb) Computerspeak: to work on a computer with great affinity and adeptness, for work or fun

Bill hacked his way through the weekend on his new computer, hardly noticing the passage of time.

2. *(verb)* Teen & College: to disassociate oneself from a person or persons quickly

I managed to hack those dweebs who kept talking to me at the party.

hacker *(noun)* Computerspeak: person who delights in the technical and creative aspect of using a computer; the opposite of gweep or user

Gil is such a hacker he won't even leave his computer for an hour.

hack attack *(noun phrase)* Computerspeak: spell of frantic programming

Josh and June worked all night, having a serious hack attack as they prepared their final exam for

advanced programming class.

hack it *(verb phrase)* General: to cope successfully

I don't know if I can hack it in the majors.

Hail Mary *(proper noun)* Sports (Football): desperation play, usually employed by the losing team, which calls for throwing a pass into a crowded end zone in hopes a teammate will catch it, used generally to mean a final, desperate effort

The last-minute proposal the consultant submitted was a bit of a Hail Mary, but she still had hopes she'd win the contract.

hair *(noun)* Surferspeak: courage

You've got hair to stay out there in those gnarly waves.

hair ball *(noun phrase)* Surferspeak: huge wave

What a hair ball! I've got to get my board out of the car.

hair stand on end *(expression)* General: to be terrified

When he heard the sound of the crash, his hair stood on end.

hairy *(adj.)* General: dangerous

I wish you'd drive more slowly on those hairy curves.

hairy eyeball, the *(noun phrase)* General: a nasty look

The minister gave me the hairy eyeball when I inadvertently laughed out loud during the service.

haken *(verb)* Surferspeak: to go surfing and then have a large meal

Billy and I are haken this after-noon.

half-baked *(adj.)* General: not serious, not well thought out
Meg concocted some half-baked plan to make money for the summer.

half the battle *(noun phrase)* General: hardest part of the work
Admitting one has a problem is half the battle in solving it.

half the pickets are missing from the fence *(expression)* General: in a diminished mental state
I've tried tor reason with Mel, but I think half the pickets are missing from his fence.

hammered *(adj.)* Teen & College: intoxicated
I was hammered last night when I got home and passed out on the couch.

hammer out *(verb phrase)* General: to create with hard work
The diplomats hammered out an agreement between the two countries.

hammock *(verb)* Entertainment: to sandwich a weak television program between two strong shows in an effort to attract the popular shows' viewers
The sitcom only benefited temporarily from being hammocked between two more popular comedies.

handholding *(verb)* Advertising, Public Relations, Business: reassuring a client
Henderson is feeling nervous

about the upcoming ad campaign, so he'll need some handholding.

handle *(verb)* Teen & College: to tolerate or cope
I can't handle Mindy's complaining anymore.

handlers *(noun)* Government and Politics: consultants and staffers who guide an individual, usually a political candidate, through the dangerous maze of press relations, image enhancement, and damage control
The candidate's handlers were slick and managed to put the best face on her many flaws.

hand-me-down *(noun)* General: something that has belonged to someone else before being given away
As kids we hated wearing hand-me-downs because they never seemed to fit.

hand-over-fist *(adv. phrase)* General: fast and in large quantities; usually refers to earning money
Queenie was making money hand-over-fist on the T-shirts she designed.

hands down *(adv. phrase)* General: easily, without a doubt
That is the best ball game I've ever seen, hands down.

hands off *(phrase)* Government, Business: purposely not involved, as a matter of policy
The conservatives prefer to see the department take a hands-off

approach to the labor dispute.

hands on *(phrase)* Government, Business: purposely and visibly involved

The President was praised for her hands-on efforts to convince the public of the need for the tax increase.

handwriting on the wall *(noun phrase)* General: indication or foretelling of something bad

Before John was fired he was severely reprimanded by his boss, so he should have seen the handwriting on the wall.

handyman special *(noun phrase)* Real Estate: property that requires repair or renovation

The cabin was a handyman special, but Sandra relished the thought of working weekends to fix up her little hideaway.

hang 1. *(verb)* General: to wait endlessly

How could you leave me hanging like that? I had to beg a ride home from someone I hardly know.

2. *(verb)* Teen & College: to relax, do nothing

I was just hanging when my dad decided it was time to mow the lawn.

hang a B.A. *(verb phrase)* Teen & College: to pull down one's pants and show one's bare buttocks as a prank

Lefty hung a B.A. out the car window.

hang in the balance *(verb phrase)* General: to be uncertain

Jody's life hung in the balance until the rescue workers arrived.

hang one on *(verb phrase)* General: to get extremely drunk; also known as: tie one on

A bunch of us really hung one on last night and didn't make it to the train on time.

hang out one's shingle *(verb phrase)* General: to open one's own business, especially a medical or law practice

After all those years of studying, it must feel great to finally hang out your shingle.

hang out to dry *(verb phrase)* General: to leave someone to his or her own defense

Quentin was fired and hung out to dry by his former colleagues after he was accused of insider trading.

hangtime *(noun)* Sports: time a ball spends in the air after being hit, kicked, or thrown, or the time a player spends in the air after jumping; *see also:* loft

The slugger hit a homerun that sent the ball into a most extraordinary hangtime, as if it might be suspended in the air forever.

hang-up *(noun)* General: problem, usually of the deep-seated, psychological variety

I finally had to deal with my hang-up about being abandoned as a child when I started thinking about having kids of my own.

hang with *(verb phrase)* Teen & College: to associate with socially; also known as: hanging out with or hanging around with
I've been hanging with the guys on the team for a while now.

happening *(adj.)* Teen & College: hip
That new restaurant is really happening.

happy as a clam *(noun phrase)* General: very content
I'm happy as a clam with my new work schedule.

happy camper 1. *(noun phrase)* Bars: person who is drunk
Don't serve that guy any more booze. He's a happy camper as it is, and we're going to have to call him a cab.
2. *(noun phrase)* General: one who is content with the state of affairs
After her grant came through, Cecile was a happy camper.

happy hour *(noun phrase)* Bars: promotional period before the dinner hour when bars attempt to attract patrons by offering free food and reduced-price drinks
Les and Laura usually skipped dinner on Thursday nights and instead visited a couple of happy hours to fill up on snacks.

hard 1. (adj.) Teen & College, Street: tough
That cop was hard, a real tough guy.

2. *(adj.)* Military: highly protected
The weapons cache was a hard target, covered with cement and disguised by foliage.

hard-and-fast *(adj.)* General: rigidly fixed
These are the hard-and-fast rules of this club, so don't even think about breaking them.

hard as nails *(adj. phrase)* General: tough, impenetrable
The judge was universally considered to be hard as nails, so lawyers were always careful to be thoroughly prepared.

hard copy *(noun phrase)* Computerspeak, Office Talk: actual printout of a document generated on a computer
Why don't you give me a hard copy of that letter so I can mark up some revisions?

hard feelings *(noun phrase)* General: resentment or anger
I don't want there to be any hard feelings between us

hardcores *(noun)* Teen & College: difficult courses
I just barely passed my hardcores this semester, and my parents are about to ground me.

hard money *(noun phrase)* Real Estate: money paid against principal on a property mortgage
The homeowners had been paying hard money against their mortgage for some time, and they now had significant equity.

hard-nosed *(adj.)* General: tough and strict

That hard-nosed Latin teacher doesn't give anyone any room for error.

hard science *(noun phrase)* Sci-fi: older brand of high-technology science fiction where the unknown quantities of fantasy and magic are controlled by the fixed laws of science

Ellen doesn't have the patience for the cyberpunk stuff being written today; she prefers hard science, the classics.

hard sell, the *(noun)* General: aggressive, energetic persuasion

The clerk really gave me the hardsell, and before I knew it I was writing out a check.

hard up *(adj. phrase)* General: deeply in need of luck, money, or some other necessity

Ziggy was so hard up for extra cash he had to work nights and weekends, in addition to his regular day job.

has a screw loose *(expression)* General: in a diminished mental state

Boggs has got a screw loose if he's thinking of running for mayor again.

has-been *(noun)* Entertainment: performer who is long past being popular

For all that fuss about Denny and the Dregheads, it didn't take them long to become has-beens.

hash *(noun)* Computerspeak: unnecessary, unwanted data

Let's clear the hash out of this report, or we'll look like we don't know what we're doing.

hash marks *(noun phrase)* Seafarers: stripes on the sleeves of the uniforms of enlisted members of the Navy; each stripe reflects a term of enlistment

There were so many admirals at the reception, a person could have gone blind starting at all the hash marks.

Hasta la vista! *(expression)* Foreign (Spanish): See you later!

I've had enough of you and your lies. Hasta la vista!

hat act *(noun phrase)* Entertainment: attractive country music performer

We could use a hat act as the headliner for the festival.

hatchet man *(noun phrase)* Government & Politics: person responsible for doing or saying harsh or unpleasant things (refers to both sexes)

The campaign's hatchet man regularly leaked rumors about the candidate's opponent.

hate like poison *(verb phrase)* General: to despise

I hate Vorelli's paintings like poison.

hat hair *(noun phrase)* Teen & College: disheveled hair; the smashed, unattractive look one can achieve by wearing a hat for too long

Don't let him see me! I've got hat hair!

hat trick *(noun phrase)* Sports (Hockey): three or more goals scored during a single game by a single player

Lefeu turned in a great performance during the semi-finals, pulling off a hat trick two night in a row.

haul ass *(verb phrase)* Teen & College: to hurry

We're going to have to haul ass if we're going to catch that train.

hauler *(noun)* Cartalk: car that can move extremely fast (from the term haul ass)

The two-door is fast, but the hatchback is a real hauler.

have a bone to pick *(verb phrase)* General: to have a conflict or argument

I have a bone to pick with you over that remark you made about me in class.

have a cow *(verb phrase)* General: to be extremely upset

Don't have a cow, Mom! I just spilled a little soda.

have a crack at *(verb phrase)* General: to try something; also known as: take a whack at

I'd like to have a crack at that video game.

have a frog in one's throat *(verb phrase)* General: to have a catch in one's voice that goes away once the throat is cleared

Kathy had a frog in her throat and had to excuse herself from the table.

have a good ear *(verb phrase)* General: to have a well-developed aural sense or aptitude

Marcus always had a good ear for new music.

have a good eye *(verb phrase)* General: to have a well-developed visual sense or aptitude

Regina has a great eye for new talent in the art world.

have a good personality *(verb phrase)* Teen & College: to be unattractive

I heard that blind date you have tonight has a good personality.

have a hole in one's head *(verb phrase)* General: to be crazy

I must have a hole in my head to invite twenty teenagers to my house for Keith's birthday party.

have a hollow leg *(verb phrase)* General: to be able to drink or eat excessively without visible repercussions

You better make more snacks for the party. Jane's coming and you know she's got a hollow leg

have an edge on *(verb phrase)* General: to have a slight advantage over

Molly had an edge on her opponent in the polls.

have a nose for something *(verb phrase)* General: to have an aptitude for finding something

You do have a nose for gossip, Corky.

have ants in one's pants *(verb phrase)* General: to be restless or anxious

Sally had ants in her pants about beginning the new writing program.

have a one-track mind *(verb phrase)* General: to be absorbed with only one subject

Wayne has had a one-track mind ever since he decided he was going to win that mathematics competition.

have a way with *(verb phrase)* General: to have a natural talent for or easy relationship with

Whenever there was a problem, the staff called on the file clerk who seemed to have a way with computers.

have been around *(verb phrase)* General: have experience; short for: have been around the block

The police officers had been around and knew every hustler in the area.

have butterflies *(verb phrase)* General: to be nervous

Eve always has the butterflies before going on stage.

have dead to rights *(verb phrase)* General: to be inarguably correct in an accusation against someone

Once a key piece of evidence was uncovered, the detective knew she had the suspect dead to rights.

have eyes only for *(verb phrase)* General: to want nothing but

The little boy ignored his other gifts: He had eyes only for the red bicycle.

have great chemistry *(verb phrase)* General: to have a naturally pleasant and fruitful relationship, to enjoy a mutual attraction; also known as: have good karma

The two leads in the musical had great chemistry and they even sang well together. ·

have guts *(verb phrase)* General: to be courageous

He really has guts if he thinks he can save that company.

have it both ways *(verb phrase)* General: to have the advantage of two positions, without having to make a choice

I'm unwilling to admit that I can't have it both ways: I want a high-quality product at a reasonable price.

have it in for *(verb phrase)* General: to feel bitter and vengeful against

After forgetting to cancel the reservations, Rudy feared his fiancee would have it in for him.

have it made in the shade *(verb phrase)* General: to have it easy

Ever since I hired that terrific secretary, I've had it made in the shade.

have no life *(verb phrase)*

Teen & College: to have a pathetic social or personal life
All I do is work. I have no life.

have one's back to the wall
(verb phrase) General: left without recourse
I had to give the customer the discount because she had my back to the wall.

have one's hands full *(verb phrase)* General: to be extremely busy
The young couple has their hands full with three small children.

have one's head in the sand *(verb phrase)* General: to choose to be ignorant
School officials have their heads in the sand about discrimination in fraternities and sororities.

have one's heart in the right place *(verb phrase)* General: to have good intentions
Ivan's heart is in the right place, but he probably isn't qualified to lead the group.

have one's name on *(verb phrase)* General: to be just right for someone
That dress has my name on it!

have one's nose in the air *(verb phrase)* General: to be snobbish
Julia has her nose in the air now that she goes to that swanky private school.

haver *(noun)* Real Estate: party who owns just the property a buyer is looking for
I'm trying to make a deal with a haver who is really gouging us on the price.

have rocks in one's head *(verb phrase)* General: to have poor judgment
Devon must have rocks in his head to think that used car he bought will run for very long.

have someone eating out of the palm of one's hand *(expression)* General: to have complete control over someone
After just ten minutes, the comic had the audience eating out of the palm of her hand.

have someone's number *(verb phrase)* General: to know someone extremely well, to know what motivates someone
Collin really has the boss' number, evidenced by the way he accurately predicts her reactions.

have the hots for *(verb phrase)* General: to be attracted to
Jill had the hots for Gino, but she was afraid to say anything.

have the last laugh *(verb phrase)* General: to be right in the end
The daring scientist knew she'd have the last laugh when she showed her colleagues the test result.

have the whammy on someone *(verb phrase)* General: to understand what motivates or moves someone

I wish he didn't have the whammy on me, because it's so easy for him to manipulate me.

have the willies *(verb phrase)* General: to be uneasy or frightened

That banging noise outside is giving me the willies.

have two strikes against *(verb phrase)* General: to be at a disadvantage

The candidate has two strikes against her: She's not bilingual and she has no diplomatic experience.

hawk *(noun)* Government & Politics: elected official who tends to favor military intervention and increases in military spending

The hawks and doves were, predictably, in disagreement over the military base closings.

hawk *(verb)* Street: to crowd someone

Why are you hawking me, Joe? Would you give me some air here?

head *(noun)* Seafarers: bathroom

When Bronson finally emerged from the head after his bout with seasickness, his shipmates started clapping.

head count *(noun phrase)* Government & Politics: way a vote appears to be turning out, through the eyes of the most interested parties

The lobbyist took a head count

on the telecommunications bill and felt confident that the results would be favorable.

headbanger *(noun)* Teen & College: heavy metal fan; *see also:* metalhead

I sit between two headbangers in English, so I have no one to talk to.

headhunter *(noun)* Business: person who looks for qualified job candidates and matches them up with suitable and available jobs

Even though Gina was happy with her position in the engineering firm, headhunters would call regularly hoping to recruit her away to a new job.

headliner *(noun)* Entertainment: featured performer of a concert, nightclub act, or other entertainment event

The Moroccan Magicians were the headliners for the benefit's extravaganza.

head over heels *(adv. phrase)* General: completely, entirely

Kitty was head over heels in love with the rock star she interviewed.

heads *(noun)* Business: mildly derogatory term for the workers in a manufacturing or assembly plant

We're short a few heads in the tool department.

head start *(noun phrase)* General: early advantage or beginning

I'd like to get a head start on that report due next week.

hear through the grapevine *(verb phrase)* General: to become aware of by listening to gossip
I heard through the grapevine that you're getting married. Is it true?

hearse *(verb)* Street: to kill
JoJo's uncle was hearsed in that burger joint hold-up.

heart of gold *(noun phrase)* General: gentle, generous nature
The neighborhood children occasionally took advantage of Mr Skeeter's heart of gold.

heart of stone *(noun phrase)* General: cold, unforgiving nature
The commanding officer supposedly had a heart of stone so the soliders avoided asking for special dispensations.

heart stops *(verb phrase)* General: to be paralyzed with fright; also known as: heart stands still
My heart stopped when I saw the special news report flash on the television screen.

heart-to-heart *(adj. phrase)* General: serious and intimate
We had a heart-to-heart talk about whether or not we should move.

heat *(noun)* Entertainment: word of mouth
The picture was getting plenty of heat from the press, which was criticizing the film's superficial

treatment of the controversial subject.

heated 1. *(adj.)* Street: extremely angry
Don't go near Ms. Roxbury because she's heated about the fight in the cafeteria.
2. *(adj.)* Teen & College: intoxicated
Bonnie's too heated to drive home.

Heather *(proper noun)* Teen & College: superficial, well-dressed female; from the movie "Heathers"
I can't believe Travis is going out with that Heather.

heavy bead *(noun phrase)* Military: most significant and costly items in the annual military budget
The admiral was willing to trade away lesser programs just to protect the heavy bead in the Navy's budget.

heavy heart *(noun phrase)* General: grief or sorrow
It is with a heavy heart I announce my resignation from this company.

heavy jack *(noun phrase)* General: large amount of money
Maurice is into his brother-in-law for heavy jack on football bets.

heavyweight *(noun)* General: important, influential person
There were a lot of political heavyweights at the legislative conference.

hedgehog *(noun)* Computer-speak: user able to use only

one program or computer system

The new assistant seems a bit of a hedgehog, so I'm not sure how useful he'll be to us in preparing this presentation.

heeled *(adj.)* Crime & Law: carrying a gun; see also: packing heat

Everyone knew that Delores was heeled, "just for protection," she claimed.

hein *(noun)* Teen & College: unattractive person, in looks and/or personality

Tricia's brother was a real hein; he would never drive her anywhere.

hella- *(prefix)* Teen & College: very

That was a hellahard physics exam, don't you think?

Hello! *(expression)* Teen & College: This is incredible!

You won the piano competition? Hello!

helter-skelter *(adv.)* General: quickly and with chaos

The large group clambered about the sinking boat helter-skelter.

hemorrhoid *(noun)* Teen & College: person so awkward or unappealing that he or she is painful to be with

I'm not sitting next to that hemorrhoid again in French lab.

Herb *(proper noun)* Street: unassertive, easily intimidated person

Let's go rough up that Herb in front of the market.

here goes *(expression)* General: I'm about to act and I hope I have good luck; also known as: Here goes nothing.

It's time for my driver's license test. Here goes.

hibernaculum *(noun)* Sci-fi: holding unit where a person artificially hibernates during deep space travel

The officer and crew slipped into their hibernacula as the technician prepared the ship for its long journey to the next galaxy.

hickey *(noun)* Wall Street: loss a broker takes when a customer fails to make a payment on a stock purchase or to turn over stock that was offered for sale.

"I got a nasty hickey from that 'great client' you sent my way," Walters complained to his supervisor.

hid *(adj.)* Teen & College: short for hideous

Mark's new haircut is totally hid.

hidden city *(noun phrase)* Travel: city where a flight stops to pick up passengers or refuel

Martha got a cheaper airfare by taking the flight down from New York to Seattle, whose hidden city was Des Moines, her destination.

high and dry *(adv. phrase)* General: without assistance

Richard realized he was high and dry in Rome after the robbery and his companions desertion.

high-and-mighty *(adj.)*
General: self-important and proud
With his high-and-mighty attitude, Mitch will never admit his mistakes.

high concept *(adj. phrase)*
Entertainment: describing a film with a simple, easily summarized plot, slim development of characters and background, and little emphasis on cinematic technique
Bart Marlowe's pictures tended to be high-concept projects.

high beams on *(expression)*
Drug World: high on cocaine
Did you see Joey at the party? His high beams were on all night!

High Frontier *(noun phrase)*
Science, Sci-fi: space, as described by those who see it as a limitless realm for exploration and human habitation
Steve grew up imagining his future would be spent exploring the High Frontier; unfortunately, he became the night manager at the Handee Mart.

high gear *(noun phrase)*
General: full energy and speed
I better get into high gear if I want to finish this story by noon.

high rider *(noun phrase)*
Cartalk: vehicle suspended high off the ground; usually refers to four-wheel drive vehicles

Billy was never happier than exploring the off-road trails in his brother's high rider.

highway robbery *(noun phrase)* General: exorbitant price
The price for that simple lamp is highway robbery!

Hill rat *(noun phrase)* Government & Politics: congressional staff person
Paul was a Hill rat for three years before going to law school.

him *(pronoun)* Military: enemy
I think we've got him where we want him. He's bound to surrender before long.

hinge on *(verb phrase)*
General: to be conditional upon
Our receiving the grant hinges on whether we convince the committee our proposal has the most potential.

HINT *(acronym)* Entertainment: Happy Idiot News Talk; the empty, often silly banter between newsreaders on local news programs
It took the new anchor a while to develop a HINT relationship with her new colleagues.

hip hop *(noun phrase)* Street: rap music
Nancy has really gotten into hip hop lately. She's becoming a regular B-girl.

hippy witch *(noun phrase)*
Teen & College: young woman who dresses in the style of the 1960s, usually in all black
Everyone thought Darla was a

hippy witch, but they liked her because she was funny and knew how to tell a story.

hit *(noun)* Drug World: dose (a single snort, puff, injection, or taste) of a drug

Todd offered me a hit, but I said I was trying to cut down.

hit a dinger *(verb phrase)* Sports (Baseball): to hit a homerun; also known as: hit a roundtripper and park it in the bleachers

Lefty hit a dinger in the third inning that almost went out of the ballpark.

hit-and-run *(adj.)* General: quick, unexpected strike and exit; usually refers to a type of car accident where the person who causes the collision leaves the scene without making contact with any of the involved parties

We just did a hit-and-run presentation of our proposal, and we're hoping the effect was dramatic.

hit a nerve *(verb phrase)* General: to raise a sensitive subject unintentionally

Wanda hit a nerve with Jake when she suggested seeing other people.

hit between the eyes *(verb phrase)* General: to make a strong, startling impression

The newspaper's sketch of the burglar hit Lonnie between the eyes; she'd seen that face before.

hit bottom *(verb phrase)*
General: to reach one's lowest point

The artist knew she'd hit bottom when she realized she hadn't lifted a brush in months.

hit it off *(verb phrase)* General: to make a great first impression and initial relationship

The new dance instructor really hit it off with his new students.

hit list *(noun phrase)* Government and Politics: a targeted group of legislators, whether singled out by special intrests groups for their approachability on a particular issue, or by opposing party for possible defeat in the next election

The trade association made up a hit list of legislators who might be persuaded to vote against the trade regulation bill.

hit man *(noun phrase)* Crime & Law: assassin; also known as: enforcer, hired gun, terminator, and trigger man

I think Tommy's brother is a hit man with the mob.

hit on *(verb phrase)* Teen & College: to make a pass at

That girl's been hitting on me all night.

hit paydirt *(verb phrase)* General: to be extremely successful

The small publisher finally hit paydirt with its new travel book series.

hit someone where he/she lives *(verb phrase)* General: to attack someone in his or her most vulnerable spot

When the judge prohibited Bryce from driving for a year, he really hit him where he lives.

hit the ceiling *(verb phrase)*
General: to become extremely angry

Constance will hit the ceiling when she finds out we didn't cover her calls while she was gone.

hit the jackpot *(verb phrase)*
General: to have great luck

Luther hit the jackpot when he met Maria.

hit the mark *(verb phrase)*
General: to succeed

I finally hit the mark with that comment.

hit the roof *(verb phrase)*
General: to become enraged

My dad will hit the roof when he sees that I scratched his car with my bike.

hit the sack *(verb phrase)*
General: to go to bed

I'll hit the sack early tonight because we're going fishing in the morning.

hit the sauce *(verb phrase)*
General: to drink alcohol heavily; also known as: hit the bottle

Henderson started hitting the sauce after he lost his biggest account.

hit the showers *(verb phrase)*
Sports: to go take a shower

I've had enough racquetball for today. Let's hit the showers.

hit the spot *(verb phrase)*
General: to be perfectly satisfactory

That lemonade really hit the spot on such a warm afternoon.

hitting *(adj.)* Teen & College: tasty

That burger is hitting tonight. I might have another.

hit up *(verb phrase)* Teen & College: to borrow something from someone

I hit up Jenson for his chemistry notes before the exam.

hog *(noun)* Cartalk: Harley-Davidson motorcycle

Everyone just stared when Letitia pulled up on a hog in her school uniform.

hold a candle to *(verb phrase)*
General: to compare well with; usually used in the negative

The critics said that the play's new lead couldn't hold a candle to the actor who originated the role.

hold court *(verb phrase)*
General: to be at the center of a gathering, as if one is a king or queen among subjects

Jimmy held court at the bar for three hours, telling jokes and buying round after round of drinks.

hold down the fort *(verb phrase)* General: to manage a situation until reinforcements arrive

Tina held down the fort at Shoe Shack until the other clerks returned from lunch.

hold one's fire *(verb phrase)* General: to refrain from confrontation

Frieda decided to hold her fire when she realized Wally had been under great pressure at home.

hold one's horses *(verb phrase)* General: to wait

Would you hold your horses? I'm just getting my keys!

hold one's nose *(verb phrase)* General: to accept with great reluctance and even disdain

The choice of qualified candidates was very slim, so Marilee held her nose and voted for the least unappealing among them.

hold one's own *(verb phrase)* General: to maintain one's position

I still have plenty of progress to make, but for now I'm holding my own.

hold one's peace *(verb phrase)* General: to keep one's reservations to oneself

Sally's parents held their peace about her daughter's friendships, hoping she would eventually choose better company.

hold one's tongue *(verb phrase)* General: to refrain from speaking

You'd better learn to hold your tongue if you want to succeed in this company.

Hold the phone! *(expression)* Teen & College: Wait a minute!

Hold the phone! You say you've got enough money for pizza?

the hole *(noun)* Crime and Law: solitary confinement in prison; *see also*: Waldorf Astoria

Both convicts were thrown into the hole for fighting.

hole in the wall *(noun phrase)* General: small, unexceptional place

Jess is living in some hole in the wall downtown.

Hollywood shower *(noun phrase)* Seafarers: long, luxurious, hot shower; term used by those at sea who must conserve water and make do with short, occasional, and generally unsatisfying bathing experiences

The ensign could think of nothing but a Hollywood shower as he prepared for his on-shore leave.

home in *(verb phrase)* Press: to bunker down and stay home

It seemed the entire population homed in as the blizzard hit the city.

homeboy/girl *(noun)* Teen & College, Street: friend or acquaintance from one's neighborhood; also known as: holmes, homes, and homie

Oh, that guy's okay. He's a homeboy, just back from a couple years in the service.

homebrew *(noun)* Sports: locally born player

Stillwell was pure homebrew, born and raised less than a mile from the stadium.

homevid *(noun)* Entertainment:

all of the electronic equipment (television, videocassette recorders, etc.) that are used for home entertainment
We're marketing the portable videotape editor to the homevid market.

hondo *(noun)* Surferspeak: derogatory term for a tourist
You can't even get near the beach for all the hondos out today.

honeymoon is over, the *(expression)* General: Brief period of initial good feelings and generosity has ended
The executive knew the honeymoon was over at the new plant when the workers organized a strike.

honk *(verb)* Teen & College: to vomit; also known as: barf, blow lunch, boot, decorate one's shoes, drive the porcelain bus, Earl, heave, hurl, ralph, shout at one's shoes, and yawn in technicolor
Michelle ran to the bathroom and honked right after her bit in the school variety show.

honker *(noun)* Teen & College: big thing
This suitcase is a honker.

hood *(noun)* Street: short for neighborhood
Remember that guy from the hood that went to West Point?

hoof it *(verb phrase)* Teen & College: to walk
I'm going to have to hoof it to work because my bike's in the repair shop.

hook 1. *(verb)* Teen & College: to understand, catch on
Did you hook on the DNA stuff in biology today?

2. *(noun)* Seafarers: anchor
Bryce let the hook down too late and missed the mark completely.

hook, line, and sinker *(noun phrase)* General: in its entirety
The audience seemed to fall for the candidate's speech, hook, line, and sinker.

hook up *(verb phrase)* Teen & College: to launch a romantic or physical relationship
T.J. was hoping to hook up with Lucinda, but she showed up at the party with another guy.

hooligan *(adj.)* Seafarers: sloppy, hasty job improperly done
That resleeving you supervised was hooligan, and this sort of work won't be tolerated.

hoover 1. *(noun)* Teen & College: remarkably big eater
Biff was such a hoover we had to go out for more snacks before the other guests arrived.

2. *(verb)* Wall Street: to acquire stocks as if sucking them up with a vacuum cleaner
All eyes of the market were on Infoco, which was inexplicably hoovering the stock of a small, unknown wire company.

hopped up 1. *(adj. phrase)* General: eager or excited
Judy was all hopped up about the track championships.

2. *(adj. phrase)* General: with many additional features

Teddy's computer was hopped up with a color monitor, modem, and a scanning device.

hop to it *(verb phrase)* General: do something quickly

I'd like to get these letters out this afternoon so let's hop to it.

hormone *(noun)* Teen & College: person who is pre-occupied with sex

Don't be such a hormone!

hornet's nest *(noun phrase)* General: complicated situation where all or most of the parties involved are angry

When Donna ordered the department reorganized, it caused a real hornet's nest.

horse 1. *(noun)* Drug World: heroine; also known as: blue sky and H.

Butch knew Carla had taken a bad turn when he found out she was on horse.

2. *(noun)* Crime & Law, Drug World: individual who smuggles drugs, money, or weapons into a prison

Frankie's spouse reluctantly acted as the horse for him and his cellmates.

horse around *(verb phrase)* General: to play in a physical manner

Winny and her brother broke their mother's favorite vase horsing around in the living room.

horse sense *(noun phrase)*

General: sound judgment

All it takes is horse sense to buy the right new car.

hose *(verb)* Crime & Law: to shoot at with an automatic or semiautomatic weapon

The group gathered in front of the house got hosed by someone in a car driving by.

hot 1. *(adj.)* Teen & College, Street: attractive, appealing, very cool

That motorcycle is hot, Jake. Can I have a ride?

hot and bothered *(adj. phrase)* General: agitated and emotional

Minnie got all hot and bothered when she received her bill from the consultant.

hot air *(noun phrase)* General: foolish nonsense

Don't ever listen to Binky. He'll give you nothing but a lot of hot air

hot bunk *(noun phrase)* Seafarers: bunk shared by sailors who work different shifts and take turns sleeping

Terrence was tired of the hot bunk routine. He wanted a nice comfortable berth where he could set up his stuff and treat it like home.

hotdog *(verb)* Sports: to show off

I hate to see you kids out there hotdogging when you should be doing your drills.

hotdogger *(noun)* General: one

who seeks attention and publicity by behaving outrageously

Smith and Jones are the worst kind of hotdoggers; all they care about is getting mentioned in the gossip columns.

hotline *(noun)* General: telephone service that helps callers with specific problems of questions

The city's new crime hotline was successful in generating new leads on the wave of robberies.

hot potato *(noun phrase)* General: difficult issue

The hot potato of the shareholder's meeting was the exorbitant salaries and perks of the senior execs.

hot shot *(noun phrase)* Drug World: powerful, sometimes lethal dose of heroin

We had to walk Janet around all night after she had that hot shot, just to keep her conscious.

hot water *(noun phrase)* General: trouble

I hope I didn't get you in hot water by dropping you off in front of the church.

house 1. *(verb)* Street: to steal money from

I housed my little brother before I left the apartment this morning.

2. *(verb)* Teen & College, Street: to succeed; from bring down the house

Jonathan housed on his first try on the SATs.

house ape *(noun phrase)* Teen & College: little child

I can't stand watching television at Marina's because there are like a million house apes running around there.

housecleaning *(noun)* Business, Government & Politics: purging of an organization of certain members for a variety of reasons, including budget-cutting, waste-cutting, behaving dishonestly or illegally, etc.

This law firm could use a housecleaning from top to bottom.

housed *(adj.)* Teen & College: confined at home as punishment; *see also:* grounded

I've been housed until Tuesday for swearing at my brother.

house of cards *(noun phrase)* General: unsteady situation

What looked to everyone like a perfect marriage turned out to be a house of cards.

house plant *(noun phrase)* Teen & College: boring person who just sits around the house

My sister never goes out anymore. She's turned into a real house plant.

housewife time *(noun phrase)* Entertainment: radio schedule period between ten o'clock in the morning and three o'clock in the afternoon

The consumer reporter found a nice niche with her radio call-in show, which was broadcast during prime housewife time.

H.O.V. *(noun phrase)* Traffic: initialism for High Occupancy Vehicle, one that carries two or more passengers and receives special traffic considerations to encourage carpooling
The van breezed along in the H.O.V. express lane on the freeway.

How ya livin'? *(expression)* Teen & College, Street: How are you?
How ya livin'? I haven't seen you in weeks.

huffer *(noun)* Drug World: individual who inhales chemical vapors to get high
He started out as just a huffer, then moved on to more dangerous stuff.

hum *(verb)* Street: to stink
Get those boots off my desk. They hum!

humint *(noun)* Military: human intelligence, which is gathered by personal effort, as distinct from sigint, or signal intelligence, which is information gathered by electronic means
The embassy's weaknesses were exposed by humint, when agents infiltrated the staff and observed operations.

hungus *(adj.)* Teen, College, Computerspeak: short for humongous; *see also:* moby
What a hungus burger! We better split it.

hunk *(noun)* General: attractive man
What a hunk Maureen's brother turned out to be!

hurl *(verb)* Teen & College: to vomit; also known as: barf, blow lunch, boag, boot, decorate one's shoes, drive the porcelain bus, earl, heave, honk, ralph, reverse gears, shout at one's shoes, spew, toss, yak, yawn in technicolor and zuke
Brenda was so sick of talking about the incident she thought she was going to hurl.

hustler *(noun)* Drug World, Crime & Law: person who sells drugs or other illegal items or services
"Gene is really just a small-time hustler," the detective allowed.

hygiene *(noun)* Computerspeak: measures taken to prevent computer virus infection
The office manager became a stickler for computer hygiene because she'd seen a system totally contaminated by a preventable virus.

hype *(adj.)* Teen & College, Street: excellent
That book we had to read this weekend for English was hype, don't you think?

hyped *(adj.)* Teen & College: excited, energetic
I was so hyped about the dance I couldn't eat my dinner.

hyperspace *(noun)* Sci-fi multi-dimensional space, where space ships travel faster than light (FTL)
The flight engineer prepared

the ship for the jump to hyper-space.

I

I can live with that *(expression)* Government, Business: somewhat unenthusiastic response to a decision that is usually the result of a compromise or consensus
While it isn't ideal, I can live with the program as amended.

ice *(noun)* Drug World: smokable amphetamine that is similar to crack but more potent and addictive
The police were disturbed at the appearance of ice on the drug market, for it caused more violent and unpredictable behavior in users than crack did.

ice cream habit *(noun phrase)* Drug World: mild drug habit, not a full-fledged addiction
Gina figured she was in no danger of becoming a basehead; she just had an ice cream habit, she told herself.

iceman *(noun)* Sports: hockey player
Warren was fondly referred to in the sports press as the Iceman from the Deep South.

idiot box *(noun phrase)* General: television; also known as: boob tube
I saw the worst movie last night on the idiot box.

idiot cards *(noun phrase)* Entertainment: cue cards used to remind performers of their lines
Cecile had a terrible memory and didn't dare do a show without idiot cards.

I heard that *(expression)* Teen & College: I agree.
You say there's not enough time to finish the lab report? I heard that.

illin' *(adj.)* Teen & College, Street: not right, stupid
Ms. Wilcox is illin' to throw us out of the library.

impact *(verb)* Government: to affect
The new garbage collection policy will certainly impact all segments of the community.

improv *(verb)* Entertainment: short for improvise
Let's improv a few lines here and see how it goes.

I'm sideways *(expression)* Teen & College, Street: I'm leaving. Goodbye.
I've got to pick up my dad at the train station so I'm sideways.

in a drought *(prep. phrase)* Teen & College: long spell without a date or a romantic or physical relationship
Ever since Jeannie broke up with me last summer, I've been in a drought.

in a fog *(prep. phrase)* General: confused
I'm sorry, I'm still in a fog about those production figures.

in a heartbeat *(prep. phrase)*

Teen & College: immediately, without hesitation

I'd take that transfer in a heartbeat.

in a holding pattern *(prep. phrase)* Air & Space: kept in a postponed landing mode, referring to airplanes being delayed from landing due to weather conditions or heavy air traffic; generally, indefinitely postponed or delayed

This project has been in a holding pattern for three weeks, but it's time to jumpstart it again.

in a grip *(prep. phrase)* Teen & College, Street: in a long time

I haven't seen Janie's sister in a grip.

in a lather *(adj. phrase)* General: upset

Mr. Wilson was in a lather because Dennis had glued his shoes to the floor.

in a nutshell *(adv. phrase)* General: briefly and concisely

In a nutshell, what we need is your public support on this issue.

in a pig's eye *(prep. phrase)* General: with no chance, extremely unlikely

Are you going to the dance with Bobby? In a pig's eye!

in a shell *(prep. phrase)* General: in a state of withdrawal or silence

It took several weeks for the therapist to bring her patient out of his shell.

in a world of one's own *(prep. phrase)* General: absorbed with one's own thoughts or environment

My brother is such an intellectual, he always seems in a world of his own.

in circles *(adv. phrase)* General: endlessly and futilely

We've been talking in circles about this problem all afternoon.

in cold blood *(adv. phrase)* General: cruelly and without feeling

The school teacher was convicted of killing his housekeeper in cold blood.

incomplete *(noun)* Teen & College: grade received for a course one simply did not finish

I got an incomplete in comparative literature because I didn't turn in that last paper.

Indians *(noun)* Military: military staff members, as opposed to the Chiefs, or the most senior officers

The Indians circulated the necessary memoranda in preparation for the strategy session.

industry *(noun)* Entertainment:Hollywood movie world, to those in the field

The actor said she never wanted to marry anyone in the industry.

indy *(noun)* Entertainment: independent television station unaffiliated with a national network

The indies were an important source of revenue to the networks because they picked up many network reruns for syndication.

indyprod *(noun)* Entertainment: independent film producer
Winston made her mark as an indyprod and soon she was being wooed by the studios.

inflatable shoe *(noun phrase)* Sports: sports shoe featuring an air pump that inflates pockets within the shoe to provide maximum support, cushioning, and custom fit
The basketball star endorsed the SneakCo's new inflatable shoe.

influence peddling *(noun phrase)* Government & Politics: use of one's contacts and position to apply persuasive pressure on those who were elected or appointed to protect the common good
Mr. Otter was accused of influence peddling when it was discovered he was lobbying his former colleagues in the administration on behalf of his clients.

infomercial *(noun)* Advertising, Media: extended-length commercial advertisement for a product, which mimics a talk show, often with a studio audience and celebrity guests enthusiastically discussing the product
Well-known, but out-of-work actors are trying to get jobs on infomercials because of the good pay and exposure.

infrastructure *(noun)* Government: elements of society's physical existence that connect and serve people and places (roads, bridges, public transportation, sewers, etc.)
The tax cuts have begun to have a negative effect on the city's infrastructure.

in full swing *(prep. phrase)* General: completely functioning
This party wasn't in full swing until Gracie arrived.

inhale *(verb)* Food, College: to eat ravenously and quickly; *see also:* scarf
Ursula inhaled her breakfast and flew out the door to get to her class on time.

in hog heaven *(verb phrase)* General: as happy as could be
I'd be in hog heaven if I could get this project done by Friday.

ins and outs *(noun phrase)* General: intricacies
I'd love to know the ins and outs of the art business.

insane *(adj.)* Surferspeak: terrific
Look at those insane waves out there.

inside lot *(noun phrase)* Real Estate: any lot other than a corner lot
The couple was happy with the condominium they'd found, which was on a prime inside lot and backed up against the woods.

intelligent document *(noun phrase)* Computerspeak: regular paper document featuring coded information that enables it to be read by a computer

The assistant's report was an intelligent document, so it could be processed into the computers at the diplomat's destination.

ink *(noun)* Advertising, Public Relations, Business, Politics: press coverage

What this campaign needs is plenty of ink to get it going again.

ink tag *(noun phrase)* Salespeople: device attached to merchandise that is meant to discourage shoplifting by spurting ink if the tag is mishandled; the tag can only be removed by a special tool

The clerk removed the ink tags from the clothing the customer was buying.

in light of *(prep. phrase)* General: as a result of

In light of recent medical reports, Brenda decided to refrain from smoking at home.

in one fell swoop *(prep. phrase)* General: with a single act

All of the lawyer's objections were dismissed in one fell swoop by the judge.

in one's mind's eye *(prep. phrase)* General: in one's memory

In my mind's eye I can see the girl who sat next to me in kindergarten but I can't remember her name.

in over one's head *(adj.*

phrase) General: involved in something beyond one's qualifications or experience

It didn't take Christine long after taking the job to realize she was in over her head.

interdisciplinary *(adj.)* Government, Education: involving and linking people or groups with different interests or backgrounds

The dean's curriculum reform proposal reflected the faculty's wishes for an interdisciplinary emphasis.

interpersonal *(adj.)* Government, Human Resources: between living, breathing people

Paul has a terrific knack with machinery but noticeably lacks interpersonal skills.

intestinal fortitude *(noun phrase)* General: strength of character, courage; also known as: guts

I hope I have the intestinal fortitude to confront Janine when she returns to the office on Monday.

into thin air *(adv. phrase)* General: entirely and without a trace

As soon as Polly made a doctor's appointment, her symptoms vanished into thin air.

in no time flat *(prep. phrase)* General: immediately

Don't worry, I'll be there in no time flat.

in seventh heaven *(prep. phrase)* General: elated

Louise is in seventh heaven over winning that scholarship.

in the air *(prep. phrase)* General: on everyone's minds

Celebration was in the air when the team returned victorious from the season championships.

in the bag *(prep. phrase)* General: with certainty

We've got this account in the bag.

in the black *(prep. phrase)* Business: out of debt, making a profit

The new software company was in the black by the third quarter of that year.

in the can *(prep. phrase)* Entertainment: film that has completed production but not yet been released

The actress was frustrated: she had two films in the can but no publicity to show for her work.

in the cards *(prep. phrase)* General: foreseeable

I'm not sure marriage is in the cards for me.

in the clear *(prep. phrase)* General: free of difficulty or blame

Drew had to wait until his finances were in the clear before he could pay his mortgage.

in the clouds *(prep. phrase)* General: in a dreamlike state

Ever since she won first place for her essay, Trudy has been in the clouds.

in the doghouse *(prep.* *phrase)* General: in trouble

I'm in the doghouse at home because I forgot to pick up my brother after school.

in the driver's seat *(prep. phrase)* General: in charge, in a position of authority

I don't think there's anyone in the driver's seat at the county office.

in the hole *(prep. phrase)* General: in debt

I'm really in the hole after playing poker last night.

in the hopper *(noun)* Government & Politics: awaiting introduction, referring to new bills deposited in a box on the House clerk's desk

We just got a new version of the insurance bill out of committee and in the hopper.

in the hot seat *(prep. phrase)* General: in a position where one is the focus of criticism or controversy

The candidate was in the hot seat after making a racially insensitive remark.

in the know *(phrase)* General: informed and aware, the opposite of ignorant; *see also:* in the loop and with it

The motel clerk was certainly in the know on the senator's extracurricular activities.

in the line of duty *(prep. phrase)* General: as a matter of course in one's job

Sleepless nights is all in the line of duty for parents of an infant.

in the loop (*prep. phrase*)
Government, Politics:
state of being informed and
aware of the inside goings-on;
see also: with it and in the know
*It was important for the junior
partners to remain collegial
with their superiors and always
to manage to stay in the loop.*

in the market for (*adj.
phrase*) General: looking to buy
*I'm in the market for a used car.
Know any good deals?*

in mothballs (*prep. phrase*)
General, Seafarers: put away in
reserve
*The mighty warship was not out
of commission, just in mothballs
for the time being.*

in the ozone (*prep. phrase*)
Food: term used by restaurant
servers to describe patrons who
are visibly intoxicated
*The guy at table number seven-
teen is in the ozone and can't
figure out his bill.*

in the pipeline (*prep. phrase*)
General: in progress
*We've got a number of projects
in the pipeline for the fall.*

in the pink (*prep. phrase*)
General: healthy, robust
*You look in the pink today. You
must have gotten a good night's
sleep.*

in the raw (*prep. phrase*)
General: naked
Barney likes to sleep in the raw.

in the red (*prep. phrase*)
General: in debt, losing money

*Five years after start-up, the
magazine was still terribly in the
red.*

in the saddle (*adv. phrase*)
General: in a position of command
*The office ran so much more
smoothly when Patrice was in
the saddle.*

in the same boat (*prep. phrase*)
General: in the same position
*All of the employees were in the
same boat when the factory shut
down after the flood.*

in the wake of (*prep. phrase*)
General: just following
*In the wake of the city riots, cur-
fews were imposed in troubled
areas until property could be
repaired.*

in the wind (*adj. phrase*)
General: probably, likely
*Dramatic changes in the cur-
riculum had been in the wind for
years.*

in the works (*prep. phrase*)
General: in progress
*A new menu was in the works for
the restaurant's summer season.*

in-your-face (*adj. phrase*)
Sports: brash, disrespectful, contentious; describing a player's attitude or behavior toward another
player
*The game was wild, full of in-
your-face exchanges, brilliant
performances, and a spectacular final minute.*

iron man/woman (*noun
phrase*) Sports: athlete who has

extraordinary endurance and who will compete to the finish, regardless of injury, weather conditions, etc.

Coach Redfield encouraged the players not to try to be ironmen, and to call time out if they were hurt or worn out.

iron out *(verb phrase)* General: to resolve or come to agreement

The committee ironed out a statement after six hours of heated debate.

irons in the fire *(noun phrase)* General: one's personal and/or professional projects

I have so many irons in the fire I don't even have time to sleep.

irrespective *(adj.)* Government: regardless

The ugly highway dividers will be constructed irrespective of the public's opinion on the matter.

Ishtar, an *(noun)* Entertainment: a stupendously expensive and therefore notorious failure; refers to a very costly, excessesively hyped film that failed miserably; also known as: a Heaven's Gate

Bart Marlowe read the film script but was afraid it would be an Ishtar, so he declined to participate.

I smell ya. *(expression)* Teen & College, Street: I understand. I know how you feel.

You don't have to say any more. I smell ya.

Isn't that special? *(expression)* Teen & College: generic sarcastic response to something that is said or done; from the popular "Church Lady" skits on television's "Saturday Night Live"

You got an A on that paper? Isn't that special?

It ain't all that *(expression)* Teen & College, Street: You have exaggerated.

That movie was okay, but it ain't all that.

It's no skin off my nose *(expression)* General: It doesn't matter to me.

Go ahead and go out with Sheila. It's no skin off my nose.

ivy pole *(noun phrase)* Medical: metal stand from which intravenous equipment is strung

The patient's ivy pole looked like a Christmas tree, all decorated with various bags and tubes.

I.V. *(noun)* Medical: intravenous solution

The patient was having trouble eating, so the doctor ordered him to be given an I.V. feeding.

J

J.O. *(noun)* Teen & College, Street: job

I can't go out tonight. I have to go the J.O. until 10:30.

jab *(verb)* Drug World: to inject heroin

"I've been jabbing for forty years," the older fellow noted wearily.

jack (*noun*) Teen & College: nothing; short for jack shit
You did jack to help us with the party.

jacked (*adj.*) Teen & College: elated
I'm so jacked about my final grade in calculus.

jacked up (*verb phrase*) Crime & Law: caught in the midst of serious legal complications, including being incarcerated, facing multiple charges, and likely multiple jail sentences, with little prospect for a positive resolution of the dilemma; also known as: jammed up
Joey's situation was so jacked up, there was little his attorney could do even to arrange bail.

jacket (*noun*) Crime & Law: prisoner's reputation
Donnelly's jacket is pretty fierce; the whole cellblock just stays out of her way.

jackfrost (*adj.*) Street: extremely cold; see also: bleedin'
It's jackfrost today. I hope we have practice inside.

jack of all trades (*noun phrase*) General: a person who is capable in many areas
Christy was a jack of all trades and always had a number of different deals in the works.

jack someone around (*verb phrase*) General: to lead someone on or play with their emotions
Don't jack me around on this. Do I have a chance at this job?

jake (*verb*) Teen & College: to cancel a commitment
Somebody told me that girl jaked me just because she heard I was a computer major.

jailhouse lawyer (*noun phrase*) Crime & Law: inmate who has made himself completely knowledgeable in matters relating to law, legal representation, and legal appeals
In his twenty years in the big house, Milo had become a savvy jailhouse lawyer.

jam 1. (*noun*) Street: noise level
The jam at the concert was unbelievable.

2. (*verb*) Military: to distort or cause interference, usually to the enemy's electronic communications
The radio operator was able to jam the airplane's transmissions before the enemy's reenforcements could arrive.

3. (*verb*) Teen & College: to be making great progress
Now that I understand the formula, I'm jamming on this algebra homework.

jarhead (*noun*) Seafarers: Marine, to a sailor
"Get a load of the jarheads prancing around the port," the sailors sniggered with disdain.

jaw (*verb*) General: to talk

incessantly
We jawed until well past midnight.

jaw jack *(verb phrase)* Street: to talk excessively
I couldn't even hear the movie because of those kids jaw jacking down in front.

jazzed *(adj.)* Teen & College: thrilled, excited
I've been jazzed for weeks about this concert.

jel *(adj.)* Teen & College: short for jealous
Naomi was mondo jel when she saw Dean with Carla.

Jeopardy champion *(noun phrase)* Teen & College: brainy sort of person who is well versed in trivia; refers to television's game show "Jeopardy"
The guy I went out with last night is cute, but he's a bit of a Jeopardy champion.

jerk someone around *(verb phrase)* General: to manipulate someone
As it turned out, Jeremy's fear that the academic bureaucracy would jerk him around was unwarranted.

jet *(verb)* Street: to leave
Let's jet this movie and check out the party at Sammy's.

jet set *(noun phrase)* Social: glamorous, wealthy, sophisticated people in society
Charlotte has been running around with the jet set ever since boarding school.

jiggy *(adj.)* Street: very cool, the best
That song is jiggy. Let's put it on our dance tape.

job lock *(noun)* Business: restricted feeling a worker has when he'd like to leave his job but cannot for fear of being without health benefits
The officials hoped that a nationwide health care plan would alleviate some of the pressures of job lock on the working population.

jock 1. *(noun)* Teen & College: avid athlete
The jocks were known to drink disgusting high-protein egg drinks on the mornings before a game.

2. *(noun)* Sports: athlete of any kind, any gender
Terry could always be found hanging around with the other jocks in the school hallway.

3. *(adj.)* Sports: athletic, or associated with athletes
None of the regular kids went near the jock table in the cafeteria because it was off limits.

4. *(verb)* Teen & College: to hang on someone; usually referring to a girl hanging on a guy
Letitia is always jocking on Monroe, even in front of her parents.

jockey for position *(verb phrase)* General: to maneuver to gain an advantage
Those account executives are

really jockeying for position within the firm.

joe *(noun)* General: coffee; an old term most recently popularized by the television show, "Twin Peaks."
Drink your joe before it gets cold.

Joe _____ *(noun phrase)* Teen & College: linked with an adjective or hour, the term refers to a male with a certain characteristic
Oh, he's Joe Popularity, all right.

Joe Blow *(proper noun)* General: anyone
So what if Joe Blow comes in and asks for your help? What will your response be?

john 1. *(noun)* General: toilet; also known as: can, jane
Quentin was in the john when the police broke down his door.
2. *(noun)* General: customer of a prostitute
The cops picked up a prostitute and a couple of johns at the motel just outside of town.

John Hancock *(proper name)* General: signature; refers to one of the signers of the United States Declaration of Independence
Just put your John Hancock right here on the dotted line of this contract.

johnny *(noun)* Teen & College: police officer; also johnny law
Slow down. I think there's a johnny parked behind those bushes.

Johnny on the spot *(noun phrase)* General: punctual person
He's always been Johnny on the spot, so something important must be holding him up.

joint *(noun)* Crime & Law: prison; *see also:* can
Jilly was going to have to spend six months in the joint for contempt of court.

jones for *(verb phrase)* Teen & College: to want something desperately
I've been jonesing for that CD for a month.

joy popper *(noun phrase)* Drug World: periodic user of hard drugs
Jim felt that he wasn't some kind of junkie, just a joy popper.

joystick *(noun)* Computerspeak: used in computer games, this inputting device gives the computer instructions at the tilt of the stick; from the World War II aviators' term for their control sticks
Josh spent so much time playing computer games, his friends kidded that he'd be buried with a joystick in his hand.

juice *(noun)* Street: power
I've got all the juice I need to take over Leroy's gang.

juicer *(noun)* Teen & College: person who uses steroids
Jules is so into his body I think he's even a juicer now.

juke *(verb)* Teen & College: to evade

I managed to juke my mom on doing the lawn this afternoon, but I know I'll have to do it tomorrow.

juku *(noun)* Foreign (Japanese): supplemental education program that prepares students to pass difficult entrance exams for private schools or higher institutions of learning

Albert attended a juku four afternoons a week for a year before taking his college entrance exams.

jump *(verb)* Seafarers: to leave without permission

The lieutenant commander had to discipline the sailor severely even though he'd only jumped ship to be with his wife while she gave birth.

jump bail *(verb phrase)* Crime & Law: to forfeit one's bail by running away and failing to appear for trial; also known as skip bail

Wendy jumped bail and flew to the Bahamas to escape being tried for murder.

jump down someone's throat *(verb phrase)* General: to attack verbally

I only asked to borrow his car and he jumped down my throat!

jumpstart *(verb)* Traffic: to start one car battery off the power of another

Mark's battery was dead so he had to call someone to jumpstart his car.

jump the gun *(verb phrase)* General: to begin too early

I don't want to jump the gun, but can I at least make some preliminary calls about this issue?

jump the track *(verb phrase)* General: to unexpectedly change the subject or plan

Let's not jump the track here, we need to stick to one thing at a time.

jump through hoops *(verb phrase)* General: to obey unconditionally

I jumped through hoops to get this promotion so it better pay off.

jump to a conclusion *(verb phrase)* General: to decide without careful consideration of facts

You jumped to a conclusion about Jack and me when you saw us dancing.

jungle rot *(noun phrase)* Medical: creeping infection of the lower pelvic region

The returning soldiers seemed well enough, though some required treatment for jungle rot.

junk bonds *(noun phrase)* Wall Street: bonds that offer exceptionally high yields due to the high risk of the enterprise

The great wealth generated in the 1980s was largely the result of excessive trade in junk bonds.

junket *(noun)* Government & Politics: trip taken by members of Congress that is paid for either by an outside party or by public funds

The legislators were chided in the press for the two-week "fact-finding" junket they took to Asia, with their entire families.

junkie *(noun)* Drug World: drug addict, or more generally, an addict of any kind

Marie had to admit she'd become a soap opera junkie, and she scheduled her lunch hour around her favorite soap.

junks *(noun)* Teen & College: swanky basketball sneakers

I still owe my mom about $20 for those junks I got last month.

junk science *(noun phrase)* Crime & Law: so-called scientific data and evidence presented by expert witnesses on either side in a courtroom trial

Many believe that junk science is harming the judicial process and contributing to the increasing costs of litigation.

jury rig *(verb phrase)* Seafarers: to make a hasty, temporary repair that will have to be properly tended to as soon as possible

We jury rigged a tow rope to get the car to the garage.

just what the doctor ordered *(noun phrase)* General: exactly what is desired or necessary

That beach vacation will be just what the doctor ordered.

K

K-12 *(noun phrase)* Education, Government: education talk for a child's kindergarten through twelfth-grade years

The publisher was pushing a K-12 reading program for the school system.

Ka-ching! *(expression)* General: imitation of the sound of a cash register ring, invoked when one senses the opportunity to make money

The hustler murmured, "ka-ching!" seeing the group of tourists approach.

kangaroo care *(noun phrase)* Medical: encouraged in hospital intensive care nurseries, in which infants are held and nurtured by mothers or others in an effort to provide essential emotional bonding in the face of high-tech medical procedures

Marta volunteered in a kangaroo-care program at the hospital, hugging and singing to tiny infants three afternoons a week.

kangaroo court *(noun phrase)* General: group of individuals who take it upon themselves to pass judgment and punishment on someone

The community of homeless people formed a kangaroo court to decide the fate of the person caught stealing from them during the night.

keep an eye on *(verb phrase)* General: to watch over

I told Molly I'd keep an eye on her class while she went to the principal's office to get a message.

keep one's chin up *(verb phrase)* General: to be courageous in the face of difficult circumstances

It was hard for Katie to keep her chin up during the graduation exercises while her father was in the hospital with a stroke.

keep one's ear to the ground *(verb phrase)* General: to pay close attention to everything one hears

I'll keep my ear to the ground for any job opportunities that come up in my company.

keep one's eye on the ball *(verb phrase)* General: to stay focused on a goal, to remain undistracted

If Joey can keep his eye on the ball during medical school, he's sure to become a fine physician.

keep one's eyes peeled *(verb phrase)* General: to be watchful for

I'll keep my eyes peeled for shoes to go with your new suit.

keep one's head above water *(verb phrase)* General: to stay away from difficulty

The clerk was making a decent salary but was just barely keeping his head above water with the bill collectors.

keep one's nose clean *(verb phrase)* General: to stay out of trouble

If you keep your nose clean for one year, all negative reports will be removed from your school records.

keep one's shirt on *(verb phrase)* General: to keep calm and be patient

Just keep your shirt on; I'll be out in a minute.

keep something under one's hat *(verb phrase)* General: to keep a secret

Can you keep this under your hat?

keep tabs on *(verb phrase)* General: to watch or check up on

Would you keep tabs on my house while I'm away?

keep up with the Joneses *(expression)* General: to compete with one's peers in trends and fashion

Ellison bought one of those huge, unsightly satellite dishes for his backyard just to keep up with the Joneses.

kennel *(noun)* Real Estate: crummy house, hardly worthy of a dog

The broker had bragged all afternoon about his "prime property," but it turned out to be just a kennel.

key *(adj.)* Teen & College: essential

Showing up at this party without a guy is key.

keyed up *(adj. phrase)*

General: agitated, nervous
Margot was very keyed up about her solo in the concert.

kick around 1. *(verb phrase)*
General: to discuss easily and informally
I'd like to kick around a few ideas with you before today's meeting.
2. *(verb phrase)* General: to go about without any plans
Let's just kick around downtown tonight and see what there is to do.

kick ass *(verb phrase)* General: to assert one's supremacy or authority with distinct force; also known as: kick ass and take names
The auditor came into the office and immediately started to kick ass and take names.

kick back 1. *(verb phrase)*
Teen & College: to relax; *see also:* chill
I'm just going to kick back tonight. No partying for me.
2. bribe
The contractor received regular kickbacks from the construction supply company.

kicked to the curb *(verb phrase)* Teen & College, Street: totally rejected
I finally got up the nerve to ask Sue Lynn out and I got kicked to the curb.

kicker *(noun)* Real Estate: loan fees
If there's one thing I can't stand about buying property, it's the

kicker I have to hand over to the bank.

kicking *(adj.)* Street: excellent
That book you loaned me was kicking.

kicking it *(verb phrase)* Teen & College: to be busy or doing something; from kicking the can
I told June I couldn't help her with her homework because I was kicking it with the guys tonight.

kick off *(verb phrase)* General: to launch
The radio station kicked off the new morning radio program with a great contest.

kicks *(noun)* Street: shoes
Did you buy those kicks at the Shoe Shack?

kick stomp *(verb phrase)* Street: to dance
I'm going kick stomping at the roadhouse tonight.

kick up one's heels *(verb phrase)* General: to celebrate or have a great time
After these exams are over, I intend to kick up my heels a bit.

kidvid *(noun)* Entertainment: children's television or video programs
That loathsome purple dinosaur has become the hero of kidvid.

killer 1. *(adj.)* Teen & College, Street: very cool
That's some killer jacket, girlfriend. Where did you get it?
2. *(adj.)* Teen & College: very difficult

I have two killer exams on Friday.

killer bees *(noun phrase)* Wall Street: support personnel, such as attorneys or public relations professionals, used by a company to battle a takeover attempt
Bestco was able to thwart the takeover, but the killer bees $2 million paid in fees seemed unacceptable to some of the stockholders.

killer cards *(noun phrase)* Teen & College: collector cards featuring the images, statistics, and grisly stories of murderers and serial killers
Jamie got grounded when his dad found killer cards on his dresser.

kill it *(verb phrase)* Surferspeak: to surf well
I guess I was killing it today.

kill shot *(noun phrase)* Sports: overly aggressive tackle, meant to impair the future performance of the player who was tackled
The defensive tackle went in for a kill shot on the ball carrier.

Kill that noise *(expression)* Street: Shut up. Stop talking.
Kill that noise, will you? I'm trying to listen to this song.

-king *(noun)* Teen & College: male with an extreme characteristic or habit
He's become a foreign film king.

kiss of death *(noun phrase)* General: certain doom
The colonel's endorsement was

the kiss of death for the candidate.

kiss up *(verb phrase)* General: to flatter someone for one's own benefit; *see also:* **apple polish**, **brownnose**, and **suck up**
You're just kissing up to Ms. Roxbury so you'll get a good grade on that paper.

klink *(noun)* General: jail; also known as: big house, cage, cooler, pen, pokey, slammer, and stir
I'd rather do a thousand hours of community service than spend one night in the klink.

kludge *(noun)* Computerspeak: complicated, unwieldy solution to a programming problem; opposite of elegant
The programmer was embarrassed at the kludge he rigged up for the program.

kneebangers *(noun)* Surferspeak: long, baggy shorts favored by surfers
Where'd you get those gnarlatious kneebangers?

kneecap *(noun)* Military: variation on the acronym NEACP (National Emergency Airborne Command Post), the jet that is ever ready to whisk the President out of harm's way when enemy missiles have been launched at Washington, D.C.
"It's nice to know that kneecap will take care of the old man, but what about the rest of us poor slobs who live in the District?" the Cabinet secretary muttered.

knife-happy *(adj.)* Medical: descriptive term for a surgeon who aggressively encourages surgical treatment over any other possible treatment

LaRue suspected her doctor was knife-happy so she decided to get another opinion.

knock *(verb)* General: to make disparaging remarks about someone or something

I wish you wouldn't knock my work in front of everyone.

knock back *(verb phrase)* Bars: to drink

Let's knock back a bunch of beers before we go to the basketball game.

knockdown *(noun)* Real Estate: kit house, partially pre-assembled and put together in pieces on the property location

Practically broke, the young couple finally settled for a knockdown on a scrappy piece of land at the edge of town.

knock-down-drag-out *(adj.)* General: riotous

That was a knock-down-drag-out fight at the pub last night.

knock oneself out *(verb phrase)* General: to make a whole-hearted attempt

Shawna knocked herself out to finish her diorama in time for the science fair.

knock someone into the middle of next week *(verb phrase)* General: to beat someone up

When a broadcaster smirked at the misguided putt, the golfer threatened to knock him into the middle of next week.

knock them dead *(verb phrase)* General: to make a successful impression

Don't worry, you'll knock 'em dead in the audition.

knotted *(adj.)* Sports: tied, referring to the score of a game

The score has been knotted for three innings now.

know all the moves *(verb phrase)* General: to be highly competent

Joey's a terrific tax lawyer; he knows all the moves.

know a thing or two *(verb phrase)* General: to be skillful, competent, and savvy; also known as: know what's what

Kendra knows a thing or two about investing in the stock market.

know enough to come in out of the rain *(verb phrase)* General: to have common sense

I don't think Jack knows enough to come in out of the rain.

know someone from Adam *(verb phrase)* General: to know someone; usually used in the negative

I don't know that guy from Adam. I've never seen him before in my life.

know like the back of one's hand *(verb phrase)* General: to be completely familiar with

Don't worry, we're not lost. I know this area like the back of my hand.

knuckle down *(verb phrase)*
General: to become serious
I've got to knuckle down and study for my exams.

knuckle under *(verb phrase)*
General: to give up
I hated to knuckle under and let Katie go out tonight, but she nagged me all day and wore me down.

KO *(noun)* Sports (Boxing): initialism for knock-out, where a boxer is knocked to the mat by his opponent and the referee counts to ten, signifying defeat; generally, refers to a decisive victory
It was a real KO for the lawyer when she won her own divorce case.

kowtow *(verb)* Foreign (Chinese): to behave in a deferential manner
I'm not going to kowtow to Charlie now just because he got that big promotion.

L

L.A. *(noun phrase)* Government & Politics: initialism for Legislative Assistant, an aide responsible for all matters dealing with legislation
Senator Dogood's L.A. was a stickler on policy matters and kept a watchful eye for consistency in his position on controversial legislation.

labor of love *(noun phrase)* General: act of affection or pleasure rather than for profit
The remodeling of the children's wing of the hospital was the philanthropist's labor of love.

lacerate *(verb)* Surferspeak: to surf aggressively and without apprehension
For such a little guy, he really lacerates those **grinders**.

laid back *(adj. phrase)* General: calm, peaceful
Everyone liked Marcia's mother because she was so laid back.

laid-back *(adj.)* Teen & College, Street: well dressed
Drew's laid-back for his interview today.

L.G.M. *(noun phrase)* Sci-fi: initialism for Little Green Men, a partly jokish reference to creatures that appeared in early science fiction
His first effort selling the story failed miserably; one editor said the L.G.M. factor made it ridiculous.

lamb *(noun)* Wall Street: inexperienced investor who is especially vulnerable to supposedly hot tips on stocks
The seasoned broker tried to advise caution to the new client, a lamb who called twice a day with some new crazy orders.

lame *(adj.)* Teen & College: stupid; *see also:* bone
What a lame excuse that is!

lame duck *(noun phrase)*

Government & Politics: incumbent legislator who has failed to be reelected but who has time left on his or her term

The congresswoman wasn't terribly influential even as an active legislator, so as a lame duck she could barely get anyone to return her telephone calls.

lamping *(adj.)* Teen & College: hanging around; from the idea of leaning up against a lamppost

We were just lamping at the mall when we saw Mark and the guys go into the movies.

land something *(verb phrase)* General: to succeed in achieving or acquiring something after much effort

I finally landed a spot on the school board.

land with a dull thud *(verb phrase)* General: to fail miserably

My idea for a new book landed with a dull thud in the editorial meeting.

Langley *(proper noun)* Government, Military: Central Intelligence Agency, referring to Langley, Virginia, where the Agency is based

Somebody at Langley should be able to fix this little problem with the Vice-President.

lap up *(verb phrase)* General: to take in with great eagerness

Saundra lapped up the critics' praise for her latest paintings.

large and in charge *(noun phrase)* Teen & College: to be the leader or boss

Sorry, kids, but I'm large and in charge tonight, and I say it's bedtime.

larger than life *(adj. phrase)* General: bigger, grander or more impressive than what one is used to

Our new housekeeper is larger than life, a real dynamo.

last call *(noun phrase)* Bars: bartender's announcement that no liquor will be served after a certain time

I'd like to order one more cocktail before last call.

last-call look *(noun phrase)* Teen & College: desperate look one gets when it is very late and no social or romantic connection has been made yet

Those guys have last-call looks but I'm not interested.

last straw *(noun phrase)* General: intolerable final act

Brenda's telling everyone I'm going to get fired? That's the last straw!

last word *(noun phrase)* General: power to make the final decision

I'd like to grant your request, but my supervisor has the last word in these matters.

latchkey kid *(noun phrase)* Press: child who returns home from school every day to an empty house because both parents work; term derived from the fact that they let themselves in with their own keys

*The community center launched a **hotline** for latchkey kids who needed help with their homework or just someone to talk to.*

later *(noun)* Teen & College: good-bye; from see you later
Later, dude—I've got to get to class now.

latronic *(noun)* Surferspeak: see you later, good-bye
Latronic, dude.

laugher *(noun)* Sports: overwhelming victory
That meet against County High was a total laugher; we placed first in every event.

laugh off *(verb phrase)* General: to dismiss lightly
Wilma could always laugh off criticism of her work because she was confident in her talent.

launder *(verb)* Crime & Law: to make legal
The drug profits became untraceable and safe to use once the cash had been laundered in South America.

lavaliere *(verb)* Entertainment (French): to attach a small microphone; from the French word for this type of microphone
Beth needs to be lavaliered now because we have thirty seconds until we're on the air.

lawyer's bill *(noun phrase)* Government & Politics: bill that would instigate considerable legal activity
The deregulation measure was a

lawyer's bill if there ever was one; some attorneys were primed the moment the bill passed.

lay scratch *(verb phrase)* Cartalk: to accelerate so quickly that skid marks are left behind on the pavement
You watch: When that race begins I'm going to lay scratch.

lay something down *(verb phrase)* Street: to explain something
Let me lay something down: I don't like you but we have a job to do.

lay day *(noun phrase)* Seafarers: a day off, usually from an extended boat race
I'd like to take a lay day but I don't want the crew to lose its momentum.

lay a finger on *(verb phrase)* General: to touch
If you lay a finger on anyone in this house, I'll call the police.

lay an egg *(verb phrase)* General: to fail miserably
The chancellor's opening remarks really laid an egg.

lay down the law *(verb phrase)* General: to issue strict orders
You knew your parents would lay down the law about using the car after you were late three nights last week.

lay it on the line 1. *(verb phrase)* General; to risk
The soldiers laid it on the line for each other during the dawn skirmish.

2. *(verb phrase)* General: to be honest

I'd like to lay it on the line for you and state my objections.

lay low *(verb phrase)* General: to be inconspicuous, to maintain a low profile

We better lay low until this scandal blows over.

lay one's cards on the table *(verb phrase)* General: to present one's position openly and honestly

Let me lay my cards on the table and then we'll talk about money.

lay to rest *(verb phrase)* General: to end

The candidate's statement at the press conference laid to rest rumors that he had been planning to withdraw from the race.

lay waste *(verb phrase)* General: to damage excessively or destroy entirely

The hurricane laid waste to the seaside mobile home community.

lead a dog's life *(verb phrase)* General: to have a difficult existence

The new recruits led a dog's life during their bootcamp training.

lead by the nose *(verb phrase)* General: to control completely

Many say the maestro's wife leads him by the nose.

Leadership, the *(proper noun)* Government and Politics: officers and ranking commitee members of Congress

The Administration appealed to the Leadership in soliciting support for the budget bill.

leaks *(noun)* Government, Politics, News: pieces of inside information intentionally or unintentionally released to the press; *see also:* backgrounder and deep background

The Watergate scandal came to public light thanks to the leaks provided by the reporters' notorious source, nicknamed "Deep Throat."

leaning *(adj.)* Government & Politics: officially uncommitted on an issue, but tending toward one side or another

The senator was courted extensively by the White House, who saw that she was leaning on the health care proposal.

leave *(noun)* Seafarers: time off; *see also:* liberty

Juanita used her leave to catch up on some errands and the latest movies.

leave a bad taste in one's mouth *(verb phrase)* General: to cause a bad impression

The sensationalistic reports of the candidate's lifestyle left a bad taste in the public's mouth.

leave hanging *(verb phrase)* Teen & College: to stand someone up

I can't believe Sue left Marshall hanging at the dance.

leave holding the bag 1. *(verb phrase)* General: to force someone to take sole responsibility or

blame by exiting the situation
Simon left his assistant holding the bag when the boss demanded to know who had mishandled the Tokyo account.

2. *(verb phrase)* General: to leave someone with no recourse
Joanne was left holding the bag when George didn't pay his share of the mortgage.

leave no stone unturned *(verb phrase)* General: to pursue every possible option
If I have to leave no stone unturned, I will find Mama's missing brooch.

leave someone to twist in the wind *(verb phrase)* General: to leave someone with no recourse and no defense
I can't believe my lawyer abandoned my case and left me to twist in the wind.

leave well enough alone *(verb phrase)* General: don't disturb present conditions
Let's leave well enough alone and stop asking your mother for advice.

leech *(noun)* Teen & College: one who is hard to get away from
Kim's such a leech when we go to parties that she even insists on dancing with my boyfriend.

left-brained *(adj.)* Medical: conceptually oriented, as opposed to linear oriented (right-brained)
I'm too left-brained to appreciate the precise order of his work.

left-handed compliment *(noun phrase)* General: compliment that ends up sounding insulting
Elaine didn't know what to think about her coworker's left-handed compliment about her proposal.

legs *(noun)* Entertainment: enduring appeal at the box office
That show still had legs, even after twelve months on Broadway.

leg to stand on *(noun phrase)* General: support for one's assertion
Go ahead and accuse me of lying, but you don't have a leg to stand on.

legwork *(noun)* General: difficult aspects of a project that are time- and labor-intensive
My assistant usually does all of the legwork on the proposals and I just fine tune the language.

Leprosy Effect *(noun phrase)* Military: tendency of a failed program to tarnish anything even slightly associated with it
The long-cancelled Ultra-Bomber program continued to have a Leprosy Effect on the legislators who supported it.

let it rip *(verb phrase)* General: to be unconcerned about the consequences
Don't worry about what everyone thinks. Just say what you mean and let it rip.

let one's hair down *(verb phrase)* General: to relax and behave in a carefree manner
I think we should all just let our

hair down and discuss our true feelings.

let sleeping dogs lie *(verb phrase)* General: don't cause trouble, don't disturb the peace
It's not worth having an argument with Mom over this. Let's just let sleeping dogs lie.

Let's cruise *(expression)* Teen & College: Let's go. Let's get out of here.
I'm sick of this party. Let's cruise.

let someone have it *(verb phrase)* General: to strike a hard blow, either verbal or physical
After Brickley embarrassed my brother in front of his friends, I had to let him have it.

let the cat out of the bag *(verb phrase)* General: to disclose a secret
Someone let the cat out of the bag and told Stan about his surprise party.

liberty *(noun)* Seafarers: time off, for members of the Navy; *see also:* leave
Cyril has some liberty coming so he's going to meet his parents in Los Angeles for the weekend.

liberty hound *(noun phrase)* Seafarers: sailor who schemes for extra time off
Cassio's bunkmates joked that he'd become such a liberty hound that they had to make an appointment to actually see him on duty.

license to print money *(noun phrase)* General: extremely lucrative endeavor

The 900-number the company launched turned out to be a license to print money.

lid *(noun)* Drug World: one full ounce of marijuana
The cops busted the rock star at customs for carrying a lid in his suitcase.

lift a finger *(verb phrase)* General: to do one's share, to make an effort; usually used in the negative
The usher didn't lift a finger when I dropped my parcels in the lobby.

light a fire under *(verb phrase)* General: to urge to action
I'll light a fire under Kirkpatrick to get his report finished on time.

lights are on, but nobody's home *(expression)* General: in a diminished mental state
I tried talking with that new librarian but I'm afraid the lights are on, but nobody's home.

lights-out *(noun phrase)* General: end, defeat
The slugger's grandslam in the ninth inning meant lights-out for the Redbirds.

lights-out factory *(noun phrase)* Technology: automated factory of the future that will be so technologically sophisticated that it could operate in the dark, without human aid
Brandon figured that if he could create a lights-out factory, he wouldn't have to worry about

paying employees' health benefits.

lightweight *(noun)* Teen & College: person who can't drink very much

We better slow down our drinking because Lauren is a bit of a lightweight.

like *(interjection)* Teen & College: term used to punctuate a spoken sentence, either to emphasize or deemphasize the preceding word or phrase

My mother won't buy me that dress for the prom because it's, like, $300.

like crazy *(adv. phrase)* General: with great energy; also known as: like mad

I studied like crazy so I could get an A on my final.

like five miles of bad road *(expression)* General: awful

That movie we saw last night was like five miles of bad road.

like nobody's business *(adv. phrase)* General: excessively

Ever since it introduced a new perfume, the company's sales have increased like nobody's business.

like two peas in a pod *(prep. phrase)* General: as alike and close as possible

The two swimmers were best friends, like two peas in a pod.

limousine liberal *(noun phrase)* Government & Politics: political liberal who enjoys the benefit of personal wealth

Conservatives were endlessly grumbling about limousine liberals who seemed so willing to spend the taxpayers money on social programs.

line *(noun)* Drug World: single dose of cocaine powder, arranged in a neat line for easy inhaling, usually through a straw

The undercover cop was afraid of sneezing and blowing away the line the dealers had prepared.

lipstick *(noun)* Cartalk: small changes, mostly for looks, made to make a new model car to look as if it has been significantly redesigned

The new four-door model looks like a major improvement from last season's, but on close inspection you can see it's all lipstick.

lit up *(verb phrase)* College, Drug World: high on alcohol or drugs; *see also:* buzzed

When Bill walked into the party, he was already lit up.

lite *(adj.)* Food: loosely used term describing food or beverage that is low in calories or fat; also known as: light and lyte

Alicia's one concession to the health and nutrition craze was to switch from regular to lite ice cream.

little black book *(noun phrase)* General: notebook containing the names and telephone numbers of one's romantic interests

The murder victim's little black book led the detective right to the most likely suspects.

live high off the hog *(verb phrase)* General: to live expensively and extravagantly

The moment Jake received his inheritance, he started living high off the hog.

live on the lam *(verb phrase)* General: to be a fugitive

The escaped convict lived on the lam for two years before being recaptured.

live hand-to-mouth *(verb phrase)* General: to exist with little money

My uncle lived hand-to-mouth for years when he couldn't work.

liveware *(noun)* Computerspeak: people who use, or work with, computers (technicians, processors, users, hackers, programmers, etc.)

Manufacturers often forget to consider liveware when designing a system.

live wire *(noun phrase)* General: extremely energetic person

Let's have Sissy do the ad; she's a real live wire when it comes to writing jingles.

living in a goldfish bowl *(verb phrase)* General: existing in a situation where there is no privacy

Royal families hate living in a goldfish bowl, where their every move is scrutinized.

living foul *(adj. phrase)* Street: without any sense of honor or loyalty

You're living foul, man, if you left her at the show with no ride home.

living large *(adj. phrase)* Teen & College, Street: doing well

One big deal and I'm living large, can't you see?

loaded for bear *(adj. phrase)* General: primed for a big confrontation

After the school budget cuts, angry parents showed up at the PTA meeting loaded for bear.

load the bases *(verb phrase)* Sports (Baseball): to put things at the best possible advantage; literally; to get an offensive player on each base

Now that we've loaded the bases, let's see if we can bat a few runs in.

load off one's mind *(expression)* General: relieved to hear that

*It's a load off my mind to hear Aunt Stella's going to **pull through**.*

lock *(noun)* Sports, Government & Politics: certain victory

The presidential candidate had a lock on the South and the Midwest, but was struggling in the Northeast.

lockdown *(noun)* Crime & Law: period when prisoners are confined to their cells all day, rather than allowed to mingle in common areas such as a tele-

vision room or exercise yard
The lockdown was into its third week and the inmates were getting mean and jumpy.

loft *(noun)* Teen & College: time spent in the air while performing a stunt on a skateboard; *see also:* hangtime
Joanie got some serious loft on that jump.

logroll *(verb)* Government & Politics: to do hard politicking, trading votes, etc., in an effort to get one's own priority bills passed
Because the jobs bill was so controversial, plenty of logrolling was going on in the cloakroom hours before the vote took place.

long drink of water *(noun phrase)* General: tall person
The bassist is a real long drink of water; she towers over the other band members.

longhair *(noun)* General: intellectual, or one with classical tastes
The rock star called himself a "longhair" because he liked to listen to classical music.

long in the tooth *(adj. phrase)* General: elderly
That dog is awfully long in the tooth to be racing around with those puppies.

long neck *(noun phrase)* Bars: beer bottle with a long, skinny neck
Never carry a long neck by the rim or the bottom of the bottle.

Always grasp it confidently by the neck.

long shot *(noun phrase)* General: only a slight chance to succeed on a risk or a wager
The actress knew she was a long shot to win the Academy Award so she didn't write a speech.

look *(noun)* Fashion: general style or trend reflected in the season's designs
The look this fall is sleek and unadorned.

look down one's nose at *(verb phrase)* General: to be scornful of
Edward had always looked down his nose at his wife's family.

lookers *(noun)* Auction World, Salespeople: derogatory term for people who shop but never bid or buy
The merchants rely on smaller staffs on Sunday, when most of the customers are only lookers.

look green around the gills *(verb phrase)* General: to appear queasy or sick
I guess you don't like sailing. You look a little green around the gills.

looking at time *(verb phrase)* Crime & Law: facing a term of imprisonment
"Just tell me if I'm looking at time here," the client asked his lawyer.

lookism *(noun)* PC: tendency to judge and evaluate people by their outward characteristics, such as attire, attractiveness, size, etc.

The large man claimed he couldn't get work because he was a victim of lookism.

look like a million bucks *(verb phrase)* General: to appear healthy and attractive and happy

After that vacation, you look like a million bucks.

look like death warmed over *(verb phrase)* General: to look tired and unhealthy

Sue came in to work today looking like death warmed over.

loomer *(noun)* Surferspeak: slow wave that gets significantly bigger as it comes in

I was tricked by that loomer and nearly drowned.

loopy *(adj.)* General: eccentric and a bit crazy

My great aunt and uncle are a loopy pair and great fun to visit.

loose *(adj.)* Teen & College: senseless and foolhardy

Driving your father's car near the ridge was loose and you know it.

Los Angelization *(noun phrase)* Government & Politics: uncontrolled growth of a city's population and traffic congestion, crime, pollution, and other such socio-economic problems

The community planners feared the Los Angelization of their city and vowed to develop a controlled growth policy.

lose it *(verb phrase)* General: to lose control of one's temper or faculties

If you don't turn down that music, I'm going to lose it!

lose face *(verb phrase)* General: to lose one's dignity or self-respect

Filing for bankruptcy made Mona feel she'd lost face among her colleagues.

lose ground *(verb phrase)* General: to get worse rather than improve

We're losing ground on this petition drive.

lose touch *(verb phrase)* General: to discontinue communication

I lost touch with my roommates soon after I left college.

lounge lizard *(noun phrase)* General: person who spends a lot of time in bars and nightclubs, looking for companionship or other diversions

Barry has a reputation as a lounge lizard in all the worst nightclubs.

lousy with something *(adj. phrase)* General: featuring something in abundance; also known as: crawling with

The beach was lousy with little kids this afternoon.

lovefest *(noun)* Government & Politics, General: mildly derogatory term for cooperation between opposing parties that appears to be mutually self-serving

The lovefest that went on at the press conference after the passage of the environmental bill seemed like just a lot of political posturing.

lowdown *(noun)* General: all the details
You better give me the lowdown on our new supervisor.

low profile *(noun phrase)* Government, Law Enforcement, Public Relations: state of being purposely out of the public eye
The judge avoids scandals by always keeping a low profile.

low rider *(noun)* Cartalk, Street: car that is structurally adjusted to ride just a few inches above the road, the vehicle of choice among many gang members
Many teens drive cars with altered suspensions, either high-riding four-wheel drive vehicles or drop-bottom low riders.

lower the boom *(verb phrase)* General: to reprimand or punish
Shel's parents lowered the boom when the principal informed them she had been skipping classes.

lowlife *(noun)* Teen & College: degenerate or despicable person
*Matt's been **hanging with** those lowlifes who stole my sister's bike.*

low-rent *(adj.)* General: of mediocre to bad quality
What kind of low-rent shop is this?

ludes *(noun)* Drug World: short for Quaaludes; also known as: quack
Bonnie was dropping ludes before her guests arrived.

LULU *(acronym)* Real Estate: Locally Undesirable Land Uses, referring to a community's resistance to such things as waste processing, landfills, nuclear dumps, etc. being located in the vicinity
The town's longstanding LULUs likely protected it from becoming the site of a waste processing plant.

lump it *(verb phrase)* General: to accept one's misfortune or mistreatment
When Bobby lost his favorite toy, his brother told him to lump it.

lump-off *(noun)* General: lazy, doltish person
You couldn't have hired a bigger lump-off to run the office while you were on vacation!

lunch *(verb)* Teen & College: to daydream or be distracted, see also: out to lunch
Juanita was lunching through the whole lecture so she'll be no help.

lunkhead *(noun)* General: a slow-thinking person
So this lunkhead finally decides where to sit and takes my chair!

M

mack 1. *(verb)* Street: to overcome someone

Johnny just macked that guy in the last lap of the race.

2. *(noun)* Street: person who is strongest or biggest

Who's the mack in this gang?

macker *(noun)* Surferspeak: huge wave

Did you see that macker? It wiped those other dudes out.

MAD *(acronym)* Military: Mutual Assured Destruction, a vital element in the theory of nuclear deterrence that holds that nuclear superpowers will not attack one another because the massive retaliation would be fatal

MAD may seem outmoded today now that the Cold War is over, but in its heyday it was the prevailing military theory of the nuclear age.

made of money *(adj. phrase)* General: wealthy

I can't buy you a car! Do I look like I'm made of money?

magalog *(noun)* Word Biz: combination magazine and catalog that possesses all the features of a magazine (articles, columns, etc.) but whose intent is simply to sell products

Jody was ten pages into it before he realized he was reading a magalog, not a regular magazine.

magic *(noun)* Computerspeak: something that is too difficult to explain or understand

I'd really like to explain how this works, but it's probably just

easier to tell you it's magic.

Magoo *(proper noun)* Teen & College: someone who is driving a car too slowly

I don't think we have enough room to pass this Magoo in front of us.

main drag *(noun phrase)* General: primary thoroughfare

All of the best shops and restaurants were on the city's main drag.

maintenance hatch *(noun phrase)* PC: manhole

The maintenance hatch was open as the workers repaired the piping below the street.

major *(adj.)* Teen & College: crucial, total, important

I think Roger will always be the major love of my life.

majors 1. *(noun)* Entertainment: top film distributors

We need a major like BigPix to give this movie the exposure it needs.

make a beeline for *(verb phrase)* General: to rush directly to

As soon as I got to the reception, I made a beeline for the refreshments.

make a day of it *(verb phrase)* General: to commit a whole day to something

Let's pack a lunch and make a day of it at the state park.

make a dent in *(verb phrase)* General: to reduce only slightly

Although Vera had been making small payments faithfully for two

years, she'd only made a dent in her credit card debt.

make a go of *(verb phrase)*
General: to make a successful venture
Let's really work to make a go of this marriage, shall we?

make a killing *(verb phrase)*
General: to make an enormous profit
We made a killing in the stock market over the last four years.

make a mountain out of a molehill *(verb phrase)* General: to make a big fuss over something of little significance
Oh, don't make a mountain out of a molehill. We only had lunch together.

make a run for it *(verb phrase)*
General: to try to escape
Let's grab our coats and make a run for it.

make ends meet *(verb phrase)*
General: to earn enough to cover expenses
We're not getting rich, but we're making ends meet.

made head or tail of *(verb phrase)* General: to understand
Can you make head or tail of this company policy memo?

make no bones *(verb phrase)*
General: to be very honest and straightforward
I make no bones about my political leanings.

make oneself scarce *(verb phrase)* General: to make a quick exit

Trudy's parents made themselves scarce when her friends arrived for her slumber party.

make one's mouth water *(verb phrase)* General: to cause one to desire
That advertisement made my mouth water for an ice cream cone.

make or break someone *(verb phrase)* General: to cause someone to succeed or fail
This debate could make or break the candidate.

make short work of *(verb phrase)* General: to defeat easily
Belinda made short work of Todd on the tennis court this afternoon.

make the grade *(verb phrase)*
General: to meet basic standards and expectations; also known as: **make the cut**
I'm sure I can make the grade at the university, but I'm no Einstein.

make waves *(verb phrase)*
General: to cause trouble or a disturbance
Try not to make waves at the council meeting this evening.

makeover *(noun)* Media: complete renovation of appearance and/or behavior
The candidate was given a total makeover that seemed to make him appear more accessible to the voting public.

mall crawler *(noun phrase)*
Teen & College: young person whose primary arena of enter-

tainment and social activity is a shopping mall; *see also:* **mall rat**

Susanna and her friends were just a bunch of mall crawlers with too much disposable income.

mall rat *(noun phrase)* Teen & College: kid who spends too much time at the mall

Jimmy was turning into a mall rat, spending every afternoon at the video arcade and pizza shop.

mall walking *(noun)* Health & Fitness: form of exercise that calls for brisk walking around an indoor shopping mall

The elderly couple went mall walking three times a week before the stores opened.

man, the *(noun)* Crime and Law: prison warden

"I swear the man has something against me," the inmate complained after a week in the hole.

Mañana *(expression)* Foreign: (Spanish): See you tomorrow.

We had a great time. Mañana.

mangled *(adj.)* Teen & College: messy, disheveled

We've been driving for hours. I must look mangled.

mark *(noun)* Crime & Law: victim or potential victim

"That's my mark," the hoodlum said, nodding in the direction of an unsuspecting shopper.

Mark 1 Mod 1 *(proper noun)* Military: earliest model of a product in development

The Mark 1 Mod 1 landing craft was a primitive vehicle compared to the sophisticated modern version.

mark time *(verb phrase)* General: to wait for something to happen

Tiffany was just marking time at bording school until she came into her inheritance.

mat *(noun)* Seafarers: primary flight deck of an aircraft carrier

There was nothing like the sight of the mat during a series of take-offs.

maul *(verb)* to kiss and grope at one another passionately

Mike and Mindy were mauling in the corner through the whole party.

max *(verb)* General: to reach one's limit; also known as: max out

Rob had maxed on his credit cards so he was forced to pay cash.

max and relax *(verb phrase)* Street: to enjoy some relaxation

I just maxed and relaxed at the beach on Saturday.

M.C. *(noun phrase)* Entertainment: initialism for Master of Ceremonies; also known as: emcee

When the M.C. introduced me, my legs froze and I couldn't go out on stage.

McGovern Democrat *(proper noun)* Government & Politics: Democrat thought to be liberal almost to the point of complete ineffectiveness; refers to Senator George McGovern, who bravely but futilely ran for President in 1972 in opposition to the United States' actions in Southeast Asia

Though she'd been derisively branded a McGovern Democrat during her campaign, the new congresswoman turned out to be an effective activist on mainstream issues.

McPaper *(noun)* Teen & College: paper written in a slapdash manner and at the last minute

Molly forgot about her assignment and had to turn in a McPaper she had written the night before.

meal ticket *(noun phrase)* General: one who provides essential financial assistance

I've got to maintain a good relationship with Aunt Sophie because she's my meal ticket.

mean business *(verb phrase)* General: to be extremely serious

Arthur failed his bar exam the first time because he didn't study, but this time he means business.

measure up *(verb phrase)* General: to meet high expectations

In my family's eyes, none of my boyfriends ever measures up.

meat and potatoes *(noun phrase)* General: most essential aspect of something

The meat and potatoes of our
publicity campaign is promotional appearances by the client.

meat market *(noun phrase)* Bars: bar that attracts singles in search of companionship

What a meat market that bar was last night! I haven't seen that much new blood since college.

meatware *(noun)* Computer - speak: human body

That all-nighter was hard on the meatware.

meat wave *(noun phrase)* Surferspeak: vehicle full of surfers

We got a meat wave going to the barbecue tonight.

mega- *(prefix)* Teen & College: large, total

I'm so stuffed from that megaburger I might explode.

megacharacter *(noun)* Fantasy: character in a role-playing game who has amassed considerable strength through the weapons and special powers he or she has acquired

It was scary to see Vince take on the mean swagger of the megacharacter he'd been playing in Fantagory—it was all too real.

megachurch *(noun)* Entertainment: church organizations that broadcast worship services on radio and television, reaching hundreds of thousands of listeners and viewers

The networks had long underestimated the vastness of the megachurch viewership.

megadeth *(noun)* Military: deaths of a million people

The nuclear exchange would surely cause megadeth, as well as untold destruction of property.

-meister *(suffix)* Teen & College: generic addition to a person's name or to a word describing the person

John, what a hairmeister you are today!

mend fences *(verb phrase)* General: to repair damaged or neglected relationships

After the scene he made in the meeting the day before, Clay had to mend some fences in his office.

mensan *(noun)* Teen & College: specifically, a member of Mensa, an organization of people with extremely high IQs; generally, a term for a smart or bookish person; *see also:* dexter, digithead, floppy disk, and pointhead

Chris is the only jock in a family of mensans.

mental *(adj.)* Teen & College: deranged, strange, bizarre

Quit looking at me like I'm mental or something.

mental giant *(noun phrase)* Teen & College: dolt

What kind of mental giant are you, giving out my telephone number to that guy?

menu *(noun)* Computerspeak: list of options under headings ranging from broad to specific

The novice couldn't figure out the next step, even though the menu made it very clear.

menuese *(noun)* Food: elaborate and often ridiculous menu descriptions of simple, basic dishes

I guess "savory ground sirloin on a fluffy sourdough roll" means hamburger in menuese, right?

mercury *(noun)* Weather: temperature; referring to the precious metal in a thermometer that indicates the temperature

What's the mercury reading today?

mess 'em up *(expression)* Teen & College: Good luck. Break a leg.

You've practiced for the recital all month. Now go out there and mess 'em up.

metal mouth *(noun phrase)* Teen & College: person who wears braces

If he weren't such a geeky metal mouth, I might consider going out with him.

MFR *(noun phrase)* Military: initialism for Memorandum For Record, a memo written for the files to make note of what was said and determined at a certain meeting

The investigators hoped to turn up some evidence against those implicated in the scandal by examining all MFRs in the file for the period in question.

M.I. *(noun phrase)* Medical: initialism for "monetary insufficiency"; referring to a patient who is clearly unable to pay for treatment

The emergency room admittance personnel were not allowed to turn away M.I.s.

mice *(noun)* Cartalk: mildly derogatory term for car customers

Because of his seniority at the dealership, Lou gets his choice of the mice.

mick *(noun)* Military: minute

I'll need about ten micks to get my stuff together before we ship out.

Mickey D's *(proper noun)* Teen: McDonald's restaurant

Sarah made a run to Mickey D's to pick up lunch for the gang.

Mickey Mouse *(adj. phrase)* General: small-time

"What a bunch of Mickey Mouse lawyers you turned out to be!" the newly convicted felon called out to his attorneys as he was led away by the sheriff.

Mickey Mouse rules *(noun phrase)* Seafarers: petty naval regulations

The sailors groused about the Mickey Mouse rules but didn't dare break them, for the punishments weren't Mickey Mouse at all.

micro *(noun)* Surferspeak: tiny wave

I'm not going out on those micros.

microbrewery *(noun)* Food &

Drink: small brewery usually combined with a restaurant that sells the brewed product on the premises

Microbreweries were sprouting up everywhere downtown and were popular among beef **aficionados.**

middle-age spread *(noun phrase)* General: tendency to gain weight and lose one's ideal figure as one gets older

The couple demonstrated exercises that combat middle-age spread.

middle of nowhere *(noun phrase)* General: remote location

I'm out here in the middle of nowhere, with no money and no credit cards, so wire me some cash right away.

middle-of-the-road *(adj.)* General: favoring a compromise or a mid-point between two opposite and extreme positions or plans

The doctor took a middle-of-the-road approach to the new drug treatment.

milicrat *(noun)* Military: military bureaucrat

No one knew better how to stall a request on procedure than a career milicrat.

milk *(verb)* Street: to take advantage of

Claire just milked that new guy for a few weeks then dropped him.

milk a wave *(verb phrase)*

Surferspeak: to ride a wave all the way to its end

There haven't been many good ones today, so I've been milking the waves.

milky *(adj.)* Street: very nice

That night with you was milky. Let's do it again.

mingling *(verb)* Real Estate: sharing ownership in property to help manage the cost

There was a lot of mingling on the oceanfront condominium units, which allowed investors to cut costs.

mint 1. *(adj.)* Teen & College: fine, excellent; *see also:* killer

That movie was mint. I could see it again.

2. *(verb)* Street: to make plenty of money

I minted on that modeling job I did last month.

MIPS *(acronym)* Computerspeak: Millions of Instructions Per Second, referring to the ability of a computer (or a person) to process information

Wesley seems a little low on MIPS today after cramming for finals all night.

mirandize *(verb)* Crime & Law: to read a suspect a statement of his or her constitutional rights, as required under the United States Supreme Court's Miranda decision.

"Go ahead and mirandize the perp," the arresting officer advised her partner.

missing a few marbles *(expression)* General: in a diminished mental state

Benny's missing a few marbles. I saw him wandering around last night totally lost.

miss the boat *(verb phrase)* General: to fail or be too late because one acted too slowly

I waited too long to sign up for the summer and missed the boat.

Miss Thang *(proper noun)* Teen & College, Street: self-important woman; can be used with affectionate sarcasm.

Well, excuse me, Miss Thang! I didn't know you owned this telephone booth.

mobile *(adj.)* Teen & College, Street: attractive

You're looking mighty mobile tonight, Mel.

mob scene *(noun phrase)* General: extremely crowded situation

The film opening was a mob scene, and the police had to be called to control the crowd.

moby *(adj.)* Teen, College, Computerspeak: enormous; *see also:* hungus; from *Moby Dick*, Herman Melville's novel about whales.

That assignment is a moby. I don't know if I'll finish it by Monday.

mole *(noun)* Crime & Law: prison inmate who secretly gathers information from the prison population and reports it to the warden

"Rocco's gonna get beat up if the guys on the block find out he's a mole," the deputy warden warned her boss.

mommy track *(noun phrase)* Business: path a woman takes when she chooses to pursue motherhood and a career

After her first child, Gretchen was back in the office and running hard on the mommy track within three months.

Monday morning quarterback *(noun phrase)* Sports: sports fan who dispenses wisdom the day after a game

Tom's carpool dreaded riding with him the day after the Super Bowl because he was such a Monday morning quarterback.

mondo *(adv.)* Teen & College: extremely, very

This suitcase is mondo heavy. What's in it?

money *(noun)* Teen & College, Street: one's best friend, also known as money grip

Hey, money, what's happening?

money to burn *(noun phrase)* General: more money than is necessary

Wendell got a big commission check, and with money to burn, he took a swanky island vacation.

monkey 1. *(noun)* Teen & College: additional love interest in someone's life

Kelly's got a monkey near her

summer house in Maine, but her boyfriend doesn't know.
2. *(noun)* Real Estate: mortgage

What's the monkey on that corner unit?

monkey around *(verb phrase)* General: to behave foolishly or to fiddle with

Don't monkey around with those switches!

monkey business *(noun phrase)* General: behavior that is unethical, illegal, or otherwise inappropriate

When it became clear that there was some monkey business going on in accounting, the auditor insisted on a full investigation.

monster fodder *(noun phrase)* Fantasy: characters in a role-playing game who are weak and used as bait or tests for hazardous maneuvers

Jamie was sick of ending up as monster fodder whenever his friends got together to play.

Montezuma's revenge *(noun phrase)* Travel, Medical: diarrhea; *see also:* Aztec two-step

Robbie was laid up for a week with Montezuma's revenge.

monthly bill *(noun phrase)* Teen & College: woman's menstrual period

I just got the monthly bill so I'm not quite myself.

monty haul *(noun phrase)* Fantasy: role-playing game where the rewards are huge compared to the significance of the acts that produce them; term comes from the popular television game show host, Monte Hall; these games are considered silly by aficionados

The kids turned up their noses at the monty haul Jennifer brought for their weekend tournament.

mooch *(noun)* Teen & College: one who borrows from others constantly; *see also:* cheeser

Quit being such a mooch and order your own french fries.

moonie *(noun)* Press: person who follows the teachings of the Reverend Sun Myung Moon

I heard that Jenny's sister was a moonie for a few years after college.

moonlight *(verb)* General: to work a second job

Actors often moonlight as waiters when there's no work.

moontel *(noun)* Sci-fi: place to stay on the moon

The moontel was as seedy an establishment as you'd find in any decaying city on earth.

mopped *(adj.)* Teen & College, Street: beaten up

Luray got mopped in that scuffle after school.

MOR *(phrase)* Entertainment: initialism for Middle of the Road, or middle class; middle-aged, middle American taste in entertainment

Let's figure how to take this highbrow script down to a MOR level.

morning after *(noun phrase)* General: aftereffects following a period of revelrous behavior; in particular a long evening of drinking alcohol

The honeymooners shopped, lounged, and dined, with no concern about the morning after.

morphing *(noun)* Computer-speak: computer animation that allows an image to change shape or color with convincing fluidity

The advertisement featured a runner morphing into a cheetah.

MOS *(noun phrase)* Advertising, News: initialism for Man on the Street, referring to an interview with a person who is randomly chosen and presumably not a professional performer

"I got some great MOS quotes for my piece on the city hall scandal," the reporter exclaimed.

mosh pit *(noun phrase)* Teen & College: open area near a concert stage where people are deposited after being carried overhead from the back of a concert crowd to the front; once there, he or she slam dances for a little while and then slips back into the crowd

Sybil met a great guy while dancing in the mosh pit at the rap concert.

most favored nation status *(noun phrase)* Government & Politics: special set of conditions and benefits extended by the United States government to another country to encourage trade between the countries

Congress voted to revoke the superpower's most favored nation status because of repeated human-rights violations in that country.

mother of all *(noun phrase)* General: biggest or best of something

Bart Marlowe's new film is the mother of all action pictures.

mother's helper *(noun phrase)* Drug World: Valium

The stressed-out detective had been getting by with mother's helper for years.

mother ship *(noun phrase)* Sci-fi: large spaceship used by smaller ships as home base; the space equivalent of a naval aircraft carrier

The small fighter raced back to the mother ship after the skirmish with a freighter of unknown origin.

motivationally deficient *(adv. phrase)* PC: careful way of describing someone as lazy, generally referring to those who aren't interested in working for a living

The social worker's report noted that the teen was motivationally deficient and needed job counseling.

mouse milking *(verb phrase)* Business, General: spending a large amount of effort for disproportionately small results

The progressive management training program was a lot of mouse milking since few participants got promoted.

mouthbreather *(noun phrase)* Teen & College: extremely stupid person

I had no idea Lisa's brother was such a mouthbreather.

move heaven and earth *(verb phrase)* General: to do everything possible

You know I'd move heaven and earth for you.

mow *(verb)* Teen & College: to eat until one might explode

I mowed last night at the Barbecue Pit.

mucho *(adv.)* Foreign (Spanish): extremely or a lot

That jacket must have cost mucho green.

muckle *(verb)* Teen & College: to eat hungrily or greedily

I muckled that ice cream cone.

Muffie and Biff *(proper noun phrase)* Teen & College: mildly derogatory name for those who dress and act like prep-school students; *see also:* preppie

Well, old Muffie and Biff are probably at the party recruiting new members for their yacht club.

mug *(verb)* Entertainment: to make humorous faces for attention

Millie's always mugging for the camera.

mule 1. *(noun)* Crime & Law,

Drug World: individual who smuggles drugs on his or her body; *see also:* **burro**

The students innocently befriended some mules in Amsterdam who were traveling to Belgrade.

2. *(noun)* Seafarers: flight deck hand on an aircraft carrier

"Don't look at me, I'm just a mule," the sailor muttered in the direction of the commanding officer.

multiculturalism *(noun)* PC: inclusive and balanced treatment of all ethnic groups in the study of history and culture

The school's new reading curriculum was applauded for its distinct commitment to multiculturalism.

multidisciplinary   *(adj.)* Government, Education: fancy word for diverse, usually used to describe panels, boards, committees, etc. to suggest there is a fair representation of several interests involved

Such a broad-ranging issue will require the study of a multidisciplinary planning committee.

mumbo-jumbo *(noun)* General: nonsense

Don't give me that legal mumbo-jumbo. Tell me what the contract really says.

munch on *(verb phrase)* Teen & College: to harass or treat unfairly

Mr. Wilgreen is munching on

Theresa again for late homework.

munchie *(noun)* Teen & College: scrape received from falling from a skateboard

Mikey got a megamunchie doing tricks in the parking lot yesterday.

munchies *(noun)* Food, Drug World: food craving, often the result of premenstrual syndrome or marijuana use

I've got the munchies so bad I'm going to the Handee Mart right now to get some chips and ice cream.

mundane *(noun)* Sci-fi: mildly derogatory term for those who have no knowledge of or interest in science fiction

Rich was the first mundane Sally had dated, and she quickly discovered they didn't have much to talk about.

mung *(verb)* Computerspeak: to destroy or irreparably harm

Incredibly, they munged the program that couldn't have been simpler to follow.

murder board *(noun phrase)* Government & Politics: nickname for the sort of hearings held by the Senate Judiciary Committee that questions Supreme Court candidates on increasingly personal, political, and philosophical matters, then votes on whether to recommend Senate confirmation

The candidate didn't fare well

before the murder board and her chances of being confirmed seemed slim.

mush-core pornography *(noun phrase)* Advertising, Entertainment: erotic bent to advertising, music, magazine features, etc., that veers deliberately close to the edge of outright pornography

The new slew of music videos were nothing less than mush-core pornography.

mushroom *(noun)* Crime & Law: victim of a stray bullet

Three mushrooms lay in the street after the shootout between the police and the bank robbers.

music to one's ears *(noun phrase)* General: something one is glad to hear

The sound of the cash register ringing was music to the owner's ears.

must-hire list *(noun phrase)* Government & Politics: certain individuals for whom gainful employment must be found anywhere in government or politics, as a return for earlier favors; a contemporary tag for the age-old method of political payback

Tending to the President's must-hire list from the campaign alone kept the personnel office busy for months.

must list *(noun phrase)* Government & Politics: those bills that must be passed during a given session, from the perspective of an interested party

The minority leader had three bills on a must list for this session.

mutant *(noun)* Teen & College: a social outcast

You can't keep hanging out with that mutant or people will start to talk.

my bad *(noun phrase)* Teen & College: my error

Sorry, I thought that seat wasn't taken. My bad.

my man *(noun phrase)* Street: one's best friend

Hey, my man's got a great car and he's letting us ride with him to the prom.

mystery meat *(noun phrase)* Food: piece of meat so doctored up that it cannot be identified

Dad loved to describe the horrible mystery meat dishes he was served in the Army.

N

nail *(noun)* Drug World: hypodermic needle

I won't take a hit without a clean nail, no way.

nail down *(verb phrase)* General: to make certain

Chad wanted to nail down the travel plans for his honeymoon a month in advance.

name is mud *(expression)* General: person who is out of favor

When my parents see I haven't mowed the lawn yet, my name will be mud.

name of the game *(noun phrase)* General: essential aspect of something

Most believe that playing is fun, but winning is the name of the game.

narbo *(noun)* Teen & College: boring person

I don't want to seem like a narbo, but I'd rather stay home and read tonight.

narc *(noun)* Teen & College: person who can't keep a secret, especially from adults; derived from narcotics cop

Craig didn't mean any harm, but he was a narc and most of the kids resented him for it.

nasty *(adj.)* Teen & College: sexy, attractive

Bonnie looks nasty today. She's probably got a hot date.

neat *(adj.)* Bars: straight liquor, no ice, no mixers

Pour me a double Scotch, neat.

neck and neck *(adj. phrase)* General: to be immeasurably close at the end of a contest

The two clerks were neck and neck when the buzzer sounded to end the grocery-bagging contest.

neck of the woods *(noun phrase)* General: neighborhood

As long as you're in my neck of the woods, why don't you stop by?

nectar 1. *(noun)* Surferspeak: beautiful

That board is nectar.

2. *(noun)* Teen & College: attractive female

Whoa, that new lifeguard is nectar!

needle in a haystack *(noun phrase)* General: something that is extremely difficult to find

Recovering that memo in these messy files will be like finding a needle in a haystack.

nerd *(noun)* Teen & College: unpopular, awkward person; *see also:* dork, dweeb, fred, geek, goob, goof, squid, and swivelneck

Dolores wasn't unpopular, but she was considered a bit of a math nerd.

nerd pack *(noun phrase)* Teen, College, Computerspeak: plastic shirt-pocket protector where writing utensils are stored

Sandra couldn't believe this kid with a nerd pack was asking her to the prom.

nerdling *(noun)* Computerspeak: unsophisticated computer programmer

"The guy in programming is just a nerdling. Don't give him a hard time."

network *(verb)* Business: to treat every encounter with another person as a possible professional contact

June really knows how to network at a cocktail party.

new age beverages *(noun phrase)* Food: naturally flavored and carbonated drinks that purport to be healthier than other traditional sodas

The Out Front Deli sold only new age beverages and organic food products.

new ball game *(noun phrase)* General: another matter entirely
After living in an apartment, buying a house will be a whole new ball game.

new blood 1. *(noun phrase)* Auction World, Business, Salespeople: new bidders or customers
The jewelry manufacturer was launching two entirely new lines this season, hoping to infuse new blood into their client base.

2. *(noun phrase)* Teen, College, Street: new members of the opposite sex to join the pool of possible partners
We've been waiting for some new blood in this club for months.

new kid on the block *(noun phrase)* General: newcomer
I'm the new kid on the block so get ready for some competition.

New News *(proper noun)* Entertainment: contemporary news coverage featuring a combination of regular reporting, celebrity consciousness, blatant commerciality, and a distinctly pop culture sensibility
The old-time journalists bemoaned the advent of New News, which had diminished the quality of serious news reporting.

New Wave *(noun phrase)* Sci-fi: brand of science fiction popular in the 1960s that stressed social and political considerations over technological and scientific ones
Walter loved Sci-fi, but had no interest in the New Wave, which he thought was too political for his taste.

newt *(noun)* Teen & College: inexperienced person
I wish I wasn't such a newt at this video game.

N.I. *(adj. phrase)* Teen & College: initialism for not interested
Jack asked me to go to the dance with him, but I told him N.I.

nibble at *(verb phrase)* Teen & College: to argue on a small scale
We nibbled at each other over who would pay the bill.

nice chunk of change *(noun phrase)* General: attractive sum of money.
You could probably get a nice chunk of change for that motorcycle.

nice do *(noun phrase)* Teen & College: ugly hair or hairstyle
Geez, that guy's got a nice do, eh?

nickel bag *(noun phrase)* Drug World: five dollars' worth of a drug
Dean couldn't believe he was stopped at the border for carrying a nickel bag.

nightcap *(noun)* Bars: late-night drink, usually following a

long evening's activities
Where shall we go for a night-cap after the opera?

nightmare *(noun)* Teen & College: extremely bad experience
Going out with that guy was a real nightmare!

night owl *(noun phrase)* General: person who has plenty of energy in the late hours of the day as opposed to the morning
Ginny's such a night owl she's been known to clean her whole house after midnight.

NIMBY *(acronym)* Real Estate: Not in My BackYard, referring to people who oppose homeless shelters, halfway houses, etc., in proximity to their property
The NIMBYs came to the city council meeting to protest the placement of group home for handicapped adults in their neighborhood.

nine *(noun)* Crime & Law: nine-millimeter semi-automatic revolver
All of the officers in the city were required to carry a nine.

nine-to-five *(noun phrase)* General: regular job, usually during the day in an office
My nine-to-five pays the bills, but it's my writing I love.

nip factor *(noun phrase)* Surferspeak: the level of chill outside
What's the nip factor supposed to be today?

nitro *(adj.)* Teen & College: excellent
That song's got a nitro beat.

nix *(verb)* General: to cancel or negate
The city nixed the plans for the upcoming rock concert in the park because of the violence and vandalism that occurred last year.

no comp *(noun phrase)* Teen & College: short for no competition
Ellen and I are up for the same part in the play, but I'm sure I'll get it, no comp.

no biggie *(noun phrase)* Teen & College: no problem; also known as: no sweat
I'll drop off your laundry for you. It's no biggie.

nobody's fool *(noun phrase)* General: sure and capable person
That Elsa is nobody's fool; she'll own this place someday.

no-brainer *(noun)* General: simple task to complete, question to answer, or problem to solve
Fixing that sink is a no-brainer.

No duh. *(expression)* Teen & College: No kidding. Tell me something I don't already know.
Winona broke up with Johnny? No duh.

NOFUN *(acronym)* Military: No First Use of Nuclear Weapons
With the President's NOFUN directive controlling the military exchange, the commanding offi-

cers believed their options were limited.

nog *(verb)* Teen & College: to touch

I nogged her on the arm, but she didn't even know I was there.

noise *(noun)* General: ridiculous nonsense

Whatever you heard about me is just a lot of noise.

nondescript*(noun)* Entertainment: casting agent's term for an actor who is so perfectly ordinary that he or she can blend inconspicuously into the background of a scene; also known as n.d.

I need about thirty nondescripts for the restaurant scene we're shooting on Friday.

nonpro *(noun)* Entertainment: individual not professionally associated with the film industry

For a nonpro, the attorney did a great job of putting together the particulars on the film's financing.

nonsizist *(noun)* PC: absence of negative judgment against a person of considerable size

Connie was careful to use nonsizist terms in her report on health problems among the overweight population.

noogie *(noun)* Kids: prank that calls for rubbing someone's head fast and hard with one's knuckle to create a burning sensation

Grant got grounded for giving his sister a noogie during church.

normal *(noun)* Fantasy: character in a role-playing game who has no extraordinary powers and has to rely on the power of other characters for protection

*Robert daydreamed about being a **megacharacter** or some other powerful being, rather than just the pathetic old normal he was.*

nosh *(verb)* Food (Yiddish): to snack

We just noshed at the cocktail party. Let's go get a real meal.

no-shows *(noun)* Air & Space, Food World: passengers (or patrons) who do not show up for a flight (or dinner) for which they have reservations

You can always count on several no-shows at a wedding reception.

no slouch *(noun phrase)* General: extremely capable, an expert

Tyrell is no slouch, so don't underestimate his ability to land that account.

nostril shot *(noun phrase)* Entertainment: camera angle unbecoming to its subject

The soap opera actress was furious to see nostril shots of her throughout the previous day's footage.

Not! *(interjection)* Teen & College: Stupid! No way!

That was a great book. Not!

not all there *(expression)* General: in a diminished mental state

Vic hasn't been all there since he was fired from his job.

Not even! *(expression)* Teen & College: No way! You're wrong! *You think you're getting an A on that lab report? Not even!*

not for nothing *(adv. phrase)* General: not insignificant *Not for nothing did the candidate call a new conference an hour before the scandal hit the newspapers.*

not have all one's switches on *(verb phrase)* General: to be in a diminished mental state *Because he moonlights as a waiter, Elliot often doesn't have all his switches on at the office.*

not having it *(verb phrase)* Street: to be unwilling to put up with something *Look, don't talk to me in that tone. I'm not having it.*

nothing doing *(adv. phrase)* General: under no circumstances *Will you babysit Tanya for an hour? Nothing doing!*

not on your life *(adv. phrase)* General: absolutely not *There's no way I'd take a vacation trip with Claire—not on your life.*

not playing with a full deck *(expression)* General: in a diminished mental state *The kids told their parents that the woman in the old house at the corner wasn't playing with a full deck.*

no two ways about it *(ex-pression)* General: absolutely no alternative way of looking at this matter *You're going to boarding school this fall, no two ways about it.*

nouveau riche *(noun phrase)* Foreign (French): newly rich *You're spending money too freely and you're acting like the nouveau riche.*

nouvelle cuisine *(noun phrase)* Foreign (French): new way of cooking, with simple ingredients, lower fat, beautiful presentation, and small portions *People who love nouvelle cuisine usually aren't big eaters.*

No way. 1. *(expression)* General: Under no circumstances. Absolutely not. *I will not allow you to stay out that late. No way.*

2. *(expression)* Teen & College: I don't believe you. Are you sure? *No way. Frieda couldn't have failed her driver's test again!*

no-win situation *(noun phrase)* General: situation with no hope for positive resolution; also known as lose-lose situation *The legal battle had become so nasty that it was a no-win situation for everybody, except the lawyers.*

No wire hangers! *(expression)* Teen & College: Please don't do this anymore!; from a well-known scene in the film *Mommie Dearest*

Not that Carpenter's album again! No wire hangers!

N.Q. *(adj. phrase)* Teen & College: initialism for not qualified

N.Q., man, I don't know anything about taking care of babies.

nuc *(noun)* Seafarers: sailor on a nuclear-powered vessel

As a nuc, special technical knowledge was required of Whitehead.

nuch *(noun)* Surferspeak: short for not much

What's going on out here? Nuch.

nuke 1. *(verb)* Teen & College: to destroy

I nuked that rosebush when I was practicing parallel parking in the driveway.

2. *(verb)* Food: to microwave; *see also:* zap

Would you mind nuking this coffee for me? It's cold.

numbers *(noun)* Entertainment: movie ticket sales

That new romantic comedy is catching on and beginning to have good numbers.

nurse *(verb)* Bars: to sip a drink over a long period of time

Jean nursed one drink the whole night.

nurse a grudge *(verb phrase)* General: to maintain a resentful feeling against someone

I'm still nursing a grudge against my Latin teacher for failing me last semester.

nutmeg *(verb)* Sports (Soccer): to dribble a ball between an opponent's legs, slipping past him or her, then regaining control of the loose ball

Scott was nutmegged twice during the game and was too humiliated to face his teammates in the locker room.

NUTS *(acronym)* Military: Nuclear Utilization Targeting Strategy, a strategy that holds that military targets, rather than cities, will be targeted for destruction in a nuclear exchange

The military strategists prided themselves on the more humane approach NUTS represented for the future of nuclear warfare.

ob *(adj.)* Teen & College: short for obvious

The answer to that problem is so ob! Can't you see it?

obscure *(adj.)* Teen & College: strange

Jamie left her uniform at home? How obscure!

O.D. *(noun phrase)* Seafarer: initialism for Officer on Deck, the officer in charge of the ship who carries out the captain's orders

It was unwise to cross the O.D., who not only gave out assignments but also signed off on a sailor's leave.

o-dark-hundred *(noun)* Military: any time in the morning before sunrise; extremely early in the morning

I can't go out tonight because

I've got to go on duty at o-dark-hundred.

odds and ends *(noun phrase)*
General: inconsequential variety of things
I've got a few odds and ends for us to snack on while we wait.

off *(verb)* Crime & Law: to kill; also known as: chill, hit, ice, lay-out, rub out, waste, and whack
"I offed the boss," the drug dealer told an associate nervously. "Now what am I gonna do?"

off and on *(adv. phrase)* General: occasionally
We corresponded off and on for twenty years before actually meeting.

off base *(prep. phrase)* General: out of line, inappropriate
What you said to my mother was way off base.

off-color *(adj.)* General: improper and in bad taste
Barney told an off-color joke at the dinner table and mother frowned.

off-load *(verb)* Government, Military: unload
After the sixteen-hour flight, the agency plans to off-load the relief supplies for the refugee camp immediately.

off one's feed *(adj. phrase)* General: ill, nauseated
No dinner for me tonight. I'm a little off my feed.

off one's hinges *(expression)* General: in a diminished mental state

Matty's off his hinges if he thinks I'm going to do a double-shift for him tonight.

off the beam *(adj. phrase)* General: mistaken
You're way off the beam if you think I had anything to do with that incident.

off the beaten path *(adv. phrase)* General: not among the usual popular and well-known choices
This restaurant is a little off the beaten path, but it's well worth the trip.

off the cuff *(prep. phrase)* General: in an impromptu manner
When the professor called on Rosie, she was forced to answer off the cuff.

off the hook *(adv. phrase)* General: absolved of responsibility or blame
You're lucky Mom got you off the hook with Dad for denting the car door.

off the top of one's head *(prep. phrase)* General: without too much thought
Off the top of my head, I can only remember the names of three people from the swimming team in high school.

off the wall *(prep. phrase)* General: wacky, crazy
I don't know how you can put up with someone who is so off the wall.

-oholic *(suffix)* Teen &

College: one who is prone or obsessed with something
You're such a snackaholic.

oilie *(noun)* Government & Politics: lobbyist for the oil industry; generally, an oil industry worker
The congressional aides knew they could always count on a decent meal when meeting with the oilies.

okey-doke *(noun)* Street: fake move
Mello tried to give an okey-doke like he was going for a gun, but nobody was fooled.

old hand *(noun phrase)* General: expert
Here, let me help. I'm an old hand at tying knots.

old hat *(adj. phrase)* General: outdated
That comedy club downtown is old hat.

old man, the 1. *(noun phrase)* Seafarer: ship's captain
Look at the old man rolling up his sleeves and working with the swabbies. What a guy!
2. *(noun phrase)* Government: a term used by upper-level Administration officials in reference to the President
"This policy proposal is in no shape to show the old man," the chief of staff scolded the undersecretary.

on again, off again *(adj. phrase)* General: fluctuating and uncertain

Leon and Margaret had an on-again, off-again relationship for years.

on a head trip *(prep. phrase)* General: to be on an egotistical high
After Jonathan was made partner in the firm, he went on a head trip that wouldn't quit.

on a mission *(prep. phrase)* Teen & College: seeking
We're on a mission for some chocolate donuts.

on a roll *(adv. phrase)* General: having a series of successes
Mr. Nokes was on a roll with his vacuum cleaner sales.

on a shoestring *(adv. phrase)* General: within a tiny budget
Darla threw a terrific party on a shoestring.

on board *(adv. phrase)* General: associated with
Luke had only been on board with the company for three months when he was fired.

on call *(adj. phrase)* General: ready at a moment's notice
As an intern, Kelly was on call at the hospital every other weekend.

once in a blue moon *(adv. phrase)* General: only very occasionally
I come to town once in a blue moon.

on cloud nine *(prep. phrase)* General: ecstatic
Gina got the department award for best customer service and she's on cloud nine.

one-armed bandit *(noun phrase)* Gambling: slot machine, like those found in gambling establishments
Gloria made twenty-five dollars playing the one-armed bandit at the Jackpot Casino.

on easy street *(adj. phrase)* General: financially comfortable
Frankly, with her salary, Susan has always been on easy street.

one foot in the grave *(noun phrase)* General: near death, in terrible shape
Barnstable has one foot in the grave and he's still going to work every day.

one for the books *(noun phrase)* General: something extraordinary; short for one for the record books
Willis's funny story last night was really one for the books.

one-liner *(noun)* Entertainment: joke told in one sentence
Jerry is so busy spouting one-liners that I can never start a serious discussion.

One's eyes are bigger than one's stomach *(expression)* General: One overestimates one's level of hunger in relation to the amount of food one can actually eat
I can't eat all these ribs. I guess my eyes were bigger than my stomach.

one's hat is on too tight *(expression)* General: in a diminished mental state

"The vicar's hat is on too tight," a parishioner complained.

one wheel is in the sand *(expression)* General: in a diminished mental state
Brock must have one wheel in the sand since he just painted his house chartreuse.

on hand *(adv. phrase)* General: nearby and available
You should always have a good first-aid kit on hand.

on hit *(prep. phrase)* Street: pleasurable or attractive
That slow song was on hit.

on-hold music *(noun phrase)* Office Talk: recorded music that plays over a telephone line while a person waits to speak with someone
Jenny was enjoying the on-hold music, which sounded like disco from the 70s.

onload *(verb)* Military: to load
The relief supplies were onloaded between bombing runs.

only one oar in the water *(expression)* General: in a diminished mental state
Liz's mom must have only one oar in the water since she just handed her over car keys to us.

on one's coattails *(prep. phrase)* Government & Politics: on the strength of a more popular and successful politician's election or reelection; referring to one successful candidate's ability to help carry others to election victory; also used generally

The new congressman well knew he'd won the election by riding on the President's coattails.

on one's high horse *(prep. phrase)* General: self-important
Gina has been on a high horse ever since winning that promotion.

on one's last legs *(prep. phrase)* General: near the end, almost expired
This ironing board is on its last legs so I'll have to get a new one.

on one's toes *(adj. phrase)* General: alert
You'll really have to keep on your toes if you want to make money in the stock market.

on one's watch *(prep. phrase)* General: during a time when one was in charge of something
The general managers were fired because profits had plummeted on their watch.

on pins and needles *(adj. phrase)* General: nervous
I'm on pins and needles waiting for the results of the tests I took at the hospital.

on-scene show *(noun phrase)* Entertainment: television program featuring footage from the scene of a crime or accident, including reports from victims and eye-witnesses
The on-scene show reported dozens of people being assisted by emergency personnel who described the horrifying details of the plane crash.

on second thought *(adv. phrase)* General: after reconsideration
On second thought, I think I will have a drink before dinner.

on shaky ground *(prep. phrase)* General: in an uncertain condition
I feel like I'm on shaky ground with my boss lately.

on the back burner *(expression)* Business, Government, General: low-priority matter doomed to suffer an indefinite delay
We've got bigger problems at the moment, so let's put that situation on the back burner.

on the ball *(adj. phrase)* General: alert and able
Greg is really on the ball and probably will get a management position in the firm.

on the bandwagon *(prep. phrase)* General: in accordance with popular taste or behavior
I guess I'll get on the bandwagon and vote for the mayor again.

on the blink *(adj. phrase)* General: broken or malfunctioning
I can't wash your clothes because the machine is on the blink.

on the block *(adv. phrase)* General: for sale; short for on the auction block

Our house is on the block because we're moving.

on the dot *(adv. phrase)*
General: precisely on time
Please meet me at three o'clock on the dot.

on the fence *(adj.)* Government & Politics: uncommitted on an issue, and waiting to see which way public opinion is turning before making a commitment
The congresswoman was still on the fence on gun control, even though her party leaders were pressuring for her support.

on the front burner *(expression)* Business, Government, General: matter that merits immediate and concentrated attention
We've got to get this deal on the front burner, or we'll lose our client.

on the house *(adj. phrase)*
General: free, courtesy of the proprietor
Please, have a drink on the house while we arrange a table for you.

on the junk *(prep. phrase)*
Crime & Law, Drug World: addicted to narcotics
Bobby's been on the junk for so long he can't remember the last time he had a steady job.

on the level *(adj. phrase)*
General: truthful
Please be on the level with me about your financial situation.

on the make *(adj. phrase)*

General: constantly looking to make a romantic or sexual connection
Tim is a nice enough guy, but he's always on the make and I hate that.

on the nose *(adv. phrase)*
General: exactly
You guessed the price of that couch on the nose.

on the pipe *(prep. phrase)*
Drug World: being addicted to smoking pure cocaine; *see also:* freebase
Jules is on the pipe. You can't count on him at all anymore.

on the rag *(prep. phrase)* Teen & College: having one's menstrual period
She said she's on the rag and doesn't want to come camping with us this weekend.

on the rocks *(prep. phrase)*
Bars: with ice
Order me a vodka on the rocks, please, while I use the telephone.

on the ropes *(adj. phrase)*
General: nearly out of luck and money
Jim's business is on the ropes, but he's trying to get a bank loan to save it.

on the spur of the moment
(adv. phrase) General: suddenly and without planning
We decided to go to Cooperstown on the spur of the moment.

on the tip of one's tongue
(prep. phrase) General: almost

remembered or spoken

That girl's name was on the tip of my tongue, but she left before I thought of it.

on wheels *(prep. phrase)* Food: to go, referring to food taken away rather than eaten on the premises

"BLT on wheels, no mayo," the waitress barked to the short-order cook.

open *(adj.)* Street: vulnerable

You were open when that guy hit on you at the party.

open-and-shut case *(noun phrase)* General: situation with a certain conclusion

Any seasoned lawyer could tell the murder rap was an open-and-shut case.

open for *(verb phrase)* Entertainment: to perform as the warm-up act for the featured performer (or headliner)

*The comic who opened for the rappers went **ballistic** when nobody clapped.*

open jaw *(noun phrase)* Travel: roundtrip in which the return trip originates at a different place than the arrival point; for example, a passenger flies from Boston to Denver but flies back from Phoenix to Boston

The open jaw the agent booked for Joan cost more than a normal round trip.

open secret *(noun phrase)* General: secret nearly everybody knows

The problems in their marriage were an open secret among friends.

operator *(noun)* General: one who always behaves with his or her own advantage in mind

By the time the cocktail party ended, the bartender had signed up twenty people for his personal fitness training program. What an operator!

O.R. *(noun phrase)* Medical: initialism for operating room

I think Dr. Lansing is in O.R., but I can page her if you like.

-o-rama *(suffix)* Teen & College: suggesting the presence of a lot of something

What a booze-o-rama that party was last night!

orange pouch *(noun phrase)* Government & Politics: receptacle for mail sent special delivery to a legislator's district

The congresswoman's letter to constituents regarding the controversial oil drilling issue was sent by orange pouch.

or what? *(expression)* Teen & College: Or am I wrong?

Is mine the best looking car in the parking lot, or what?

OTE (Overtaken by Events) *(expression)* Government, Military: made moot or obsolete by time and subsequent developments

Although the subcommittee was once considered crucial, it is currently being phased out as OTE.

other side of the coin *(noun phrase)* General: opposing point of view

Do you think there might be another side of the coin in this S&L scandal?

other end of Pennsylvania Avenue, the *(phrase)* Government & Politics: used by the White House and Congress in oblique reference to one another

The President half-joked to the reporter that she should go ask the folks at the other end of Pennsylvania Avenue about the fate of the budget.

out 1. *(verb)* General: to expose someone's secret to the public; originally from the practice of exposing the sexuality of gay people; *see also:* go public

The senator was outed as a blatant womanizer when several female staffers reported to the press his unwelcome advances over the years.

2. *(adj.)* Street: crazy

That guy's just out! Did you see him crash into the wall?

out cold *(adj. phrase)* General: unconscious

Dan was out cold when his buddies discovered he'd fallen from the ladder.

out in left field *(adj. phrase)* General: entirely wrong

Martin was way out in left field when he thought I'd support him.

out in the cold *(adv. phrase)* General: not included

Meg was angry because she was left out in the cold when the wedding was being planned.

out like a light *(adv. phrase)* General: in a fast, deep sleep

As soon as Craig's head hit the pillow he was out like a light.

out of hand *(adv. phrase)* General: out of control

The crowd at the concert got out of hand after the main act came on stage.

out of here *(prep. phrase)* Teen & College: gone

The bell rang and she was out of here.

out of it *(prep. phrase)* General: dazed, distracted

I'm sorry I didn't hear you. I was out of it.

out of one's league *(adj. phrase)* General: caught in a situation where one is surrounded by people who are more skillful, experienced and sophisticated than oneself

The budding writer enjoyed rubbing elbows with famous novelists, but realized she was out of her league.

out of the blue *(adv. phrase)* General: unexpectedly

The money Tory needed to pay his tuition came from out of the blue, and just in time.

out of the loop *(phrase)* Government, Politics: state of being uninformed of inside goings-on

The surest sign of the aide's demise was his coworkers suc-

cessful efforts to keep him out of the loop.

out of thin air *(adv. phrase)* General: from nothing or nowhere
Darren always seemed to be able to get tickets to the best shows out of thin air.

out to lunch *(adj. phrase)* General: absentminded, extremely distracted; *see also:* lunching
I'd never work with Viv because she's really out to lunch.

outsert *(noun)* Advertising: self-contained and detachable advertising supplement within a newspaper or magazine
The cosmetics company's expensive outsert in the leading magazines featured samples and coupons for its new line of colognes and perfumes.

outsider art *(noun phrase)* Art: art produced by those not considered part of the mainstream
The traveling crafts show featured a rich sampling of outsider art, from handmade quilts to folkloric woodcuts.

outtake show *(noun phrase)* Entertainment: program consisting of a series of homemade and/or professional video clips strung together around a common theme
The terrific new outtake show called "Sports Goofs and Blunders" features homemade videos of wacky local sporting events.

overkill *(noun)* Military, General: more destructive power than could possibly be necessary; in general use, excessive
John's thank-you letter to the person who finally hired him was definitely overkill.

overnights *(noun)* Entertainment: ratings for a single night of television
The network was happy with the overnights brought in by the new, flashy sitcom it had broadcast.

over one's head *(prep. phrase)* General: beyond one's ability to understand
That calculus test was way over my head.

oversight *(noun)* Government: defensive term for a mistake
After offering apologies for the oversight, the director was forgiven for the millions lost through careless disregard.

over the edge *(expression)* General: to the point of emotional chaos
The death of her father sent Susanna over the edge.

over the hill *(adj. phrase)* General: beyond one's prime years of youth and vigor
When Gwendolyn couldn't keep up with the younger joggers, she really felt over the hill.

over the top *(adj. phrase)* General: extreme, even outlandish
The television evangelist's delivery was way over the top, but he was still very convincing.

P

PAC *(acronym)* Government & Politics: Political Action Committee, an organization created to promote a specific political agenda through a combination of lobbying and fundraising
A good PAC would be essential in getting the civil rights bill passed.

pack heat *(verb phrase)* Crime & Law: to carry a gun; *see also:* heeled
The small-time hood was more dangerous now that he was packing heat.

pain in the neck *(noun phrase)* Teen & College: source of irritation
What a pain in the neck that customer was!

paint *(noun)* Sports (Basketball): free-throw lane, which is usually a different color from the other floor markings
I caught the pass in the paint and handed it off to Checkers, who threw it in.

paint oneself into a corner *(verb phrase)* General: to get oneself into a situation that is difficult to get out of
You really painted yourself into a corner by offering to throw a party for Shane without her mother's permission.

palm off *(verb phrase)* General: to trick someone into taking something or believing something
I could scream at Henry for palming off these terrible tickets on us when he knew we hated that kind of show.

pan a show *(verb phrase)* Entertainment: to review a show negatively
That critic killed the show when she panned it on the evening news.

pan out *(verb phrase)* General: to have a positive result, to succeed
I hope the new office manager pans out because we really need someone reliable in charge.

panic *(noun)* Drug World: temporary shortage of heroin
Everyone blamed the panic uptown on the recent police busts.

paperless book *(noun phrase)* Computerspeak: book published as readable on a computer, for great range in reference and research
The medical encyclopedia was featured as a paperless book for doctors who used computers.

paper profit *(noun phrase)* Wall Street, Business: expected profit on a security that has not been delivered, or on an uncompleted transaction
Unfortunately, Storm based his projected income on paper profits that never materialized.

paper pusher *(noun phrase)* Government & Politics: em-

ployee who has no authoritative power but merely implements policy by writing/receiving/filing memos, reports, etc.; also known as: pencil pusher
Insecure administrators often surround themselves with obsequious paper pushers.

paperweight (*noun*) Office Talk: low-level office worker with responsibilities that do not require high qualifications
The boss's son doesn't know the business at all; he'll just be a paperweight in the office.

par for the course (*noun phrase*) General: just what one expected
The morning train was late, but that's par for the course.

Pardon me for living! (*expression*) General: sarcastic apology for interfering in another's affairs
Well, pardon me for living! I was just trying to help you get ready for your dinner party

parker (*noun*) General: buttocks
Get your parker over here and tell me about your trip.

parley (*verb*) Street: to relax, to calm down; *see also:* **chill**
Parley, John! Just ignore that jerk.

party favors (*noun phrase*) Teen & College: drugs that turn up at social events
I wonder if there'll be any party favors tonight?

Party on! (*expression*) Teen &

College: Have a great time!; *see also:* Rock on!
I see you guys are ready to go out. Party on!

pass muster (*verb phrase*) General: to meet standards, expectations, or approval
I hope I pass muster with your family at dinner tonight.

pass the buck (*verb phrase*) General: to divert responsibility or blame onto someone else
Gorman always manages to pass the buck when the quarterly sales figures are low.

patch (*noun*) Crime & Law: percentage of the proceeds of a crime that must be given to corrupt police officers for protection from arrest
"We lost more than half our profits taking care of that patch," the drug dealer complained to associates.

pat down (*verb phrase*) Crime & Law: to frisk
The suspect was patted down, then handcuffed to the car door handle.

pathography (*noun*) Word Biz: popular sort of biography which highlights a subject's failings, scandalous behavior, brushes with the law, etc.; also known as trash biography
The royal couple was the subject of yet another best-selling pathography.

patrol (*verb*) Teen & College: to wander aimlessly while deciding an evening's course of action *Barbara and her friends patrolled Broadway while they figured out which movie to see.*

pay lip service *(verb phrase)* General: to make an empty show of support or loyalty
Morton promised to serve on the protest committee, but he was only paying lip service to our cause.

pay-off *(noun)* General: reward
After all these years of hard work, isn't it nice to finally see the pay-off?

payola *(noun)* Entertainment: bribes paid to radio stations to guarantee air time for a record
The payola scandal set the record industry on edge, for there were few that were not implicated in some way.

payroll adjustment *(noun phrase)* Business: euphemism for the firing of an employee
Half of the accounting department were the victims of the company's payroll adjustment program.

pay the freight *(verb phrase)* General: to take responsibility for an expense
I volunteered to pay the freight for my nephew to go to Greece because I knew it was a once-in-a-lifetime opportunity and didn't want him to miss it.

pay through the nose *(verb phrase)* General: to pay an excessive amount

If you don't order your airline tickets ahead of time, you can really pay through the nose in the end.

p.c. *(adv. phrase)* Government & Politics: initialism for Politically Correct, a term for taking a position, political or otherwise, which is offensive to no one
The actor came off in the interview as the picture of p.c., having dabbled in social causes and activism for years and now sharing the limelight with his favorite candidate.

pea brain *(noun phrase)* General: dolt
Mark parked in the handicapped spot and got a ticket. What a pea brain!

peace dividend *(noun phrase)* Government & Politics: extra federal funds that are available because defense spending is reduced during peacetime
Legislators claimed that money would be available for additional unemployment relief due to the current peace dividend.

Peacekeeper *(proper noun)* Military: MX missile of the United States
All the top generals argued the Peacekeeper was their weapon of choice in case of invasion.

peace up *(noun phrase)* Street: good-bye
Hey, man, I'll see you next week. Peace up.

pea shooter *(noun phrase)* Military: low-caliber gun
That pea shooter isn't going to do me any good in battle.

pecking order *(noun phrase)* General: relative rank or status of people in a group
I'm not sure of the pecking order in my office yet, so I better be nice to everybody.

peeps *(noun)* Teen & College: parents; *see also:* rents
What do the peeps think about your summer plans?

pencil in *(verb phrase)* Government, Business, Social: to make tentative plans
I'm not sure if I'll be able to make it, so just pencil me in for lunch.

people meter *(noun phrase)* Entertainment: electronic device used in some television viewers' homes to measure their response to programming
The new actcom didn't fare well on the people meter in its first three weeks on the air.

performance panache *(noun phrase)* Advertising: qualities of excellence, power, and style conveyed in the advertising of certain products
The ads for the luxury sedan said nothing new about the car but simply peddled performance panache.

permahold *(noun)* Office Talk: state of a caller being put on hold for an extended period of time in hopes that she or he will just hang up
I've had this guy on permahold for twenty minutes and he just won't get the message.

person of size *(noun phrase)* PC: large or overweight person
The successful model was proud to be a person of size.

personality *(noun)* Entertainment: television or radio performer who doesn't play a character but simply him or herself
The talk show host was a popular television personality and was asked to be the grand marshal of the Christmas parade.

pessimal *(adj.)* College, Computerspeak: awful; made-up word for the opposite of optimal, which is an actual word
My performance on that exam was pessimal.

pet the cat *(verb phrase)* Surferspeak: to surf a wave crouched down on the surfboard while moving one's arms carefully to maintain balance
Jordy can pet the cat like a real pro.

peter out *(verb phrase)* General: to dwindle, then expire
Efforts to generate new business had petered out over the last few months.

phase in *(verb phrase)* Government: to begin to implement a program or policy
The new director hopes to phase

in a variety of cost-cutting measures.

phase out *(verb phrase)* Government: to begin to dismantle a program or policy
The consultant suggested that the candidate phase out the anti-communist rhetoric he had relied on for years in his public addresses.

phase zero *(noun phrase)* Government, Military: very beginning
Phase zero of the assault will be the establishment of a beach-head position.

phat *(acronym, noun)* Teen & College, Street: Pretty Hips And Thighs, referring to a physically attractive woman
"We're hoping we'll come across some phat at the party," the youths noted.

phoner *(noun)* Entertainment: radio interview conducted by telephone rather than in person
The publicist couldn't get the client to the station in time for an in-person interview, so they had to settle for a phoner.

photo opportunity *(noun phrase)* Government & Politics: even staged for the express purpose of allowing photographs to be taken; also used generally
There will be a photo opportunity following the President's remarks.

phreak *(verb)* Computerspeak, Crime & Law: to illegally access another party's telephone lines
By the time the perps were apprehended, they had made $7,000 worth of calls to 900-numbers by phreaking in an empty office building on weekends.

physical *(adj.)* Sports: overly aggressive, too rough
Those players walked in prepared to play a physical game and weren't disappointed.

pick-me-up *(noun)* General: something used to revive one's spirits or energy
Shopping is a good pick-me-up when I'm feeling down.

pick someone's brain *(verb phrase)* General: to converse with someone at length in order to learn more about a certain subject
I'd like to pick your brain for ten minutes on that health legislation.

pick up your face *(expression)* Teen & College: You should be embarrassed for the stupid thing you did.
I can't believe you broke Mom's favorite lamp messing around like that. Go pick up your face.

piece 1. *(noun)* Cartalk: junky car
The car's trade-in value was unarguably low, mainly because it's such a piece.

2. *(noun)* Crime & Law: handgun
The police couldn't arrest Smith who had a permit for the piece

they found under his car seat.

piece of cake *(noun phrase)*
General: easy; also known as
cake; *see also:* cakewalk
*That French assignment will be
a piece of cake.*

pig out *(verb phrase)* Teen,
College, Food: to overeat
*I totally pigged out on Mrs.
Leone's baked ziti.*

pigeonhole *(verb)* General: to
categorize
*Don't pigeonhole Dave as just a
lawyer. He has a lot of other interests.*

piggyback *(adv. phrase)* General: carried atop one's shoul-
ders or back
*Darlene carried the boy piggy-
back while holding her parcels
in her arms.*

pigheaded *(adj.)* General: stubborn
*Don't be so pigheaded. We have
to come to an agreement now.*

pigskin *(noun)* Sports (Football): football
*Let's toss the pigskin around for
a little while.*

pin down *(verb phrase)* General: to get someone to make a
commitment
*I'd like to pin down Shep on
whether he's attending the conference or not.*

pinch *(verb)* Crime & Law: to
arrest; *see also:* bag, bite, bust,
and collar
*The night manager finally got
pinched for stealing from the cash*

*register after the store's video se-
curity monitor got it on tape.*

pinch hit *(verb phrase)* Sports
(Baseball): to fill in for someone; literally, to bat in place of
someone else
*Sally is out sick today, so I'll
have to pinch hit for her at the
seminar.*

pink-collar *(adj.)* Press: element of the workforce applied to
low-level clerical workers (usually female)
*The pink-collar employment fig-
ures were on the decline, mostly
because of more temps being
employed.*

pinner *(noun)* Teen & College:
thin person
*I've seen Allison talking to that
pinner who's the captain of the
track team.*

pipe dream *(noun phrase)*
General: unrealistic, unattain-
able wish
*Poncho sent away for tourist in-
formation about Europe, but the
trip he had in mind was just a
pipe dream.*

piss and moan *(verb phrase)*
General: to complain
*You've been pissing and moan-
ing about that broken gate for a
month*

pissed *(adj.)* Teen & College:
angry, irritated; also known as:
pissed off
*I was pissed when I found out I
was going to miss my mother's
birthday party.*

pissing match (*noun phrase*)
General: argument
I got into a pissing match with Yvonne over the overdue accounts.

piss or get off the pot (*verb phrase*) General: to make a decision
You better piss or get off the pot because I'm ready to roll on this project now.

pit 1. (*noun*) Wall Street: area where commodities are traded; *see also:* floor
Normally calm and well-mannered people often turn into frantic lunatics when they report for work in the pit.

2. (*noun*) Medical: emergency room of a hospital
"That was a rough night in the pit," the resident noted with exhaustion. "We had a gunshot wound and a carful of crash victims."

pit stop (*noun phrase*) Travel: place along the way on a trip where one takes a break to use the bathroom or to grab a snack; from the car racing term
On the way to the state tournament the team made a quick pit stop at Mickey D's.

Planet X (*proper noun*) Sci-fi: imaginary tenth planet in the solar system
The hypothetical Planet X is the setting for many adventures in space and time.

plastic 1. (*adj.*) Teen & College: phony, artificial
I know you don't like hanging out with that crowd because most of them seem so plastic.

2. (*noun*) Business, General: credit cards
"I'd like to pay with plastic, if you don't mind," the tourist said, heaving innumerable items on the counter.

play by ear (*verb phrase*) General: to improvise
I'd like to have you over for dinner Friday night, but let's just play it by ear.

play cat and mouse (*verb phrase*) General: to tease
Barton has said she'll release me from my contract, but she may be playing cat and mouse with me.

play down (*verb phrase*) General: to take emphasis or attention away from
We've decided to play down the prime minister's visit to the United States for security reasons.

played (*adj.*) Teen & College, Street: expended; short for played out
This party is played. Let's get out of here.

player (*noun*) Teen & College: one who toys with others' emotions, usually by leading them on or by cheating on them
I wouldn't go out with Troy if I were you—he's just a player.

play hardball (*verb phrase*) General: to take a rough, aggressive approach

Those detectives are playing hardball on that homicide and have **clammed** *up.*

playing chicken *(verb phrase)* Cartalk, Business: to engage in a dangerous game in which two cars drive toward each other on a direct collision course, and the first driver to veer away is considered the chicken; commonly used to refer to a determined struggle of wills

You can wait out that salesman on the price because he's just playing chicken with you.

play into someone's hands *(verb phrase)* General: to make oneself vulnerable to the advantage of someone else

The out-of-towner played right into the **hustler's** *hands when he said he was looking for a good time.*

play off *(verb phrase)* General: to pit forces or entities against each other to one's own advantage

Young Charlotte played her parents off each other when she wanted something new.

play one's cards right *(verb phrase)* General: to behave to one's advantage

If you play your cards right, you may just get that extra ticket to the game.

play oneself *(verb phrase)* Street: to kid oneself

Don't play yourself, Joanie.

Maybe Ronnie's not telling you the truth.

play the field *(verb phrase)* General: to avoid settling down to a single commitment, especially with regard to romantic relationships

Tina had been playing the field for so long, the idea of marriage had become foreign to her.

play up *(verb phrase)* General: to highlight or emphasize

Let's play up the dramatic aspect of this story.

play with fire *(verb phrase)* General: to take dangerous risks

You're playing with fire when you go into business with Roscoe.

plex *(noun)* Entertainment: movie cinema featuring multiple screens; short for multiplex

Bart Marlowe's new movie was playing in 80 percent of the plexes across the country.

plug *(verb)* Advertising, Public Relations: to publicly endorse or be seen using a product so as to benefit exposure and sales of the product

Talk show interviews are often nothing more than opportunities for guests to plug their latest book or movie.

plum *(noun)* Government & Politics: prestigious or important government position which is given out at the political discretion of the President

The new President was quick to

reward his allies with plums like the ambassadorship to Bermuda.

plumber *(noun)* Medical: urologist

Don had no choice but to visit a plumber. He'd been uncomfortable for weeks.

P.M.S. monster *(noun phrase)* Teen & College: menstruating female

I'm such a P.M.S. monster today I don't even want to go to class.

podmall *(noun)* Real Estate: small-scale neighborhood shopping center; also known as: a strip center

A new ice cream shop was about to open in the Riverdale podmall.

points 1. *(noun)* Entertainment: percentage partnership in a movie or theatrical production

The movie's investors counted on their points bringing in a return, at least after the release of the video.

2. *(noun)* Real Estate, Banking: percentage of a mortgage charged by the lender as a fee for making the loan; one point equals one percent of the total mortgage

The bank agreed to a slightly higher interest rate on the loan instead of charging points.

pointless pollution *(noun phrase)* Ecology: environmental contaminants produced when technology has developed more ecologically sound alternatives

The burger chain abandoned its unbiodegradable styrofoam packaging as pointless pollution and switched to recycled paper wrappers.

poison pill *(noun phrase)* Wall Street: device used to make a deal or takeover less appealing and more difficult to achieve

After frantically trying to hold off the takeover attempt, the board finally determined that a poison pill would be the company's last chance.

pokey *(noun)* General: jail; also known as: bighouse, cage, cooler, klink, pen, slammer, and stir

You're going to find yourself in the pokey if you don't straighten up and fly right.

policy *(noun)* Government, Business: proscribed position on a matter

We expect all employees to adhere to company policy regarding dress code.

policy wonk *(noun phrase)* Government & Politics: mildly derogatory term for an individual who is most concerned with the specific details of public policy

The candidate always ended up sounding like a policy wonk whenever he was interviewed on television.

polish off *(verb phrase)* General: to finish

We polished off two bottles of wine with dinner.

polish up *(verb phrase)*
General: to improve
I would like to polish up my Italian before we go on our trip.

polluted *(adj.)* Teen & College: intoxicated
You were so polluted at that dance last night I bet you don't even remember my name.

pollution rights *(noun phrase)* Government & Politics: concept that allows corporations to pay a community for the right to pollute its environment, in the belief that this financial burden will induce corporations to reduce their pollution levels
Chemi-Ko recently paid Dintyville $4 million dollars for the pollution rights to emit a certain quantity of toxic vapors into the air every day.

po-mo *(noun)* Art: short for postmodernism
VanGel's early works were distinctly po-mo, but he later moved on to other styles.

pond scum *(noun phrase)* Teen & College: contemptible person; *see also:* scum-sucking pig
How could you dump her like that? You're pond scum!

poop, the *(noun)* General: information; also sometimes refers to inside information or gossip; also known as: the scoop, the skinny
What's the poop on those flight changes?

porcupine provisions *(noun phrase)* Wall Street: legal devices used to deter takeovers
The stock purchase plan was sprinkled with porcupine provisions.

pork barrel *(noun phrase)* Government & Politics: fictional deep well of public funding into which legislators habitually reach for money to pay for pet projects in home districts
The congressman was the master of pork barrel politics, securing all manner of federal funding for special projects back home.

poser *(noun)* Teen & College: one who tries unsuccessfully to latch onto a group by dressing or acting like them
Nina is such a poser that she bought hundreds of dollars of clothes just to look like us.

posse *(noun)* Teen & College: group of friends, usually with an interest in common; *see also:* squad
The posse from the football team took over the lunchroom every time they walked in.

possie *(noun)* Teen & College: group of girlfriends; *see also:* squad
Elizabeth was watching videos with her posse when Josh called.

postcard pressure *(noun phrase)* Government &

Politics: heavy constituent mail on an issue, especially the type generated by special interest groups

The postcard pressure the senator is getting is really swaying her vote on the housing bill.

postnup *(noun)* Crime & Law: short for postnuptial agreement; a contract between spouses that lays out the financial terms of a divorce should it ever occur

Anne's postnup set a generous percentage of assets and income to her husband.

potatoes in one's ears *(noun phrase)* Kids: dirty ears

Yuck, Kyle's got potatoes in his ears

pound 1. *(noun)* Crime & Law: .357 handgun; term refers to heft of the weapon

The guy had two pounds and an Uzi that he was selling from the back of his car.

2. *(verb)* Food & Drink, Teen & College: to consume an entire beverage in a single drawing

I pounded a couple of shots, then went to the reception.

pound the pavement *(verb phrase)* General: to search aggressively for employment or business

I've been pounding the pavement for three months and haven't made a sale yet.

power breakfast/lunch/ dinner *(noun phrase)* Politics, Food: meeting that takes place over a meal among important officials, politicians, businesspeople, etc.

The reporter spotted the senator and the agriculture secretary having a power breakfast in the hotel dining room.

powerhouse *(adj.)* General: extremely successful in a field or activity

The team's new hitter is a powerhouse: three homeruns in one game.

powers that be *(noun phrase)* General: those in positions of authority

The powers that be told me that you're not to be trusted.

preacher's car *(noun phrase)* Cartalk: car without fancy options

You can save money on a basic model if you don't mind driving a preacher's car.

preemie *(noun)* Medical: prematurely born infant

Though Alexander had been a preemie, he caught up in normal development by his second birthday.

prenup *(noun)* Crime & Law: short for prenuptial agreement, a contract signed between two parties planning to marry that outlines financial terms of a divorce settlement should a misfortune occur

Both Dan and Rachel were strongly opposed to the idea of a prenup against the advice of

their parents, accountants, and lawyers.

preppie *(noun)* Press: one who attends or has attended a prep school

Molly looks like such a preppie in that blazer and khakis.

press pool *(noun phrase)* Government & Politics: collection of reporters covering a certain aspect of government exclusively

The White House press pool waited all morning for the announcement about the President's weekend travel plans.

pretty *(adj.)* Teen & College: stupid, ridiculous

This is really pretty—I lost my keys and nobody's home.

pre-woman *(noun)* PC: young female; used in place of girl

The Institute sponsored a poetry reading for pre-women from certain inner city areas.

prickly *(adj.)* General: sensitive

You've always been a bit prickly on the subject of your in-laws.

primo *(adj.)* Foreign (Italian): first, best, ultimate

That dinner was primo, Dad, truly excellent.

private sector *(noun phrase)* Government: real world of business or private enterprise, or anything outside of government; also known as: public sector

After failing to be reelected, many senators return to their lucrative positions in the private sector.

program *(noun)* Government, Military: all-purpose term for a policy, expenditure, legislative effort, etc.

The school lunch program appeared to be the only item in the bill that was not destined to be cut.

promise the moon *(verb phrase)* General: to make promises that are not possible to fill

Some exotic tour companies promise travelers the moon, then fail to deliver.

prop art *(noun phrase)* Art: short for propaganda art, or art with a prevailing political content

Madame M's performance pieces were panned by the critics as angry, distorted prop art.

prophet of doom *(noun phrase)* General: one who constantly predicts the worst

Stephens was a prophet of doom who never let the other board members get optimistic about the foundation's future.

props *(noun)* Street: weapons or guardians used for protection

I had my props with me when I went to Rosie's funeral.

prune *(noun)* Government & Politics: person who has held a plum position in government for a significant amount of time

An old prune like me won't like losing a post in Paris with the change in administrations.

pseudo *(noun)* Teen & College: phony person, one who is trying too hard

I can't believe you'd cheat on me like that. What a pseudo.

psych *(expression)* Street: Just kidding! That was a joke!

I heard you didn't make the soccor team. Psych!

psycho *(noun)* Teen & College: weird person

Who is that psycho lurking around the restrooms?

psychotic *(adj.)* Teen & College: excellent

That ride at the Aqua Universe was psychotic.

public sector *(noun phrase)* Government: government—all branches, all levels, from federal to local

Ideally, all those employed in the public sector should consider themselves accountable to the taxpayer.

public trough *(noun phrase)* Government & Politics: taxpayers' dollars that pay off consultants, contractors, and corporations, etc., hired by the government

The newspaper wrote a scathing editorial about the high-priced consultants feeding at the public trough.

puffing *(noun)* Real Estate: exaggerated or misleading assertions sometimes made in an effort to sell a piece of property

If you really want to buy a house, listening to that broker's puffing will only confuse you.

pull a _____ *(verb phrase)* Teen & College: to behave in a similar manner as someone or something

It looks like she's going to pull a Greta Garbo and stay in her room.

pull a boner *(verb phrase)* General: to make a mistake that has significant consequences

The driver pulled a boner when he made an illegal U-turn and ran into a pick-up truck coming from the other direction.

pull an all-nighter *(verb phrase)* Teen & College: to remain awake all through the night, usually finishing a paper or project

I'm going to have to pull an all-nighter to finish my thesis.

pull it off *(verb phrase)* General: to succeed, to be convincing

I'm not sure I'm going to be able to pull it off in this disguise.

pull one's leg *(verb phrase)* General: to trick someone into believing something, just for fun

Clancy was pulling my leg when he said he got a call from the White House.

pull one's weight *(verb phrase)* General: to make a fair contribution, to do one's fair share of work

Todd was released from his contract because he wasn't pulling his weight on the team.

pull out all the stops *(verb phrase)* General: go to all extremes

Let's pull out all the stops and

throw a huge party for graduation.

pull rank *(verb phrase)* General: to exercise one's superior position

Everyone was shocked when Manny suddenly pulled rank and started giving people orders around the office.

pull something out of a hat *(verb phrase)* General: to conjure up, as if by magic

I just pulled those numbers out of a hat, but they sounded okay, didn't they?

pull strings *(verb phrase)* General: to use one's influence

I think I can pull some strings and get your son a summer job at the beach.

pull the chicken switch *(verb phrase)* General: to panic

Carol pulled the chicken switch when she couldn't see Tommy in the pool.

pull the plug 1. *(verb phrase)* Medical: to remove a terminal or comatose patient from life support systems

I'm going to instruct the doctor to pull the plug if things go back after surgery.

2. General: to quit or abort an activity

Are you sure you want to pull the plug? I think this business could take off in a couple years.

pull the rug out from under *(verb phrase)* General: to upset one's plans or position

You really pulled the rug out from under me when you announced you were closing the business.

pull through *(verb phrase)* General: to recover from an injury or illness

I'm glad to see Clarissa pulled through after her cancer operation.

pump *(verb)* Drug World, Street: to sell

I think Winnie's pumping Hawaiian weed this week.

pump it up *(verb phrase)* Teen & College: to turn up the volume on live or stereo music

I love this song. Could you pump it up?

pump up *(verb phrase)* Health & Fitness: to lift weights for an immediate effect on the appearance of one's muscular structure

I want to pump up for the publicity photograph.

punchline *(noun)* Entertainment: closing line of a joke

The bored audience couldn't wait for the comedian to get to the punchline.

puppy *(noun)* Teen & College: thing

What a disgusting joke! You're a sick puppy.

push someone's buttons *(verb phrase)* General: to know just what to say or do to irritate or anger someone

My sister will be pushing my

buttons within minutes of her arrival—we argue whenever we see each other.

push the envelope *(verb phrase)* General: to push something almost beyond its limit

The performance artist's show pushed the envelope with its controversial subject matter and profane dialogue.

push the panic button *(verb phrase)* General: to become frightened and panic

Dolly pushed the panic button when she heard noises coming from the basement.

put it in high gear *(verb phrase)* General: to hurry, to speed up

Kerry had to put it in high gear to make it to the lecture on time.

put one's finger on something *(verb phrase)* General: to identify the answer to a question or problem

I think you've put your finger on why Joan is always late for school.

put one's foot down *(verb phrase)* General: to prohibit; in some cases, to be firmly against

If I don't put my foot down on Saturday cartoons, the kids won't leave the house until noon.

put one's foot in one's mouth *(verb phrase)* General: to say something rude, inappropriate, or embarrassing; also known as: put one's foot in it

I really put my foot in my mouth when I asked Sharon if she'd lost weight.

put one up to *(verb phrase)* General: to persuade someone to do something

Who put Kyle up to stealing that gun?

put on one's thinking cap *(verb phrase)* General: to set one's mind to solving a problem

I've got to put on my thinking cap and figure out how to pay for the new furnace.

put on the feed bag *(verb phrase)* General: to eat

I can't wait to put on the feed bag. I'm starving.

put on the map *(verb phrase)* Advertising, Public Relations: to give an unknown product or personality high public profile status through promotion and/or advertising

The retractable phone cord is sure to put our telecommunications company on the map.

put the bite on *(verb phrase)* General: to ask for something

Marcia put the bite on me to babysit this weekend.

put the pedal to the metal *(verb phrase)* Cartalk: to push the car accelerator as far as it will go

You better put the pedal to the metal if we want to get there first.

put two and two together *(verb phrase)* General: to reason toward a conclusion

It was only a matter of time before Vince put two and two together and figured out Olivia was working two jobs.

put words in one's mouth (*verb phrase*) General: to make an unfounded claim about what someone else thinks or believes
I never said I believed in reincarnation; you're putting words in my mouth.

Q

Q. (*noun*) Entertainment: recognizability
Blanche Whiting hasn't had a decent role in years, but thanks to her work in commercials, she still has a remarkably high Q.

quarter (*noun*) Drug World: twenty-five dollars' worth of a drug
Lisa picked up a quarter on her way to the party.

queef (*verb*) Teen & College: to pass gas
Milton queefed just as he stood up to do his trumpet solo.

-queen (*noun*) Teen & College: female with an extreme characteristic or habit
I'm trying not to be such a pizza queen.

queer (*adj.*) Teen & College: embarrassingly stupid; weird
That card he sent me for my birthday was so queer.

queeve (*verb*) Teen & College: to run out of momentum; term

usually used in reference to skateboarding
I make it all the way to the end of the run and then I queeve.

quick fix (*noun phrase*) Government: immediate, though, in the end, an inadequate and incomplete solution; *see also:* applying a band-aid
The emergency relief provided after the hurricane was just a quick fix for the devastated community.

quimby (*noun*) Surferspeak: jerk
What are you going out with that quimby for?

quit cold turkey (*verb phrase*) General: to give up a habit at once, without any gradual weaning
I quit doing the daily crossword puzzle cold turkey. It was beginning to control my life.

R

R & D (*noun phrase*) Government, Business: common abbreviation for the research and development department of a company or enterprise
The recession forced the industry to cut back on its R & D, causing its technology to fall behind on the international market.

R & R (*noun phrase*) General: initialism for Rest and Relaxation, especially after a long spell of hard work

Priscilla just came off a double shift at the hospital and all she could think of was a weekend of R & R.

rabbit food *(noun phrase)* Food: fresh, uncooked, and un-adulterated fruit and vegetables
I ate rabbit food for a week and still didn't lose weight.

race norming *(noun phrase)* Education, PC: practice of adjusting the scores on standardized tests to reflect the relative rank of the person taking the test within the test score norms of his or her own race
The private school had an unspoken policy of race norming when considering the test scores of its applicants.

rack *(verb)* Teen & College: to sleep
I'm probably going to rack late tomorrow, so don't call me until noon.

rack monster *(noun phrase)* Teen & College: one who requires or demands plenty of sleep
Darlene is such a rack monster I'm sure she'll never show up for her first class on time.

rack one's brains *(verb phrase)* General: to search one's memory
I racked my brains trying to remember where I left those keys.

rad *(adj.)* Teen & College, Kids: very cool, impressive; short for radical
No one could believe the rad suit Mr. Knight wore to the dance.

rage *(verb)* Teen & College: to have a great time
We raged on Friday at the frat party.

ragging 1. *(adj.)* Teen & College: well dressed
Joanie was ragging for the graduation party her parents threw.
2. *(verb)* Teen & College: complaining, harassing
I wish Coach would quit ragging on me about getting a haircut.

rags *(noun)* Teen & College: clothing
"Nice rags," Dean said to his sister approvingly.

raider *(noun)* Wall Street: individual who rushes in and acquires other companies by buying large amounts of stock
Few of the notorious corporate raiders from the 1980s managed to emerge in the 90s with their fortunes and reputations intact.

railroad *(verb)* General: to force something to happen through wit or intimidation
I will not let you railroad me into a trip I can't afford.

railroad flat *(noun phrase)* Real Estate: apartment whose floor plan requires one to walk through one room to get to the other
The young women decided against renting the railroad flat because they needed more privacy.

railway thinking *(noun phrase)* Sci-fi: belief that the events of history (on a grand and personal scale) repeat themselves

"But that's just indulging in a bit of railway thinking," the professor admitted to the roomful of students.

rainmaker *(noun)* Business: one thought to be a creative leader in developing business

Sheena was widely regarded as a rainmaker among the city's top executives.

raise eyebrows *(verb phrase)* General: to cause surprise or disapproval

The controversial industrialist's contribution to the candidate's campaign raised a few eyebrows in the press.

rake it in *(verb phrase)* General: to earn plenty of money

The Snyders have hired a housekeeper, gardener, and nanny, so I guess they must be raking it in now.

rake over the coals *(verb phrase)* General: to criticize

The graduate professors didn't like Sally's new painting, and they ruked her over the coals in their report.

ralph *(verb)* Teen & College: to vomit; also known as: barf, blow lunch, boag, boot, decorate one's shoes, drive the porcelain bus, earl, heave, honk, hurl, reverse gears, shout at one's shoes, spew, toss, yak, yawn in technicolor, and zuke

Dean tried to make it home but finally had to pull the car over and ralph on the side of the road.

rampage *(verb)* Teen & College: to search frantically

I've been rampaging for red shoes to go with my new dress.

ramscoop *(noun)* Sci-fi: spaceship that converts the hydrogen it collects in space into energy

Milo's ramscoop was a dependable ride but couldn't begin to generate the power needed to jump to hyperspace.

rancid *(adj.)* Teen & College: awful

What a rancid couple those two make.

random *(adj.)* Teen & College: out of the ordinary

This random guy comes up to me and asks me to dance.

rank 1. *(verb phrase)* Teen & College: to insult; also known as: rank out

Bo just stood there without saying anything while Ronnie ranked him.

2. *(verb phrase)* Teen & College: to back out of a commitment

Minas promised he'd play tennis this afternoon, but he ranked out at the last minute.

3. *(adj.)* Teen & College: disgusting

Marvin's sneakers are rank. Let's get rid of them.

ranker *(noun)* Teen & College: person who backs out of a commitment

Gwen says she's not going to dance with us. What a ranker.

rap sheet *(noun phrase)* Crime & Law: computer-generated printout of an individual's entire criminal record

The suspect had a rap sheet a mile long, and the detectives were pretty sure this was the character they were looking for.

rap someone's knuckles *(verb phrase)* General: to give a mild punishment

I got my knuckles rapped for forging my boss's signature on that letter.

raring to go *(adj. phrase)* General: ready for action

I got a great night's sleep and I'm raring to go.

rat *(verb)* Crime & Law: to inform or testify against another party; see also: belch and sing

The gang leader didn't even worry whether his loyal lieutenants would rat.

rat boy *(noun phrase)* Drug World: person in a drug community who has an ability to test the purity and potency of a drug, acting as a human experiment

The Weasel was the neighborhood rat boy, and nobody could read a new load better than him.

rate *(verb)* Seafarer: to deserve

"You don't rate a second dessert, never mind a shore leave, you miserable swabbie," the officer barked.

rat race *(noun phrase)* General: daily grind of work, eat, sleep, etc.

The rat race in New York is really getting me down.

rattle around *(verb phrase)* General: to be somewhere, though one is not sure quite where

I think there's some money rattling around in my purse.

rattle someone's cage *(verb phrase)* General: to irritate someone

Oh, great—it's Monday, and here comes the boss to rattle my cage.

raunchy *(adj.)* Teen & College: disgusting

What a raunchy meal this is.

raw *(adj.)* Surferspeak: terrific

That new guy has some raw moves.

raw deal *(noun phrase)* General: unfair arrangement or conclusion

You go to the beach and I stay home and babysit? What a raw deal!

razor boy/girl *(noun phrase)* Sci-fi: unpleasant cyberpunk character who menaces others with cybernetic appliances such as razor claws or other moderately empowering devices

Vera's friends started calling her "razor girl" for her extraordinary manicure and contentious demeanor.

reach for the sky *(verb phrase)* General: to try to attain one's dream

Marla decided to reach for the

sky, so she moved to Hollywood to become a powerful studio executive.

read between the lines (verb phrase) General: to understand someone's meaning by correctly imagining what was left unsaid
You have to read between the lines a bit to understand what the countess's letter is saying.

read my lips (expression) General: listen closely to what I am saying in case you didn't hear me the first time
Read my lips, class. No late assignments.

read someone the riot act (verb phrase) General: to chastise someone
If that babysitter lets those kids stay up until midnight again, I'm going to read him the riot act.

Reagan Democrat (proper noun) Government & Politics: modern, conservative sort of Democrat who voted for Ronald Reagan for president in 1980 and 1984, and who continue to reflect a tendency toward conservatism on a number of issues in public opinion polls
There are still plenty of Reagan Democrats in public office who are pulling the Democratic party away from traditional liberal positions.

reality check (noun phrase) General: examination of one's thoughts and motives to determine whether one is being realistic or just hopeful
Whoa, we've got to have a reality check here. We don't even have that new account yet.

reality programming (noun phrase) Entertainment: television shows featuring real people in real situations
There was a rash of reality programming on the networks' fall schedules: two ride-with-the-cop shows, a ride-with-the-ambulance show, and a courtroom-based program.

ream (verb) Teen & College: to treat unfairly
I'm sick of getting reamed by that professor just because he doesn't like me.

rear admiral (noun phrase) Medical: proctologist
Jim had put off the appointment long enough. The time had come to visit the rear admiral.

rear-ender (noun) Traffic: accident where the front of one car hits the back of another
My father hurt his back in that rear-ender on Carlton Avenue.

rebirthing (noun) Psychology: New Age therapeutic technique where memories of birth are supposedly stimulated by an enforced breathing technique similar to hyperventilation
Corinne attended a weeklong rebirthing seminar in the mountains.

red-eye (noun) Air & Space: late-night, coast-to-coast flight

If you want to make the meeting in Los Angeles on time, you'll have to take the red-eye from New York.

redlining *(verb)* Real Estate: illegal lending policy that does not allow loans for property in certain areas; used to control the racial composition of neighborhoods

The bank was heavily fined when it was proven that they were redlining to keep Hispanic families from moving into the previously all-Irish neighborhood.

red pipe *(noun phrase)* Medical: artery, as opposed to a blue pipe, which is a vein

Walters is scheduled for major surgery to repair his red pipes.

redshirt 1. *(verb)* Sports: to keep a college player from competing for a season in order to take advantage of his or her eligibility to play the following season

Watson was redshirted with the understanding he'd be the starting player in his position the next year.

2. *(verb)* Education: to delay a child's enrollment in kindergarten so that he or she would have more time for emotional and physical development before entering school

The counselor recommended that Winston be redshirted for a year because he seemed emotionally young for his age.

redundancy of human resources *(noun phrase)* Government, Business: unnecessary employees; usually when a company department discovers its work load could be handled easily by fewer employees

Payrolls can always be cut back by a concentrated effort to identify a company's redundancy of human resources.

reek *(verb)* Teen & College: to stink

Tell Beau to get out of my car. His feet reek.

reeker *(noun)* Medical: stinky patient

Someone give number 2B a sponge bath, please. She's a real reeker.

ref *(noun)* Sports: referee

The ref blew his whistle furiously, but the players continued to fight.

reg-neg *(verb)* Government & Politics: short for regulatory negotiation, which is the practice of adjusting government regulations to suit an interested party

The paper companies reg-negged a deal with the government on air emissions standards.

regular guy *(noun phrase)* General: likeable, unpretentious person

Oh, you'll like Joe. He's a regular guy.

rehab *(verb)* Real Estate: to rehabilitate or renovate

As soon as we rehab the apart-

ment the new tenants can move in.

reinvent the wheel *(verb phrase)* Government, Business: to attempt to resolve or refine something already considered to be in an acceptable form
The analyst's suggestions pleased the stockholders, but the board was aware that she was just reinventing the wheel.

rents *(noun)* Teen & College: short for parents; *see also:* peeps
My rents are going away for the weekend, so I can't have the car.

repeat offender *(noun phrase)* Crime & Law: individual caught and punished for committing the same crime over and over
Dolly was certainly looking at time since the judge never let repeat offenders off easy.

repetitive strain injury *(noun phrase)* Medical: occupational injury resulting from the strain imposed on muscles in the hands, wrists, or necks, while engaged in repeated actions such as typing or working with small instruments or machine components
Repetitive strain injuries affect people in many jobs, from butchers to machine and computer operators.

reskilling *(verb)* Government, Business: to retrain, usually referring to new job skills for workers laid off in other fields
The revival of western Penn-

sylvania's economy is credited to the reskilling of so many former steel industry employees.

retool *(verb)* Military: to repeat an action
Let's retool on programming those coordinates. I'm not sure we've got them right.

revenue enhancement *(noun phrase)* Government & Politics: term used instead of tax or taxes, because tax has become a dirty word in the vocabulary of the legislator looking to be re-elected
The proposed oil tax was a particularly unpopular method of revenue enhancement and was soundly defeated by lobbyists from the oil industry.

revenue shortfall *(noun phrase)* Government: deficit, more money spent than was taken in
Ambitious election-year programs often become victims of revenue shortfall.

revolving door *(noun phrase)* Government, Politics: practice of certain government employees to shift constantly between public service to private employment according to opportunities
Jumping from senator to industry exec to vice-president, Stephens had proved himself master of the revolving door.

rhyme or reason *(noun phrase)* General: logical explanation
There's no rhyme or reason to

Derrick's evacuation plan.

rice burner *(noun phrase)*
Cartalk: Japanese-made vehicle
U.S. auto sales have slumped from all the rice burners on the market.

ride 1. *(noun)* Teen & College:
car
Your brother's got a cool ride.

2. *(verb)* Teen & College: to haunt or harass
My uncle's been riding me about not going to college.

ride herd on *(verb phrase)*
General: to guard closely
I had to ride herd on a dozen third-graders at the museum.

rider *(noun)* Teen & College:
derogatory term for an uninvited guest or tag-along
I'm not taking you and all your rider friends to the movies with me and that's final.

ride shotgun 1. *(verb phrase)*
Teen & College: to ride in the front passenger seat of a car
Get in the back seat. I'm riding shotgun this time.

2. *(verb phrase)* General: to defend
I had to ride shotgun for Henderson in that meeting today.

ride the boards *(verb phrase)*
Advertising: to drive around an area and survey the collective effect of billboards
The sales representatives spent the afternoon riding the boards.

riding high *(adj. phrase)* General: at the peak of popularity

After winning the World Series, the Redbirds were riding high.

RIF (Reduction in Force)
(noun phrase) Government, Military: decrease in staff size through layoffs; always the result of government budget cuts
The true decline of the nation's military presence in Europe will begin with extensive military and civilian RIFs.

riff *(noun)* Entertainment: a musical sequence (as on a guitar); also imitation or version of someone else's performance
Vee did a splendid riff of an old Miles Davis favorite.

right-brained *(adj.)* Medical:
linear oriented, as opposed to conceptually oriented; opposite of left-brained
I think I have trouble with the professor's sweeping lectures because I'm right-brained.

right hand doesn't know what the left is doing, the
(expression) General: to be unaware of the actions of those with whom one should be in close contact
I'm not surprised that both of us ordered birthday cakes for Sean. It seems like the right hand doesn't know what the left is doing anymore.

right off the bat *(adv. phrase)*
General: immediately
I knew I liked you right off the bat.

right out of the chute *(adv.*

phrase) General: brand new
Don't be critical of my new story because it's right out of the chute.

rim shot *(noun phrase)* Entertainment: old-time term for a gag in which the drummer emphasizes the punchline of a comedian's joke
The hip young comic delivered a series of rim shots in imitation of nightclub comics from the old days to the delight of the older adults in the crowd.

ring a bell *(verb phrase)* General: to cause to remember
Her name doesn't ring a bell, but maybe I'd recognize her if I saw her.

ringer *(noun)* Sports: illegal player
The team was penalized when it was discovered they had a ringer on the field.

ring the register *(verb phrase)* Business: to realize a profit
Finally I'm ringing the register with this new product I'm selling.

rip 1. *(noun)* Teen & College: bad deal; short for rip-off
I've only had this car a month and the transmission died. What a rip!

2. *(verb)* Cartalk: to drive extremely fast; short for rip up the road
I was ripping down Route 9 when I saw the cop's flashing lights.

ripped *(adj.)* Teen & College: intoxicated

I had no idea I was so ripped last night.

roadblock *(noun)* Advertising: complete saturation of an advertising medium or media with simultaneous advertisements for a product; seen as a way to deflect competitive advertising and to ensure consumer exposure to the product
We're going to do a roadblock for Fizz Cola on the networks tonight.

road dog *(noun phrase)* Teen & College: best friend
Mom, Vinnie's my road dog, so be nice to him.

road hog *(noun phrase)* General: person who monopolizes the road, making it difficult for other drivers to maneuver or pass
Bella was a terrible road hog, and other drivers were always beeping their horns at her.

roadkill *(noun)* Traffic: animal casualties caused by traffic and left along the roadway
There was an unprecedented incidence of roadkill on the scenic highway that spring.

road show *(noun phrase)* Entertainment: touring production of a theatrical or musical show
Cecil was gone for six months doing a road show in Europe.

rob *(verb)* Teen & College: to ridicule someone with a witty remark
Wow, you robbed that guy! He

won't be bothering you any-more.

rob Peter to pay Paul *(verb phrase)* General: to resolve a matter at the expense of another; refers to the New Testament characters from the Bible

I don't want to dip into my retirement account to pay off my credit cards. It's a little like robbing Peter to pay Paul.

rob the cradle *(verb phrase)* General: to become romantically involved with someone who is very young, or who is much younger than oneself

Ivy is really robbing the cradle going out with that high school guy.

rock *(noun)* Drug World: portion of a larger quantity of cocaine, broken off in hard, uneven pellets

"Please, just give me a little rock, to tide me over?" the druggie pleaded.

rock on *(expression)* Teen & College: Have a great time!; *see also:* Party on!

It's Friday night! Let's rock on!

rock one's world *(verb phrase)* Teen & College: to upset the status quo

I warned you that getting chummy with Ellen was going to rock your world.

rock the boat *(verb phrase)* General: to disturb the status quo

Let's not rock the boat by push-

ing Reese to pay the money she owes us.

rod *(noun)* Crime & Law: handgun; *see also:* equalizer, heat, and piece

Don't make a move. I've got a rod in my pocket.

roids *(noun)* Health & Fitness, Medical: steroids

Marcel was accused of using roids to bulk up for the competition.

roll around *(verb phrase)* General: to come at a regular time

When spring rolls around, Tanya gets excited again about gardening.

roller *(noun)* Drug World, Street: police or police car; derived from the way patrol cars drive slowly through areas known for drug selling

The peddler spotted the roller as it rounded the corner looking for suspects.

roll out the red carpet *(verb phrase)* General: to give preferential treatment

The town rolled out the red carpet when the soccer team returned from winning the league championship.

roll over *(verb phrase)* Crime & Law: to become a government witness

It wasn't until his former assistant rolled over that the Wall Street big shot knew he'd go to jail for inside trading.

rope *(noun)* Drug World: marijuana cigarette; also known as: spliff and stick

I couldn't believe Terence was standing there smoking a rope right in front of a cop!

ropes, the *(noun)* General: a thorough knowledge of standard procedure

I've got to learn the ropes on my new job before I ask for a special assignment.

Rose Garden strategy *(noun phrase)* Government & Politics: a presidential campaign strategy that calls for the incumbent president to base his credentials on the fact that he is already undeniably in power

The last president continually tried to use Rose Garden strategy to divert attention away from his failings.

rough up *(verb phrase)* General: to treat badly, usually in a physical manner

Those thugs roughed up Raoul and me when we left the bar.

rounder *(noun)* Crime & Law: a street criminal who's always "around" at hotels, bars, and nightclubs, organizing gambling, drug sales, or prostitution; a concierge of the crime world; *see also:* steerer

Billie the rounder was never more than a whistle away when someone was looking for action.

royal *(adj.)* Teen & College: utter

You are a royal pain in the neck.

R.P.G. *(noun phrase)* Fantasy: initialism for Role-Playing Game, a game that lacks the usual gimmickry of board games, but rather has a certain set of rules and guidelines, and lays out a fictional narrative for players to enact an adventure

Wallis was infinitely more comfortable in the R.P.G. world than in the awkward role she had to play in real life.

rubber duckie *(noun phrase)* Seafarers: inflatable raft towed behind a ship as a decoy to the enemy's radar-guided missiles

Sometimes the sailor managed to sneak in a nap in the ship's rubber duckie.

rubberneck *(verb)* Traffic: to slow down and gawk at a car wreck or other roadside spectacle

There were terrible rubbernecking delays in traffic caused by the overturned semi-truck.

rub it in *(verb phrase)* General: to tease or constantly remind someone of something that bothers them

I know I lost the contest; you don't have to rub it in.

rub off on *(verb phrase)* General: to have an effect on

I hope your good luck rubs off on me and I get the job I want.

rude *(adj.)* Teen & College: very cool, impressively so

Those cowboy boots are so rude.

rug *(noun)* General: toupee

What an awful rug Mrs. Meyer's husband wears!

rug rank *(noun phrase)* Military: officer whose rank is high enough to warrant a rug on the floor of his or her office

The officer enlisted twenty years ago and had worked his way up to rug rank the hard way.

rule *(verb)* Teen & College: to be the best

Bobby's new motorcycle rules.

rules lawyer *(noun phrase)* Fantasy: derogatory term for a role-playing game player who memorizes the games rules in order to quote them when needed for defense during the game

Will had become such an annoying rules lawyer that his pals hardly called him to play anymore.

run against the clock *(verb phrase)* General: to be working within tight time constraints

We're running against the clock to finish this report for tomorrow's meeting.

run away with *(verb phrase)* General: to succeed easily

The young equestrian ran away with all the honors in the contest.

run circles around *(verb phrase)* General: to outperform

I'm not worried about the competition because I know this staff can run circles around them.

run-down *(adj.)* General: in an exhausted or worn-out condition

I've been feeling run-down for weeks and I don't know what's wrong.

run into the ground *(verb phrase)* General: to do or use something to excess until it no longer functions

You've run this business into the ground and now we're broke.

run in the family *(verb phrase)* General: to be an inherited characteristic

Poor vision runs in our family.

run it up the flagpole *(verb phrase)* General: to try out an idea before actually implementing it

Let's run the new customer service program up the flagpole in the main store before we make a formal announcement.

run-of-the-mill *(adj.)* General: ordinary

For all of its rave reviews, that book seemed to me rather run-of-the-mill.

run scared *(verb phrase)* General: to take certain measures because one is desperate

Joan is running scared because she's getting audited.

run-through *(noun)* Entertainment: rehearsal

Let's just do one more run-through before the opening tonight.

running two quarts low *(expression)* General: in a diminished mental state

The judge who gave that repeat

offender a slap on the wrist must be running two quarts low.

rush *(verb)* Teen & College: to behave with hostility or violence

Glen was furious about losing the game and rushed all the reporters.

rush hour *(noun phrase)* Traffic: prime commuting hours of the morning and evening

I dread driving to the airport during rush hour.

S

sack *(verb)* Sports (Football): to tackle the quarterback

Tommy sacked the quarterback on the first play of the game.

sacred cow *(noun phrase)* General: someone or something that must not be spoken badly of

Dad's inventions are a sacred cow in our house.

safe seat *(noun phrase)* Government & Politics: incumbent's seat not likely to be lost in a reelection campaign

The senator's was considered a safe seat, so no party money was added to his campaign coffers.

safety net *(noun phrase)* Government & Politics: financial assistance provided to those in need by a combination of Social Security, welfare, Medicare, and veteran's programs

The New Deal Democrats believed that every American deserved to be protected by the government's safety net of social programs in the event of personal catastrophe.

Safirism *(noun phrase)* Word Biz: term coined by political columnist and sometime-etymologist William Safire; *see also:* telepundit

One could always read the signs of the times in every Safirism that came out of his writing.

Sagebrush Rebels *(proper noun)* Government & Politics: loose coalition of Western legislators who actively monitor the control of huge pockets of federal land in the region

The Sagebrush Rebels were upset that the government planned to force ranchers to pay for the right to use federal land to graze their cattle.

salami attack *(noun phrase)* Computerspeak, Crime & Law: computer crime in which the perpetrator secretly uses the computer to perform an illegal act in several small increments (like thin slices of salami)

The pennies Swit had been siphoning from each employee's pension fun had begun to add up, but his year-long salami attack was finally uncovered by programmers.

Sally *(proper noun)* Teen & College: overly meticulous female, from the movie *When Harry Met Sally*

She's nice but kind of a Sally, so I'm not sure we'd be good room- mates.

sandwich *(noun)* Real Estate: lease involving a landlord, an original tenant, and a subletting tenant

Once Beau signed the sandwich, he was free to pack his stuff and move to Norway for his year- long sabbatical.

sandwich generation *(noun phrase)* Press: people who are taking care of their children and elderly parents at the same time

Members of the sandwich gener- ation face different conflicts and stress than those with simpler demands on their time and emo- tions.

sanitize *(verb)* Government, Mil- itary: to edit out the parts of a doc- ument or statement that might be damaging or sensitive in nature

The strategy memo was classi- fied top-secret, but a sanitized version was distributed among the Cabinet members.

sap *(noun)* Street: lies

Don't give me sap now. Tell me the truth.

Sappnin'? *(expression)* Teen & College: What's happening?; *see also:* Wassup? and Zup?

*Hey, **dude**, sappnin'?*

save one's breath *(verb phrase)* General: to refrain from speaking because one's words will be ignored

I'm just going to save my breath because I know you'll do what you want to.

save for a rainy day *(verb phrase)* General: to put aside money for unexpected needs or emergencies

Luckily, I've been saving for a rainy day, so I can afford to re- place my car's transmission.

save the day *(verb phrase)* General: to rescue from certain defeat

The team was dying when Paolo came into the game and saved the day, scoring three in a row.

say a mouthful *(verb phrase)* General: to say something of pointed significance

When Laurie noted that management seemed to be about to make a big move, she said a mouthful.

say hello *(verb phrase)* Cartalk: in a car race, to bump the car ahead in order to tell the driver to move over and make room for passing

Looks like the only way to change lanes here is to say hello to the driver just ahead.

say one's piece *(verb phrase)* General: to say what one thinks about a certain matter

After Naomi said her piece to her supervisor, she stormed out of the room.

say the word *(verb phrase)* General: to indicate willingness or approval

Just say the word and I'll transfer Smitty to another department.

say uncle *(verb phrase)* General: to acknowledge defeat

When all the votes had been counted, the candidate had no other choice but to say uncle.

scab *(noun)* General: worker who crosses the picket line of a striking union

The factory was able to stay open during the strike because there were plenty of scabs willing to work.

scalp tickets *(verb phrase)* Entertainment: to buy tickets to a performance and resell them for a profit

Kate was reprimanded by a police officer for scalping right in front of the theater.

scam 1. *(verb)* Teen & College: to lie

Billy managed to scam his way out of trouble with Roy one more time.

2. *(verb)* Teen & College: to assess people as potential sexual partners

Beau was shamelessly scamming every girl at the party.

scamming on *(verb phrase)* Teen & College: flirting with

Matthew was scamming on Maureen, and right in front of Lisa!

scandalous *(adj.)* Street: attractive

You are looking scandalous tonight, Sonny.

scare the living daylights out of *(verb phrase)* General: to frighten

The sudden power failure scared the living daylights out of me.

scare up *(verb phrase)* General: to search for until one finds

I think we can scare up enough food for dinner tonight.

scarf *(verb)* Teen, College, Food: to eat ravenously and quickly; *see also:* inhale

Micah scarfed the burger, then ordered another.

scary *(adj.)* Teen & College: unattractive

That guy who keeps asking you out is kind of scary, isn't he?

scenario-dependent *(adj. phrase)* Military: conditional upon a certain succession of events

The nuclear missile launch was strictly scenario-dependent, and until five crucial conditions existed, no final order could be issued.

scenery *(noun)* Business: board of directors apparently chosen for their unblemished reputations and respected status

The company's financials weren't great but because of the scenery the investigators looked the other way for quite some time.

schizo *(adj.)* Teen & College: bizarre

That wild-haired lady at the salad bar in the cafeteria is sort of schizo.

Schwing! *(expression)* Teen & College: invoked at the sight or thought of an attractive woman; from the popular skit, "Wayne's World," on television's "Saturday Night Live"

Did you see the photo of Madonna on the cover of rolling stone? Schwing!

Sci-fi *(noun)* Sci-fi: Science Fiction; devoted fans prefer to call it "science fiction;" also known as: s.f. and skiffy

Thanks to the Star Wars movies, sci-fi became popularly recognized in the late 1970s.

scoob *(verb)* Teen & College: get some food

I'm starving. Let's scoob.

scoop 1. *(verb)* Teen & College: to kiss

Jennilee scooped Roger right in front of his sister.

2. *(verb)* Teen & College: to make a pass at; also know as: scoop on

Lisa scooped on Wendell the minute she walked in the door.

scope *(verb)* Teen & College: to hunt something down, to evaluate; also known as: scope out

Let's scope this party for bettys for a while.

scorch *(verb)* Teen & College: to move quickly

I was scorching on my algebra homework until I got to the last problem.

score 1. *(verb)* Drug World: to buy

I'd like to score some weed tonight for the party.

2. *(noun)* General: truth

Now that Derrick knows the score about Abigail maybe he'll get smart and dump her.

scrambler *(noun)* Entertainment: electronic device used by television cable companies to keep customers from watching premium pay channels without paying for them

The MegaCable Company decoded its scrambler to offer viewers a free weekend of the Horror Channel.

scratch *(verb)* Sports: to cancel one's participation in a sporting event

The top-seeded player in the tournament had to scratch because of a muscle strain.

scratch one's back *(verb phrase)* General: to do someone a favor

If I scratch Jenna's back this time, maybe one day she'll scratch mine.

scratch the surface *(verb phrase)* General: to discover or understand something superficially

There seem to be some irregularities in the bookkeeping, but I think we're only scratching the surface.

screw 1. *(noun)* Seafarers: boat's propeller

The screw got tangled in some underwater cable and the boat was out of commission for two days.

2. *(verb)* General: to treat unfairly; also known as: screw over

Wally got screwed when he traded in his watch for a new one.

screw up *(verb phrase)* General: to make a mistake or make a mess of; also known as: flub up, mess up, and trip up

How could you screw up the bookkeeping like that? We're sure to get audited.

screwy *(adj.)* General: odd and a bit crazy

We tolerated his occasionally screwy behavior because he was such a warm and funny person.

scrounge *(verb)* Teen & College: to find or borrow

I've got to scrounge something to wear to dinner tomorrow night.

scrounge around *(verb phrase)* General: to hover around in hopes of being the recipient of someone's goodwill

She's been scrounging around all afternoon, hoping we'll invite her to dinner.

scrub 1. *(noun)* Teen & College: slob

What a scrub! Would you please take a shower?

2. *(noun)* Sports: poor, last-string performer

The team was so far behind, the coach just removed all the

starters from the game and put in the scrubs.

scrut *(verb)* Surferspeak: to eat ravenously

I'm going to scrut tonight!

scum rock *(noun phrase)* Entertainment: brand of rock that features an amalgam of influences, from heavy metal to bluegrass and evokes working-class values and imagery

U.B. Waddell has been at the forefront of scum rock for years and still remains a blue-collar hero.

scum-sucking pig *(noun phrase)* Teen & College: contemptible person; *see also:* pond scum

You scum-sucking pig! I don't ever want to speak to you again.

scurb *(noun)* Teen & College: person who skateboards on streets and curbs, usually in a suburban setting

Ryan's not a bad little boarder for a scurb.

scuz ball *(noun phrase)* Teen & College: grubby person who could use a bath and some clean clothes

Tasha looks like a scuz ball today. What's up?

search and destroy *(verb phrase)* Military: order that technically calls for searching for a target then destroying it, but commonly means simply destroy and move out

Walters flew a midnight search

and destroy mission over the rebels' camp in the jungle.

search me *(expression)* General: I don't know. How should I know?

You're asking me where Denise is? Search me.

seatwarmer *(noun)* Government & Politics: individual appointed to a vacant seat in the Senate or House to finish an unexpired term, and who is meant to fill the seat without expectation of running for the office in the next election

After his death, the governor appointed the senator's son as a seatwarmer so the party could line up a strong candidate for the fall election.

Secdef *(noun)* Military: shortened version of Secretary of Defense

The Secdef ordered a complete review of all personnel procedures.

second strike *(noun phrase)* Military: the offense's military response to the defense's retaliatory strike caused by a nuclear first strike

The senior officers knew there would be no hope of survival if the exchange required a second strike.

second wind *(noun phrase)* Sports: second burst of energy after a long period of exertion

Once I caught my second wind, I had no trouble finishing the race.

security blanket (noun phrase) General: something or someone that one relies upon to provide comfort and reassurance

Melanie's security blanket in case of emergency is her healthy savings account.

see someone about a horse *(verb phrase)* General: to use the toilet; also known as: see someone about a dog

Excuse me, I've got to see someone about a horse.

seed money *(noun phrase)* Government, Business: initial financing used to launch an enterprise

Rebuilding the inner cities depends on making seed money available to community-based developers.

see eye-to-eye *(verb phrase)* General: to concur

I think we see eye-to-eye on how to handle Danny's behavior problem.

see red *(verb phrase)* General: to be enraged

The doctor was seeing red over the slanderous article in the newspaper.

see stars *(verb phrase)* General: to be nearly unconscious

When Nora hit her head on the cupboard door, she saw stars.

see the light *(verb phrase)* General: to come to an agreement or realization, after a period of misunderstanding

I used to think Jackie was a great

guy, but now I've seen the light.

selected *(verb)* Military: promoted to a higher rank

The corporal was selected for his leadership qualities under stress.

selected out *(verb phrase)* Military: to be fired

No one could understand why the project supervisor was selected out when she had done nothing but excellent work.

sell a bill of goods *(verb phrase)* General: to deceive

Too bad that phony stockbroker sold you a bill of goods when you gave him your savings.

sell like hotcakes *(verb phrase)* General: to sell rapidly, one right after the other

Those handmade picture frames sold like hotcakes at the festival.

send someone packing *(verb phrase)* General: to force someone to leave

The school authorities debated punishing the ringleaders of the demonstration by expelling them and sending them all packing.

send to the showers *(verb phrase)* Sports: to remove someone from a game completely; generally, to fire someone

Once the company's huge stock losses were announced, it wasn't long before the CEO and several other high-ranking officers were sent to the showers.

serious *(adj.)* Teen & College:
plentiful or intense

Those are serious curls you're wearing today.

set one's teeth on edge *(verb phrase)* General: to grate on, to make one wince with irritation

That endless bickering is setting my teeth on edge.

set the world on fire *(verb phrase)* General: to do something notorious or noticeably significant

I'm not setting the world on fire as an accountant, but I'm making a decent living.

sev's *(noun)* Teen & College: Seven-Eleven convenience store

I'm going to Sev's to get a soda.

sex worker *(noun phrase)* PC: prostitute

The foundation volunteer distributed health and disease control information among the sex workers in the pier area.

shade *(verb)* Street: to criticize or verbally abuse someone

That big guy was shading the store clerk when the fight broke out.

shadow gazer *(noun phrase)* Medical: radiologist

The physician waited for the shadow gazer's report on the x-rays before reporting the findings to the patient.

shaft, the *(noun)* General: unfair, shoddy treatment

Sue really gave me the shaft — I lent her my car when hers was in the shop, and now that I have a flat tire, she won't give me a lift.

shag 1. *(verb)* Teen & College: to pull someone up in the air by his or her underpants; *see also:* give a wedgie

I shagged my brother before he went out on the court for his big game.

2. *(adj.)* General: terrific

Steve's new mountain bike is totally shag.

shake down *(verb phrase)* General: to elicit money from someone by threatening harm

The eighth graders were punished for shaking down the neighborhood children.

Shall we spin 'em or wonk 'em? *(expression)* Government & Politics: question one asks when determining the best response to a politically difficult question; translated: Shall we manipulate the questioner with clever catch phrases or shall we overwhelm the questioner with boring but intimidating expertise?

The press pool wants to discuss the President's budget initiative. Shall we spin 'em or wonk 'em?

shark *(noun)* Wall Street: individual who attempts the unwelcome takeover of a company; *see also:* black knight

Peters was becoming infamous as a shark cruising the waters of the plastics industry.

shark repellent *(noun phrase)* Wall Street: legal and/or strategic efforts made by a company to fend off an unwelcome takeover

The savvy corporate attorney advised her client to rely on plenty of porcupine provisions for shark repellent.

shed crocodile tears *(verb phrase)* General: to feign sorrow

Lillian shed crocodile tears when her boss said he was leaving.

shellback *(noun)* Seafarers: sailor with an impressive amount of experience, including having crossed the equator at least once

Martinson was a shellback, and the young sailors often came to him for advice.

shelve a project *(verb phrase)* Entertainment: to put aside or suspend production on a project

Since your television pilot got shelved, what will you do next?

shermed *(adj.)* Drug World: high on PCP

Mitch is so shermed he doesn't even recognize me.

shine on *(verb)* College, Crime & Law: to ignore

When that kid started bugging me, I just shined him on without looking up.

shiner *(noun)* General: black eye; also known as: mouse

Terry came home with a shiner and got grounded for a week.

ship over *(verb phrase)* Seafarers: to reenlist in the Navy

Watson decided to ship over rather than face what to do next in his career.

shirts vs. skins *(phrase)* Sports: condition where two teams are distinguished by one wearing shirts and the other playing shirtless; usually occurring in informal games arranged on the spur of the moment among male players only
They found enough kids to play shirts vs. skins for a couple of hours at the public courts.

shock jock *(noun phrase)* Entertainment: radio disc jockey whose trademark is making rude or offensive remarks on the air
Someone tried to run the station's shock jock over with a truck after he spent an entire program making mean remarks about cats.

shoe *(noun)* Crime & Law: detective in plainclothes
Don't look up now. That guy's a shoe.

shoegazers *(noun)* Entertainment: musicians so absorbed in their technique that they rarely look up or engage with the audience in any way
The trio was good enough, but they were all shoegazers and couldn't capture the heart of the audience.

shoot down *(verb phrase)* General: to reject or defeat
I don't appreciate your shooting down my proposal before I've had a chance to defend it.

shooter *(noun)* Bars: straight shot of liquor usually drunk in one gulp; also known as: hooter
Laverne ordered a round of vodka shooters to celebrate her big promotion.

shoot from the hip *(verb phrase)* General: to be startlingly direct or to behave impulsively
I better warn you before we talk: I shoot from the hip.

shoot off one's mouth *(verb phrase)* General: to blather
Why don't you give us a break and quit shooting off your mouth for a while?

shoot one's wad *(verb phrase)* General: to spend all of one's money
I shot my wad at the casino last night.

shoot the breeze *(verb phrase)* General: to have a casual conversation; also known as: shoot the shit
We were just shooting the breeze for a while on the sea wall.

shoot the works *(verb phrase)* General: to spare no expense
Let's shoot the works on our New Year's Eve party.

shorts *(verb)* Teen & College: to pull down someone's gym shorts, whether or not he or she is wearing anything underneath
I was so mad at Bobby for shortsing the new kid I wouldn't speak to him for two days.

shot in the arm *(noun phrase)*
General: encouragement or in-spiration
Your kind words were a real shot in the arm.

shot in the dark *(noun phrase)*
General: unlikely chance that something will succeed
It's just a shot in the dark, but we may get the contract.

shottie *(noun)* Street: short for shotgun
Winchell just sold a shottie for his older brother.

Shot who? *(expression)* Teen & College: Excuse me? What did you say?
Shot who? You think I'm going out with Amanda?

shoulder surfer *(noun phrase)*
Crime & Law: thief who lurks around airports and similarly congested public areas appropriating (and eventually selling) telephone credit card numbers by watching over the shoulder of a person making long-distance calls on a public telephone
Liza was scammed by a shoulder surfer who made ten calls to Asia, all charged to her number.

shove something down one's throat *(verb phrase)*
General: to force someone to accept something
It looks like Congress will shove a tax increase down our throats again.

showboat *(verb)* General: to perform or behave in a grand, flashy manner
Why were you showboating in that meeting? Are you trying to get a promotion?

show one's true colors *(verb phrase)* General: to reveal one's real nature or loyalties
When Sam sided with Henderson in the meeting, he showed his true colors.

show the door *(verb phrase)*
General: to ask someone to leave
If you can't speak respectfully to me, I'll have to show you to the door.

show time *(noun phrase)*
Sports: especially brilliant performance or period of play for an athlete
It was show time last night at the Garden when Isaacson scored forty-seven points.

shred *(verb)* Teen & College: to perform extremely well
I shredded my driver's test.

shrink *(noun)* Medical: psychotherapist, psychologist, or psychiatrist; short for "head shrinker"
Polly was afraid to go a month without seeing her shrink because she had deep anxiety.

shuck and jive *(noun phrase)*
General: deceitful nonsense
Don't give me that shuck and jive! What really happened to my car?

Shut up! *(expression)* Teen & College: You're lying!

Shut up! You saw Tina Turner on the street?

sick and tired *(adj. phrase)*
General: exasperated
I'm sick and tired of picking up your dirty socks all the time.

sick and wrong *(adj. phrase)*
Teen & College: terrible, unimaginable
I'm not driving cross country with my family. The whole idea of it is sick and wrong.

sick as a dog *(verb phrase)*
General: extremely unwell
Ms. Roxbury has been sick as a dog for a week now.

sideline *(verb)* Sports: to remove a player from a competition
Coach sidelined Jacobs for swearing at him at halftime.

sight gag *(noun phrase)* Entertainment: joke or routine that relies on visual comedy
The new comedian was a quiet intellectual and didn't use sight gags to buffet his act.

sigint *(noun)* Military: signal intelligence, which is gathered by electronic means, as distinct from humint, or human intelligence, which is gathered by actual intelligence agents
Murphy worked as a decoder in the sigint unit at the sub base.

sign off on *(verb phrase)* Government & Politics, Military: to give formal or informal approval of an action
Benson signed off on the firing

of the ten clerks but later denied any involvement.

Silicon Valley *(proper noun)*
Computer Industry, Media: nickname for an area in Southern California where much of the American computer industry is clustered; "silicon" refers to the silicon chip vital to computer technology
"I may head out to Silicon Valley to find a job," said the hopeful college senior.

silver lining *(noun phrase)*
General: hidden benefit; from the saying, Every cloud has a silver lining
Let's look for the silver lining in this situation.

simmer down *(verb phrase)*
General: to calm down
Now just simmer down and tell me what happened.

simp *(noun)* Teen & College: dolt, simpleton
That guy is failing junior English for the third time. What a simp.

sing *(verb)* Crime & Law: to inform or testify against another party; *see also:* belch and rat
The mob boss was finally convicted after the federal officers convinced the capo to sing.

sing a different tune *(verb phrase)* General: to change one's position
Ever since her parents bought her a car, Elena is singing a different tune about studying.

single *(adj.)* General: not involved with someone
I've been single for months.

sinker *(noun)* Food: dense, filling dish
That pot pie was a real sinker. Now I need a nap.

sink one's teeth into *(verb phrase)* General: to work on, or think about, something in a serious or meaningful way
I'd like to work on a project I could really sink my teeth into.

sitcom *(noun)* Entertainment: situation comedy program, where each episode is based on a new comic situation acted upon by the show's regular cast of characters
The new sitcom was a flop and was cancelled after just six episodes.

sitting duck *(noun phrase)* General: vulnerable person
If you don't confront this problem with your coworker, you'll be a sitting duck when it comes time for your review.

six of one, half dozen of the other *(expression)* General: it makes no difference
You can ride with me or not. It's six of one, half a dozen of the other.

six-pack Republican *(noun phrase)* Government & Politics: common Republican, not one of the fabled elitist, pinstriped kind
The president had populist appeal and knew he could attract a good number of six-pack Republicans.

size up *(verb phrase)* General: to assess a situation
I sized up the competition and decided we had a good chance to win the game.

size the vic *(verb phrase)* Crime & Law: to assess a potential victim
The pair had a system where one would size the vic, the other would set up the scam.

sizzle *(noun)* Advertising: image; from the old advertising rule: Sell the sizzle, not the steak
Let's put some sizzle back into this brand. Its sales have gone flat.

skanky *(adj.)* Teen & College: disheveled, in slight need of a bath, even disgusting
That guy at the gas station was too skanky.

skate on thin ice *(verb phrase)* General: to risk getting into a bad situation
You're already skating on thin ice with Mom and Dad, so don't be late again tonight.

skate rat *(noun phrase)* Teen & College: one who spends too much time on a skateboard
Pinky's little brother is a skate rat and never comes home from the school parking lot until after dark.

skegging *(adj.)* Surferspeak: very fun
That barbecue was skegging last night.

skeleton in the closet (*noun phrase*) General: longstanding secret that causes one great shame
Our family has too many skeletons in the closet for any of us to run for public office.

skid-bid (*noun*) Crime & Law: time served in prison
I've done my skid-bid and now I'd like to get on with my life.

skin (*noun phrase*) Sports: money payable to a player based on performance
The golf partners made their bets in the morning and handed over the skin to the winner at the end of the afternoon.

skin alive (*verb phrase*) General: to chastise harshly
I'll be skinned alive if I don't get the car home for my mom before five o'clock.

skin and bones (*noun phrase*) General: extremely thin, describing a person or animal
That old dog turned up on our doorstep all skin and bones.

skin flick (*noun phrase*) Entertainment: movie that revolves around sex and nudity
Does your mother know you see skin flicks?

skin it (*verb phrase*) Surferspeak: to surf without a wetsuit
I think I'll just skin it today since the water seems warm.

skins 1. (*noun*) Seafarers: waterproof oilskin outerwear
The fishers donned their skins just as the storm broke out.

2. (*noun*) General: dollars, money; also known as: cabbage, coin, dough, green, jack, lettuce, and simoleons
Do you have any skins I can borrow? I'm broke.

skippie (*acronym*) Press: School Kid with Income and Purchasing Power
Toy and clothing companies have begun to appeal more aggressively to skippies, a vital segment of their market.

skirt-chaser (*noun*) General: man who is incessantly in pursuit of female companionship
Morty's such a skirt-chaser that none of the women in the office will take him seriously.

skitcom (*noun*) Entertainment: television comedy program featuring a series of unrelated comic skits
Carol Burnett was a pioneer of the skitcom format.

skunk works (*noun phrase*) Business: group within a corporation whose job it is to come up with new ideas
Though Ed had hoped to become a top exec in the main office, he ended up a part of the skunk works.

skylark (*verb*) Seafarer: to shirk duties; *see also:* goldbrick
The sailor was adept at skylarking without the slightest notice of his coworkers.

slacker (*noun*) Teen & College: aimless sort of person, who has few interests or commitments

With no plans for college or a job, Jimmy B. was just a slacker waiting for something to happen.

slam *(verb)* Teen & College: to insult, usually in front of others

Did you see Jed slam Jolene in the cafeteria today?

slammer *(noun)* General: jail; also known as: big house, cage, cooler, hole, klink, pen, pokey, and stir

Sarina had to spend the night in the slammer for starting a fight in the restaurant.

slamming *(noun)* Teen & College: slam dancing, an extremely physical form of dancing that calls for dancers to bump into each other forcefully

*I got a **mega**-bruise on my thigh last night from slamming at the concert.*

slap-down *(noun)* Teen & College: humiliation

The score Lila received for her skating routine was a real slap-down.

slap in the face *(noun phrase)* General: stinging insult

Calling me a hack was a real slap in the face.

slap on the wrist *(noun phrase)* General, Crime & Law: extremely lenient punishment for a crime or other misdeed

The school board was angry that the principal let the kids go with just a slap on the wrist for damaging the school building.

slaps *(noun)* Teen & College: flip-flops, or thong sandals

I won't go into that creepy shower at school without wearing my slaps.

slasher movie *(noun phrase)* Entertainment: film featuring excessive violence for the sake of violence

*Bart Marlowe actually got his start as an actor with a **bit part** in a horrible slasher movie.*

slave *(noun)* Computerspeak: computer that is controlled by another

Sally was frustrated by the limitations and delays caused by her computer being a slave to her supervisor's.

sleazebag *(noun)* Teen & College: unethical person and a loser

Can't you find a better person to date than that sleazebag?

sleeper *(noun)* Entertainment: movie that is an unexpected success

That sweet romantic comedy turned out to be the sleeper of the season.

slice up *(verb phrase)* Teen & College: to criticize

Mr. Cartwright sliced up my writing assignment and gave me a D.

slim chance *(noun phrase)* General: little or no possibility; *see also:* fat chance

I think we only have a slim

chance of getting that federal grant.

sling it (*verb phrase*) General: to tell lies

All the staffers knew the chief was slinging it about the consequences of information leaks just to scare them.

slip of the tongue (*noun phrase*) General: something that is said unintentionally or misspoken

Arnie certainly didn't mean to insult you; it was just a slip of the tongue.

slot (*noun*) Entertainment: standard time period in a television programming schedule

The young actor's new show had been assigned a prime slot on Thursday nights.

slow-and-go (*adj. phrase*) Traffic: erratic, characterized by much stopping and starting

Traffic was slow-and-go for about three miles, then cleared up after that.

small potatoes (*adj. phrase*) General: insignificant

The owner of Daley's Department Store thought the new boutique that opened in the same mall was just small potatoes.

small-time (*adj.*) General: petty; also known as: two-bit

You're just a small-time **hood** and you always will be.

smart aleck (*noun phrase*) General: impudent person; also known as: **smart ass**

Some smart aleck in the theater kept making loud remarks so I could barely hear the film's dialogue.

smart car (*noun phrase*) Technology: automobile with a computer system that provides such information as current location, best driving routes, general traffic tips, and indicators

The prototype for the smart car debuted at the auto show to much acclaim.

smash mouth (*noun phrase*) Teen & College: passionate kissing

There was a lot of smash mouth going on at the movie theater last night.

smart money, the (*noun phrase*) General: informed predictions of those who would be in position to know something

The smart money says the Bammer won't last three rounds in the fight tonight.

smell a rat (*verb phrase*) General: to be suspicious

There's no evidence that someone broke into my files, but I smell a rat in the office.

smiley (*noun phrase*) Teen & College: buttocks crack visible when one's pants are slipping down; also known as: working man's smile

When the attendant bent over, his smiley sent the carload of teenagers into hysterics.

smoke (*noun*) General: cigarette; also known as: butt, cig, and drag

I'm dying for a smoke. Do you have one?

smoke and mirrors *(noun phrase)* General: deceptive persuasion

Frank called his lawyer when he made a surprise visit to his newly-acquired farm and discovered the deal was all smoke and mirrors.

smoking *(verb)* Teen & College: looking terrific

Did you notice Joe was smoking on the beach the other day?

smoking gun *(noun phrase)* Government & Politics: guilt

Due to the efforts of the FBI, no one in the Cabinet was left holding a smoking gun in the latest scandal.

smooth operator *(noun phrase)* General: charming, clever, and often manipulative person

It was only after the fire was put out and the cash was missing that the others discovered what a smooth operator Harry was.

snag *(verb)* Teen & College: to steal

I snagged Violet's lipstick from her purse.

SNAG *(acronym)* Teen & College: Sensitive New Age Guy; a fellow who is nice and willing to express his emotions

Trish is dating a SNAG from her kiddie lit class. I wonder what it's like after dating Rocko.

snake *(verb)* Teen & College: to steal

Lou snaked a few grapes from the basket on the table.

snakebit *(adj.)* Sports: luckless

Trudy was starting to seem snakebit and no one would pick her for a team in gym class.

snake-check *(verb)* Government & Politics: to examine the possible results and consequences of a plan before it is implemented

I'd like to snake-check this policy thoroughly before we present it to the committee.

snap 1. *(verb)* Teen & College: to renege on a promise

Chip snapped on me the moment he had to come up with the money for the payoff.

2. *(verb)* Street: to pick on or harass

Why are you snapping on me like that?

snapper *(noun)* Teen & College: one who has broken a promise

Sarah always offers to help but then never shows up. What a snapper.

snarf *(verb)* College, Computerspeak: to help oneself to, usually without permission

I just snarfed Warren's lecture notes. I'm sure he won't mind.

sniff *(verb)* Drug World: to inhale narcotics, either the fumes of certain chemicals or a solid powdered drug such as cocaine

I'd like to sniff a few lines before we go to the concert.

sniffer *(noun)* Government & Politics: mildly derogatory term for an environmentalist; short for **posy sniffer**

The sniffers were protesting the fast food restaurant's styrofoam packaging.

snipe *(verb)* Advertising: to paste up advertising posters in public areas, such as building exteriors, subway walls, etc.

The movie posters had been sniped all over the city by morning.

snort 1. *(verb)* Drug World: to inhale a powdered drug, usually by a tiny spoonful

We snorted in the car, all the way to Canada.

2. *(noun)* Drug World: single dose of powdered cocaine, usually inhaled with the aid of a tiny spoon

Artie gave Spin a snort just before he went out on stage and collapsed.

snow bird *(noun phrase)* Press: Northerner who spends the winter in the South

Grandpa was happy to retire and become a snow bird.

soak *(verb)* General: to charge a lot of money

Those resorts really soak you for those stupid little items you forget at home.

soap *(noun)* Entertainment: short for soap opera, television's daytime drama format

Shelley played a nurse on a soap for a couple of years before making it big in prime time.

sob story *(noun phrase)* General: story that causes pity

The store manager listened to the young man's sob story and then offered him a job.

soc (pronounced sosh) *(noun)* Teen & College: one who is considered extremely socially active but somewhat superficial; plural is soshes

The campus soshes and the alumni association organized the homecoming weekend activities.

so far, so good *(expression)* General: up until this point, everything seems fine

We're at the mouth of the cave now and no one got hurt. So far, so good.

soft *(adj.)* Military: unprotected

The civilian population was the soft target in the multi-level attack.

soft money *(noun phrase)* Real Estate: money paid against interest only on a loan

Julia's payments were so low she was still paying soft money against her mortgage years later.

soldier *(noun)* Crime & Law: employee of organized crime; *see also:* button man, goodfella, goombah, and wiseguy

Dino's been a soldier with the mob for a year now.

solid (adj.) Street: okay, good enough
So you'll help me babysit Friday night? Solid.

solo (noun) Fantasy: role-playing game where a person can play alone against a proscribed set of conditions and characters
When Skye couldn't get a group together for D & D, she just played solo in her room all weekend.

something fierce (adv. phrase) General: intensely
I wanted to go to that ice cream social something fierce.

something the cat dragged in 1. (noun phrase) General: unexpected party who has just entered a room
Well, look what the cat dragged in!

2. (noun phrase) General: someone who looks a little ragged and untidy
You look like something the cat dragged in. Go wash your face!

song and dance (noun phrase) General: insincere or even untrue excuse or story
Lisa gave me some song and dance about how her dog ate her homework.

soufflé (noun) Medical: person who has fallen or jumped from a high location
"There was nothing we could do for the souffle," the residents soberly agreed.

sound bite (noun phrase) News: snip of a quote used within the context of a news report
These days the candidates talk in sound bites so that they will sound good in print.

sounds (noun) Teen & College: music
Let's turn on some sounds here and find something to eat.

soup (noun) Seafarers: thick fog
We've run into some soup here. Let's switch to full radar.

souped (adj.) Street: self-important and conceited
Kendra is so souped she can't even see that people don't like her.

soupe de jour (noun phrase) Foreign (French): current style; literally, soup of the day; *see also:* flavor of the week
*That new actress sure is **hot**, the soupe de jour.*

souped-up (adj.) General: improved with extra performance-enhancement features
Tricia was driving her brother's souped-up car when she was detained by the police.

sour grapes (noun phrase) General: bitter jealousy
*I heard that Louise is **trashing** me to everyone, but I think it's just sour grapes because I won the contest.*

space (verb) Teen & College: to be in another world, to not be paying attention; *see also:* zone
I was spacing through most of

algebra this afternoon and never heard the assignment.

space cadet (noun phrase) Teen & College: perpetually distracted, dizzy person; *see also:* airhead and trip-out

I don't mean to seem like a space cadet but what was the assignment again?

space opera (noun phrase) Sci-fi: high-action, super-exciting science fiction adventure story

Doris enjoyed a good space opera for a weekend's diversion.

spaceship ethic (noun phrase) Sci-fi: moral code that asserts that all members of society must cooperate to survive, as is necessary in a spaceship setting

We follow a spaceship ethic at Acme because the office is small and the pressure intense.

spank (verb) Teen & College: to beat someone decisively in a contest

I spanked Minas in our pool game this afternoon.

spare tire (noun phrase) General: extra flesh on one's waist; also known as: love handles

When I saw Patrick at our class reunion I couldn't believe the spare tire he had!

spark plug (noun phrase) General: one who brings great energy and enthusiasm to every situation

We could really use a spark plug in this office to get everyone ex-

cited about their work again.

spazz 1. (verb) Teen & College: to become agitated or extremely excited

Joanne spazzed when she heard that the Cruds were coming to town.

2. (noun) Teen & College: one who tends to be extremely excited

Jenn is such a spazz she knocked my soda off the counter.

speak of the devil (expression) General: here is the person who was just being discussed

Well, speak of the devil, Bob, we were just wondering where you've been.

spear (verb) Sports (Hockey): to use one's stick against another player

Leroy had to sit in the penalty box for spearing Whitman.

special (noun) Entertainment: any type of program not on the regular television programming schedule

The network's Mother's Day special brought in unexpectedly high ratings, thanks to the celebrity guests.

sped (noun) Teen & College: slow-witted person

Why are you acting like such a sped? Pay attention!

speedball (noun) Drug World: combination of cocaine and heroin; *see also:* Belushi cocktail

Somebody shot Vince a speedball that almost killed him.

spend down *(verb phrase)*
Government & Politics: process of reducing one's assets and income to a point which qualifies one for Medicaid
The social welfare worker alleged that the elderly woman was spending down by dispersing her property among family members.

spew *(verb)* Teen & College: to vomit; also known as: barf, blow lunch, boag, boot, earl, heave, honk, hurl, ralph, reverse gears, shout at one's shoes, toss, yak, yawn in technicolor, and zuke
I was tickling the kid I was babysitting for last night and he suddenly spewed all over me!

spike 1. *(verb)* Sports (Baseball): to slide into a base with the spikes on one's shoes facing up in an attempt to harm the player defending the base
One of the meanest baserunners in baseball, Ty Cobb was never above spiking the second baseman to beat the tag.
2. *(verb)* Sports (Football): to slam the football down in the end zone after scoring a touchdown
The league officials had banned spiking and other effusively celebratory acts that might take place in the end zone.

spikes *(noun)* Teen & College: shoes
Where did you get those excellent spikes?

spill one's guts *(verb phrase)*
General: to tell everything
Marty spilled her guts to her best friend about her problems at home.

spin *(noun)* Public Relations, Politics, Media: calculated slant on the discussion of an issue or event
With the right spin, an automobile manufacturer's recall could be seen as a benevolent public-interest gesture.

spin control *(noun phrase)*
Public Relations, Politics, Media: effort to keep an issue or event regarded and reported with a certain slant
The company's efforts at spin control backfired when the truth behind the scandal came to light.

spin doctor *(noun phrase)* Public Relations, Politics, Media: individual charged with attempting to control the way an issue or event is regarded
Acme will need their best spin doctor to get through the recent hazardous waste scandal.

spitting image *(noun phrase)*
General: uncanny likeness
My little sister is the spitting image of that girl on the detergent commercial.

splash *(noun)* Bars: just a hint of water or soda added to a drink
Make mine a Scotch with a splash of soda and a twist, please.

splatter movie *(noun phrase)*
Entertainment: gory, bloody film
It's been suggested that young people can become inured to the effects of violence by watching too many splatter movies.

splatterpunk *(noun)* Sci-fi: strain of science fiction featuring an ultra-violent, amoral, hopeless environment
Jeremy's mother was horrified to discover the cache of splatterpunk novels under his bed.

split hairs *(verb phrase)* General: to argue about small details
Let's not split hairs on this contract. I'll give you whatever you're asking for.

sponge *(noun)* Food & Drink: person who drinks a lot of alcohol
The guy at the end of the bar is a sponge, so don't let him get in his car when he leaves.

spoof *(noun)* Entertainment: satire
That spoof of the presidential debates was hilarious.

spooged *(adj.)* Teen & College: sticking straight out in any direction, usually referring to hair
Donna had her hair spooged on top and slicked back on the sides.

spoon-feed *(verb)* General: to explain something slowly and carefully
I had to spoon-feed the reporter those labor statistics.

sport *(verb)* Teen & College: to wear
Those are some serious shoes you're sporting, Missy.

sport climbing *(noun phrase)* Sports: simulated experience of mountain climbing, whereby the participant climbs a constructed vertical surface that features footholds and various levels of climbing challenge
Gloria sprained her knee learning sport climbing at her health club.

spread *(noun)* Sports: number of points by which one team is favored to win over another; important figure among bettors
What's the spread on Friday night's game?

spread it on thick *(verb phrase)* General: to tell lies and half-truths in order to persuade
I'm going to have to spread it on thick to get some extra vacation days from my boss.

spread oneself too thin *(verb phrase)* General: to involve oneself in too many commitments
I've spread myself too thin this summer and I have no time for myself.

spring for *(verb phrase)* General: to pay for
I'll spring for a new surfboard if you get straight As on your report card.

sprout *(noun)* Ecology: one who has undeveloped opinions about environmental matters
The sprouts in the crowd didn't

oppose the proposal to finance a clean-up of the river area, but they didn't support it.

sprouthead *(noun)* Food: vegetarian

Julie's such a sprouthead she won't even eat eggs anymore!

sprung on *(verb phrase)* Teen & College: attracted to

I'm sprung on that new kid in my gym class.

spud *(noun)* Teen & College: jerk

Jason's a spud and no one will choose him for a lab partner.

squad *(noun)* Teen & College, Street: group of friends; *see also:* posse and possie

I'm having my squad over after school today.

square *(noun)* Street: cigarette

Get me some squares at the corner, will you?

square up *(verb phrase)* Street: to calm down; *see also:* take it light

If you don't square up, you're going to have a stroke.

squash that *(verb phrase)* Teen & College: never mind, forget it

Since I can't borrow my mother's car to go to the movies, I guess we can just squash that idea.

squat 1. *(noun)* General: nothing; short for diddly squat

I don't owe you squat, so quit bugging me.

2. *(noun)* Crime & Law: minor car accident staged so that a fraud-

ulent injury claim can be made

"This isn't a wreck, it's a squat, and if either one of you make an insurance claim, I'll see you in court," the officer said to the two drivers.

squeaky clean *(adj. phrase)* General: beyond reproach, with an impeccable reputation

The position needs to be filled by someone who is squeaky clean, to counter the department's corrupt reputation.

squeal rule *(noun phrase)* Government & Politics: state or federal regulation requiring that parents of a patient eighteen years old or younger be notified if the patient requests an abortion or contraceptives; enforceable only if the medical facility receives public funds

The youth council staged a protest on the day the legislature was to debate the squeal rule.

squeegee people *(noun phrase)* Traffic: people in urban areas who descend upon cars when stopped at traffic lights and offer (or demand) to clean the cars' windshields for a small fee

The squeegee people were out in force near the congested entrance to the toll bridge.

squid *(noun)* Teen & College: unpopular, awkward person; *see also:* dork, dweeb, fred, geek, goob, goof, nerd, and swivel-neck

Clarice felt bad because her new friends thought Sheryl was a squid and wouldn't talk to her.

squid tank *(noun phrase)* Teen & College: computer center at school, referring to the unfair impression that computer afficionados are usually **squids**, or awkward, unpopular people

Janine took a peek in the squid tank to look for her friend Chantal.

squish *(noun)* Government & Politics: term applied to conservatives who cannot fully commit on many traditionally conservative issues

The senator had run as a full-fledged conservative, but later proved to be a squish who could never be counted on for support.

S & S *(proper noun)* Fantasy: initialism for Swords and Sorcery, a strain of fantasy fiction that features monsters, scantily clothed women, and barbarians for main characters; also known as heroic fiction

After reading S & S stories, my son sometimes has trouble shifting back to the real world.

stab in the back *(verb phrase)* General: to betray

I can't believe that after all I've done for him, he'd stab me in the back like that.

stack *(verb)* Street: to make plenty of money

My brother is stacking now that

he's got his own law practice.

stack the cards *(verb phrase)* General: to create a situation purposely advantageous or disadvantageous to someone

I think my colleagues stacked the cards against me, so I better not expect the partnership.

stall *(noun)* Crime & Law: person who distracts the victim during a robbery, while the **hook** actually steals the money or items

The stall in the robbery was a charming young man with an English accent who so captivated his victims that they didn't know they had been robbed until hours later.

stand up and be counted *(verb phrase)* General: to make one's position known

If we're going to win this fight with City Hall, plenty of people are going to have to stand up and be counted.

stand-up comic *(noun phrase)* Entertainment: comedian who performs his or her routine alone

I've always wanted to be a stand-up comic, but I'm not sure how to get started.

stand on one's own two feet *(verb phrase)* General: to be self-reliant

After depending on my family so much during my illness, it feels good to stand on my own two feet again.

stars in one's eyes *(noun phrase)* General: unconditionally hopeful or positive feeling about someone or something

I warned you not to get stars in your eyes about Chris so you wouldn't get hurt!

start from scratch *(verb phrase)* General: to begin at the beginning, usually not for the first time

Okay, let's start from scratch. Exactly what did you see when you opened the door?

stash *(noun)* Drug World: individual's supply of drugs designated for personal use

The dealer never touched his stash while he was selling.

stats *(noun)* General: short for statistics; usually refers to sports-related subject

The stats on the batter coming to the plate are impressive.

state-of-the-art *(phrase)* Industry, Business, Government, Military: as current or contemporary or technologically advanced as possible

The plane features state-of-the-art laser tracking components.

stay up until all hours *(verb phrase)* General: to remain awake until very late

Jessie was staying up until all hours every night working on her chemistry project.

steal one's thunder *(verb phrase)* General: to say something someone else was about to say

I was about to talk about the as-

tronauts' courage and commitment, but my colleague here has stolen my thunder.*

steal the show *(verb phrase)* General: to be the most appealing and popular participant in a performance

That new understudy stole the show last night.

steel belt *(noun phrase)* Press: Midwestern region of the United States that produces steel

The candidate didn't have much of a chance of winning the steel belt states where the effects of the recession were so deeply felt.

steel collar worker *(noun phrase)* Business, Technology: industrial robot

The plant manager knew that two of the seven departments could be replaced by steel collar workers.

steerer *(noun)* Drug World: person who doesn't actually sell drugs but puts buyers in touch with sellers; see also: rounder

Dana worked weekends as a steerer to support her growing habit.

stellar *(adj.)* Teen & College: terrific

The whole evening was stellar.

step on it *(verb phrase)* General: to move more quickly

The drugstore closes at eight o'clock so we better step on it.

step on someone's toes *(verb phrase)* General: to offend or embarrass someone

I don't want to step on any toes, but this office is a mess and I'm in charge of straightening it out.

step out on someone (*verb phrase*) General: to be unfaithful, to cheat

Jan felt more confident about her relationship with Chris after their mutual promise not to step out on each other.

stew in one's own juice (*verb phrase*) General: to suffer the consequences of one's own actions

You went and told everyone about our problem and now you have to stew in your own juice.

stick-in-the-mud (*noun*) General: boring, unadventurous person

He won't want to go mountain climbing with us; he's just a stick-in-the-mud.

stick one's neck out (*verb phrase*) General: to take a risk

I stuck my neck out for you by giving you that recommendation and you've done nothing but make me look bad.

stick one's nose into (*verb phrase*) General: to meddle with

How dare you stick your nose into my private affairs!

stick out like a sore thumb (*verb phrase*) General: to be overly conspicuous

In these jeans I'll stick out like a sore thumb at that fancy restaurant.

sticker shock (*noun phrase*)

Cartalk: startled reaction a car shopper has when confronted with the high price of the vehicle

We're still interested in this family van, but I'll admit to having a bit of sticker shock.

stick to one's knitting (*verb phrase*) General: to tend to one's own affairs

No matter what anybody else does, you just stick to your own knitting and be home by ten o'clock.

stick-um (*noun*) Sports: sticky substance that some athletes use to improve gripping ability or the chances of hanging on to a ball one has caught.

Wiley's statistics on passes caught improved dramatically after he started using stick-um.

sticky fingers (*noun phrase*) General: tendency to steal or borrow without permission

Don't leave Lenny's little brother alone in the store because he's got sticky fingers.

stink (*adj.*) Street: great, exceptional

Charlie got a real stink cycle.

stinky rich (*adj. phrase*) General: extremely wealthy

The Carters had become stinky rich speculating on real estate.

stock (*noun*) Street, Rap: boyfriend or girlfriend

"That is some serious stock," the youths noted of their friend admiringly.

stoked *(adj.)* Teen & College: excited, enthusiastic
I'm stoked about going to the beach for the weekend.

stomp on *(verb phrase)* Drug World: to dilute the potency of a drug by mixing it with a similar-looking nonnarcotic substance; also known as: step on; *see also:* burn and cut
This weed has been stomped on by that cheating supplier of mine!

stoner *(noun)* Teen & College: marijuana-smoking, fairly delinquent youth
Evan's parents had no idea he'd been hanging around with the stoners at school for months.

stone sober *(adj. phrase)* General: completely sober
I wouldn't worry about Lance. He's been stone sober for a month.

stop on a dime *(verb phrase)* Cartalk: to stop at the least notice
This car has great control. It'll stop on a dime.

strack *(verb)* Street: to become psychologically prepared to engage in a contest or conflict
The gang stracked at D.C.'s house until they headed across town for the party.

straighten up and fly right *(verb phrase)* General: start behaving properly
I better straighten up and fly right or I'm going to get expelled from school.

straight man *(noun phrase)* Entertainment: person in a comedy team who plays his or her lines seriously
Jerome was always remembered as Jocko's straight man.

straight shooter *(noun phrase)* General: honest, forthright person
I like working with Johnson because he's such a straight shooter.

straight up *(adj. phrase)* Bars: no ice or other drink additions
Robert ordered three bourbons, straight up, and carried them back to his table in the corner.

stress *(verb)* Teen & College: to have anxiety, to worry; also known as: stress out
I've been stressing ever since I sent in my application.

strike oil *(verb phrase)* General: to succeed overwhelmingly, to have extraordinary luck
We really struck oil when we hired Diana to manage new accounts.

strike out *(verb phrase)* Sports (Baseball): to fail; literally, to fail to get a hit or otherwise get on base
I really struck out on my sales calls this afternoon.

string along *(verb phrase)* General: to lead someone to believe something by being deceitful or not telling the entire truth
Gretchen strung Bill along for years before she finally told him

she didn't really want to marry him.

strip a car *(verb)* Crime & Law: to steal all reuseable or resalable parts off a car
I had my new car for just one month before it was stripped on the street.

stroke *(verb)* General: to flatter
The director knew both leads were going to need to be stroked after a difficult morning of rehearsals.

strongarm *(verb)* General: to force someone to do something
Coach strongarmed Lefty to study for his exams.

stuck on *(verb phrase)* General: to be in love or infatuated with
It's obvious that Matt is stuck on Naomi.

stuck-up *(adj.)* General: conceited
Shelly and Sheila decided they didn't like Brenda anymore because she was stuck-up.

studly *(adj.)* Teen & College: masculinely attractive
Is that new bank teller studly, or what?

stuff 1. *(noun)* Business: wide variety of fringe benefits that can be a part of an employment package
Martinson's stuff included a company car, health and retirement benefits, a pension plan, and the right to use the company's beach condominium.

2. *(noun)* General: courage and capability
Dilly's got the stuff to win that marathon on Friday.

stuffed shirt *(noun phrase)* General: uptight, boring person
What a stuffed shirt he turned out to be!

stump *(verb)* Government & Politics: to campaign and politic, traveling around giving rousing speeches; term refers to the stump of a tree from which candidates from the old days gave speeches in small towns
Senator Dogood was happiest when he was stumping, shaking hands with constituents, and attending benefits.

stunting *(noun)* Entertainment: special ploys used by networks to attract additional viewers during crucial ratings periods
The string of true crime movies the network ran in February was very effective during stunting.

styling *(adj.)* Surferspeak: surfing well
I was styling on those last two waves.

substandard housing *(noun phrase)* Government: slum
The decaying urban zone can be improved immediately by tearing down the substandard housing.

suburbs, the *(noun)* Sports: (Basketball): long distance from the basket
You could always count on

Freeman to make a crucial shot from the suburbs.

suck *(verb)* Teen & College: to be bad

You got kicked off the team? That sucks!

suck face *(verb phrase)* Teen & College: to kiss deeply and passionately; *see also:* box tonsils

I saw them sucking face down by the boardwalk last night.

sucking one's flava (pronounced flay-vuh) *(verb phrase)* Teen & College, Street: imitating one's style

I'm not telling you where I got this outfit because you keep sucking my flava.

suck up *(verb phrase)* General: to flatter someone shamelessly; *see also:* apple polish, brownnose, and kiss up

You're sucking up to me just to get a good seat at the awards dinner.

sudden death *(noun phrase)* Sports: tie-breaking technique that calls for awarding the win to the first team or player to score

The excitement built in the stadium as the hockey game went into sudden death.

sue someone's pants off *(verb phrase)* General: to sue someone for everything they have

If you violate that copyright, I'll sue your pants off.

suicide squad *(noun phrase)* Sports (Football): special team called in for kickoffs; referred to as such for their increased chances of being injured

Sharkey chose to play for the suicide squad rather than retiring before he was ready.

sunbelt *(noun)* Press: southern area of the United States, which has hot summers and mild, sunny winters

The Keatons moved to the sunbelt from New England after retiring.

superstation *(noun)* Entertainment: television station that broadcasts to a large local market as well as nationally through cable television systems

The ads ran frequently on the superstation's regular movie schedule.

Sure, Bill! *(expression)* Teen & College: I don't believe you

You got a full-time job for the summer? Sure, Bill!

sure thing *(noun phrase)* General: certainty; also known as: sure shot

Grover felt that getting the government assignment should be a sure thing.

surviving spouse *(noun phrase)* Government, Social: widow or widower

As a surviving spouse, you are entitled to receive Social Security benefits early, but at a reduced rate.

swabbie *(noun)* Seafarers: sailor of the lowest rank

The swabbies grumbled among themselves over the unglamorous duties they were regularly assigned.

swallow one's pride *(verb phrase)* General: to be humble
I'm going to have to swallow my pride to ask my in-laws for a loan.

swallow something whole *(verb phrase)* General: to believe something without reservation
Dick said he didn't falsify the documents and his boss swallowed it whole.

swear a blue streak *(verb phrase)* General: to curse excessively
I don't like the kids to be around Uncle Norbert because he swears a blue streak.

swear off *(verb phrase)* General: to vow to give up
I've sworn off cigarettes for a month.

sweat 1. *(interjection)* Teen & College, Street: wow
Sweat, what a terrible story.
2. *(verb)* Street: to badger someone or to crowd someone
You're always sweating me, Mom. Please leave me alone.

sweat blood *(verb phrase)* General: to make a great sacrifice or effort
I had to sweat blood to get you those tickets to the show.

sweat like a pig *(verb phrase)* General: to perspire profusely
After ten minutes on the rowing machine, I'm sweating like a pig.

sweep off one's feet *(verb phrase)* General: to stir strong, uncontrollable feelings in someone
Iris was swept off her feet within hours of meeting Mack.

sweeps *(noun)* Advertising, Entertainment: crucial periods during which television programs are rated based on the size of the audience; these ratings determine the value of advertising time during the programs
During the April sweeps, the networks broadcast the most popular movies and spectacular specials in order to grab more ratings.

swim against the tide *(verb phrase)* General: to struggle to do something that is not the norm
The minister was swimming against the tide with his new congregation by trying to arrange a community outreach program.

Swoon! *(expression)* Teen & College: Wow, what an attractive person!
Did you see that star who just walked by? Swoon!

swooner *(noun)* Wall Street: stock that is overly influenced by news of any kind
"It's too much of a swooner for me," the client explained to his broker, adding he didn't want to buy it.

swoop on *(verb)* Teen & College: to show immediate interest in
Mark swooped on my sister the minute he met her.

system, the *(noun)* Crime & Law: judicial and correctional complex; seen by criminals and inmates as the true adversary
The ex-con always complained it was the system that failed.

T

tab *(noun)* Drug World: single dose of LSD; *see also:* dose
The three brothers popped tabs after the party and not one of them could remember the way home.

table from hell *(noun phrase)* Food: restaurant servers' description of a table of patrons who has become intoxicated and unruly
"The table from hell over there spilled the entire pitcher of water," the waiter hissed to the busperson.

tablehop *(verb)* Social: to move from table to table at a social event, looking for the most interesting or promising companionship
Maureen tablehopped during the wedding reception, upsetting the carefully arranged seating plans just to network.

tag *(noun)* Street: one's name or nickname
Margie's tag is M-Girl.

tagger *(noun)* Crime & Law: graffiti vandal
The police knew that Tango was the tagger they were looking for, but they couldn't come up with the evidence to prove it.

tail between one's legs *(noun phrase)* General: feeling of defeat
After the debate Gina went home with her tail between her legs.

take *(noun)* General: perspective or understanding
So what's your take on the company's new payroll policy?

take a back seat *(verb phrase)* General: to be assigned or accept a lesser position
I'm tired of taking a back seat to you in every department meeting.

take a bath *(verb phrase)* General: to suffer a severe financial setback
Uncle Willie really took a bath when the factory went bankrupt.

take a beating *(verb phrase)* General: to endure a severe loss, usually financial
We really took a beating during the holidays, which is usually our best season.

take a bull by the horns *(verb phrase)* General: to confront something directly and forcefully
Why don't you just take the bull by the horns and ask her to marry you?

take a chill pill *(expression)*

Teen & College: Calm down. Cool it.

Mom, would you just take a chill pill? I was only five minutes late.

take a leak *(verb phrase)* General: to urinate; also known as: take a whizz

Pull in at the next gas station because I've got to take a leak.

Take a midol! *(expression)* Teen & College: stop being so difficult!; refers to the pain relief medicine called Midol, used by women during their menstrual periods

Would you just take a midol and shut up? I'm trying to figure a way out of this situation.

take a nose dive *(verb phrase)* General: to turn bad suddenly

The business took a nose dive when the nearby military base closed.

take a picture *(expression)* Teen & College: Stop staring!

"Hey, take a picture, why don't you?" Jillian barked to the man who'd been staring at her for ten minutes.

take a rain check *(verb phrase)* General: to postpone

Can I take a raincheck on dinner tonight?

take by storm *(verb phrase)* General: to approach something boldly and with great confidence, with the results being unquestionable success

It seemed the new band was taking Europe by storm.

take care of business

1. *(verb phrase)* General: to complete something extremely successfully

I can't believe you fixed Stinky's car! You really know how to take care of business.

2. *(verb phrase)* General: to do something unpleasant because it is an obligation

Listen, I don't like turning these kids into the police for shoplifting; I'm just taking care of business.

take downtown *(verb phrase)* General: to beat or beat up

Once we get our new faxes installed, we'll be able to take the competition downtown.

take down at the knees *(verb phrase)* General: to be severely punished; from the criminal method of punishing someone by shooting or crushing his or her kneecaps

Mom and Dad took me down at the knees for lying to them about where I was going.

take five *(verb phrase)* Entertainment: to take a brief break

Why don't you let the cast take five so they can rest?

take for a ride *(verb phrase)* General: to take advantage of

That salesperson took you for a ride when he convinced you that horrible television was such a bargain.

take gas *(verb phrase)* Surfer-speak: to be treated roughly by a wave while surfing; *see also:* eat the cookie, get biffed, get lunched, get pounded, get prosecuted, and toad

I sure took gas on that one. Just let me catch my breath.

take it down a thousand *(expression)* Teen & College: Calm down!

I've got this thing under control, so why don't you take it down a thousand.

take it in the neck *(verb phrase)* General: to be harshly punished or injured

If you don't pay that guy the money you owe him, you're going to take it in the neck.

take it light *(verb phrase)* Street: calm down; *see also:* square up

If those guys don't take it light soon, there's going to be a big brawl.

take it to the street *(verb phrase)* General: to seek the public's opinion on a matter

The President decided to take his tax program to the street.

take it with a grain of salt *(expression)* General: to not believe something entirely

I appreciate your telling me what you heard, but I'll take it with a grain of salt.

take no prisoners *(verb phrase)* General: rigid, uncompromising approach; from a vaguely military notion that a true conqueror fights to kill the enemy rather than just to capture the enemy

Mary Jo had a tough reputation and was known to take no prisoners in contract negotiations.

take off one's hat to *(verb phrase)* General: to show someone respectful recognition for their accomplishments

I've got to take my hat off to you for training that dog so well.

take one's medicine *(verb phrase)* General: to accept one's punishment

When Charlie's mother found out he had lied, he had to take his medicine and give up his motorcycle for a month.

take-out *(noun)* Food: food that is prepared on the premises of a restaurant and taken home to be eaten

I don't feel like cooking tonight, so let's order take-out.

take someone down a notch *(verb phrase)* General: to cause someone to feel less successful or confident

The boss really took Jeffrey down a notch when he berated him in front of his colleagues.

take someone for a ride *(verb phrase)* General: to deceive someone

After watching her boss make empty promises to fellow employees, Maryann vowed never to take anyone for a ride in such a disgusting way.

take someone to the cleaners *(verb phrase)* General: to get all of someone's money by legal or illegal means

The shady broker took my grandparents to the cleaners with a phony investment scheme.

take the bait *(verb phrase)* General: to be gullible

Don't take the bait when she tells you her car broke down again.

take the Fifth *(verb phrase)* Crime & Law: to rely on the Fifth Amendment of the United States' Constitution to protect oneself from incrimination during an investigation or trial; also known as: plead the Fifth

If someone asks me where I was last night, I'll have to take the Fifth.

take the rap *(verb phrase)* General: to take the blame

I'm not taking the rap for your sloppy work.

take the words right out of one's mouth *(expression)* General: to say what someone else was just thinking or was about to say

Shall we go get some pizza for dinner? You took the words right out of my mouth!

talent *(noun)* Entertainment: any sort of performer, famous or completely unknown

I'd like to pay the talent as little as possible for the voice-over on that ad.

talk big *(verb phrase)* General: to boast or speak in grand terms

Dylan is always talking big, so

don't believe too much of what he says.

talk someone's ear off *(verb phrase)* General: to talk incessantly to someone; *see also:* bend someone's ear

Peter talked my mother's ear off during the graduation ceremony.

talk to the seals *(verb phrase)* Surferspeak: to vomit in the ocean

Did you see Skeghead talk to the seals just now?

talk trash *(verb phrase)* Sports: to engage in an aggressive, contentious verbal exchange with an opponent in an effort to upset his or her concentration

The two had been talking trash the previous quarter and finally came to blows near the end of the game.

talk until one is blue in the face *(verb phrase)* General: to continue talking even though no one is listening

Listen, I could talk until I'm blue in the face, but you're still not going to take my advice.

Tank, the *(noun)* Military: conference room used by the Joint Chiefs of Staff; also known as: the Gold Room

The assistant delivered lunch to the officers meeting in the Tank.

tape watchers *(noun phrase)* Wall Street: small investors who keep track of their investments by watching the market transaction tape, which runs continuously through the duration of a market day

Lauren had become something of a tape watcher since she began investing her savings last year.

tard *(noun)* Teen & College: dolt

Ellen is such a tard, she left her bookbag on the bus.

taste *(adj.)* Surferspeak: attractive, appealing

That new waitress is taste. I think I'll ask her out.

taste of one's own medicine *(noun phrase)* General: treatment that mirrors the way one treats others; usually used in reference to the bad treatment one gives others

I'd like to give that horrible gossip columnist a taste of her own medicine.

taxi squad *(noun phrase)* Sports (Football): players who fill in for injured teammates

Jameson got plenty of playing time, even though he was a member of the taxi squad.

team Xerox *(verb phrase)* Teen & College: to cheat from someone by copying their answers; refers to the Xerox brand photocopy machine and service team

I had to team Xerox on the vocabulary quiz because I forgot to study.

tear it up *(verb phrase)* Teen & College: to have a great time

We really tore it up at the dance last night.

teaser *(noun)* Advertising, Entertainment: announcement meant to arouse interest, and only vaguely and briefly referring to the product or event it is promoting

Between the detergent commercial and the carpet shampoo ad, the station ran a teaser for the afternoon talk show subject: male strippers.

teaser rate *(noun phrase)* Real Estate, Banking: appealingly low first-year rate for a mortgage, used to attract borrowers to adjustable-rate mortgages

The young couple went to BigBuck Bank for the mortgage on their first home, having been attracted by its good teaser rates.

techie *(noun)* Computerspeak: technician

Janet didn't bother to explain the problem to the puzzled user since it was something only a techie could understand.

technotrash *(noun)* Computerspeak: highly skilled and intelligent technician who is a social misfit

Nobody could touch Brad's work as a professional, but socially, he was technotrash.

teepee *(verb)* Teen & College: to cover something with toilet paper

The football team teepeed the coach's car after they won the big game.

telepundit *(noun)* News, Entertainment: television commentator; a Safirism

The conservative telepundit raged about the increase in government spending on welfare programs.

tell it like it is *(verb phrase)* General: to tell the honest truth

Doug's coworkers appreciate him because he tells it like it is.

temp *(noun)* Office Talk: temporary worker, hired to fill in for absent employees or to help out with a heavy work load

Right now I'm a temp, but I'm looking for a full-time job.

tenner *(noun)* General: ten dollar bill

I found a tenner in my jeans pocket so I'm buying lunch.

ten-four *(adv.)* General: all right; from the term used by citizen's band radio users when indicating an affirmative response

Cooper, will you take the garbage out now? Ten-four, Mom.

term limits *(noun phrase)* Government & Politics: movement that promotes the limitation of terms an elected official can serve

The election reformer worked tirelessly for term limits, believing that elected individuals would not serve properly if they could ostensibly rule forever.

terrorist art *(noun phrase)* Art: anti-establishment art featuring violent images and unconventional forms

The sociologist studied the painter's terrorist art for its

reflection of urban decay.

test the water *(verb phrase)* General: to try to get a sense of someone's reaction before saying or doing something

I'd like to test the water with my parents about borrowing their sailboat for the weekend.

Texas disease *(noun phrase)* Business: savings and loan failures that have reached epidemic proportions

There are few banks in the country that haven't suffered from the Texas disease.

thang *(noun)* Teen & College: thing or activity; *see also:* **Miss Thang**

Hey, what's your thang, man? Do you play basketball?

That will be the day! *(expression)* General: That will never happen!

That'll be the day if I ever see that money again.

That's what your mouth says. *(expression)* Street: You have no idea what you're talking about. You're lying.

That's what your mouth says, but you don't know anything about my brother.

thick *(adj.)* General: dense, slow-thinking, unaware

Mr. Flaherty is so thick he never even noticed we weren't in class today.

thin *(adj.)* Sports: without enough players in reserve

The coach knew the team was

going to be playing thin that day, but he had to hope for the best.

thingy *(noun)* General: something one doesn't know the name of; also known as: whaddayacallit, whatchamacallit, whatsit, and whosit

Could you go get that thingy that we use to lock the windows?

thin-skinned *(adj.)* General: easily hurt or irritated

It's really difficult to joke around with you because you're so thin-skinned.

thinking man/woman, the *(noun phrase)* Press: someone who puts intellectual requirements before aesthetic requirements; term not used to describe an individual, but a collective or hypothetical person

Jackie wanted to change her image from starlet to the thinking woman's hero.

thirst *(verb)* Street: to pine for something

I'm thirsting for that leather skirt at Daley's.

thrash 1. *(verb)* Teen & College: to perform well on a skateboard

Brian was thrashing at the exhibition.

2. *(verb)* Teen & College: to excel at something

Those new guys thrashed at the band tryouts.

3. *(noun)* Entertainment: loudest, most extreme form of heavy metal music

Brian's mother couldn't understand how he could listen to that thrash all the time.

thrasher *(noun)* Teen & College: skateboarder; *see also:* boarder

If Jimmy doesn't want to be a thrasher all his life, he'd better start studying.

threat tube *(noun phrase)* Military: path of an incoming enemy missile

The antinuclear weapons were developed to intercept incoming missiles in the threat tube.

three sheets to the wind *(adj. phrase)* General: intoxicated

After just two beers Dyan was three sheets to the wind.

three-humped camel *(noun phrase)* Military: efforts of the three branches of the Armed Services when working together on a project

The proposed cuts were the three-humped camel created by the budget committee at the Pentagon.

through the mill *(prep. phrase)* General: through a difficult experience

Mrs. Bates has been through the mill this year with the illness of her husband.

through thick and thin *(adv. phrase)* General: through easy times and difficult times

We've been friends through thick and thin since third grade.

throw a fit *(verb phrase)* General: to become angry or extremely agitated

My grandmother threw a fit when we talked about having her come live with us.

throw attitude *(verb phrase)* Teen & College: to behave rudely

Don't throw attitude around me, man.

throwaway *(noun)* Advertising: promotional handbill distributed with the assumption that the consumer will only look at it very briefly before discarding

The advertising campaign included some old-fashion and personal touches: sandwich boards and throwaways.

throw in the towel *(verb phrase)* General: to give up

I'm exhausted emotionally and financially from this legal battle. I'm almost ready to throw in the towel.

throw one's weight around *(verb phrase)* General: to use one's influence or position ostentatiously

The owner of the restaurant came in last night and threw his weight around in front of his friends.

throw out on one's ear *(verb phrase)* General: to be ejected

Tyrone showed up at the party without an invitation, but he was quickly thrown out on his ear.

throw someone a curve *(verb phrase)* Sports (Baseball): to do or say something unex-

pected; literally, to pitch a tricky ball to a batter

Please don't throw me a curve in front of the client today.

throw someone to the wolves *(verb phrase)* General: to put someone in a position where they are vulnerable and in danger

The partners decided to throw their philandering colleague to the wolves and called the police.

throw the book at *(verb phrase)* General: to punish severely

The judge is going to throw the book at Coral for violating her parole.

thumb a ride *(verb phrase)* General: to hitchhike; also known as: hitch a ride

I'll thumb a ride to the movies and meet you there.

thumbs-up *(noun phrase)* General: approval; *see also:* OK, the, and nod, the

The lab supervisor gave Barry a thumbs-up on the experiment he'd proposed.

thunder *(verb)* Teen & College: to perform well

I plan on thundering today at the track meet.

ticked off *(adj. phrase)* General: irritated

I've been ticked off for weeks over that court summons I received.

ticker *(noun)* General: heart

I've got to take it easy because I've had a bad ticker for years.

ticket puncher *(noun phrase)*
Military: individual who takes
assignments for the good appearance they will make on a
professional resume
*Worthington wasn't a special-
ist at all, just a ticket puncher
who managed to turn up on
every high-profile commission.*

tied up in knots *(verb phrase)*
General: to be worried or anxious
*Arnie was all tied up in knots
waiting for his test scores.*

tie the knot *(verb phrase)*
General: to get married
*Linda and Bart planned to tie the
knot at the end of the summer.*

tie the President's hands
(verb phrase) Government &
Politics: to challenge or stand in
the way of the Administration's
intended course of action on a
matter; also, generally, tie one's
hands
*The Republicans were accused
of trying to tie the President's
hands on the budget.*

tight 1. *(adj.)* Teen & College:
close-knit
My gang is really tight.

2. *(adj.)* Health & Fitness: describing great muscle tone
*That girl on the Stairmaster is
tight.*

3. *(adj.)* Teen & College: mean,
stingy
*How could your dad be so tight
and not let you use the car?*

tight-ass *(noun)* Teen & College: person preoccupied with
following rules without much
humor
*That bartender is such a tight-
ass! I just wanted one more drink
before closing time.*

tighten one's belt *(verb
phrase)* General: to live in a
more frugal fashion
*After Uncle Ned lost his job, the
family had to tighten its belt for
a while.*

tighten the screws *(verb
phrase)* General: to increase the
pressure
*The Internal Revenue Service
announced plans to tighten the
screws in collecting back taxes.*

timebomb *(noun)* Computerspeak: instruction built into a
computer program that destroys
all data at a predetermined time
in the future; a technique employed mainly by computer criminals or serious troublemakers
*The temps were angry at their
dismissal and arranged a timebomb to destroy the system's
data long after they were gone.*

time frame *(noun)* Government, Business: period of time
under consideration
*There was no mention of a time-
frame so the reporter had to ask
about the deadline on the story.*

time is ripe *(expression)* General: it is the most advantageous
time
*The time is ripe to make a bid on
the failing airline.*

time of one's life *(noun phrase)* General: wonderful experience
Emily had the time of her life at summer camp.

time-out *(noun)* General: break
I need to take some time-out before I start my new job.

tin *(noun)* Crime & Law: police officer's badge; a cop; *see also:* badge
A couple of tins are coming up the block and they look mad.

tinsel teeth *(noun phrase)* Teen & College, Kids: orthodontic braces
Sonya was sure her popularity would plummet when she got tinsel teeth.

tip the scales *(verb phrase)* General: to have a crucial effect or influence
The dismal annual report tipped the scales, and the board voted to reduce the size of the company.

toad *(verb)* Surferspeak: to be treated roughly by a wave while surfing; *see also:* eat the cookie, get biffed, get lunched, get pounded, get prosecuted, and take gas
Damon got toaded out there today.

to a T *(adv. phrase)* General: exactly
That swimsuit fits you to a T.

to be into 1. *(verb phrase)* General: to owe
I'm into my mom for about five hundred bucks already.
2. *(verb phrase)* General: to be interested in
I've been into astrology for several years.

to be wise to someone *(verb phrase)* General: to be aware of someone's hidden motives and actions
My mother's always been wise to Rachel and her sneaky ways.

to boot *(adv. phrase)* General: additionally, on top of
After losing the baseball account, the ad firm lost the perfume line to boot.

to death *(adv. phrase)* General: to the greatest extent possible
I love you to death and would do anything for you, except that.

toe the line *(verb phrase)* General: to be careful to obey the rules
Ginny had to toe the line for the entire summer after she got caught driving her mother's car in the middle of the night.

toilet *(noun)* Entertainment: small-time comedy club or nightclub, as referred to by the comedians who perform there
"I got booed out of that toilet in Cincinnati," the aspiring comedian said, "and I'm never going back."

tools of ignorance *(noun phrase)* Sports (Baseball): catcher's equipment
"I know it's not a glamorous job, but my wife thinks I look

cute in my tools of ignorance," the catcher joked to reporters.

too rich for my blood *(adj. phrase)* General: too costly or much swankier than one is used to

Wow! This club is beautiful! It's too rich for my blood.

toot one's own horn *(verb phrase)* General: to call attention to one's accomplishments or qualities

I don't want to toot my own horn, but I have several merit awards in my field.

top banana *(noun phrase)* General: chief, the boss; *see also:* big cheese, head honcho, and top dog

Raul always knew he'd be the top banana someday.

top cat *(noun phrase)* Travel: passenger on a Concorde jet

Two top cats from the office are going to Paris next week.

top dog *(noun phrase)* General: the boss; *see also:* big cheese, head honcho, and top banana

Everyone knew it was just a matter of time before Nelson became top dog at the advertising firm.

top-drawer *(adj.)* General: of the highest quality

Those linen shirts are exquisite, really top-drawer.

topline *(verb)* Entertainment: to be featured as the top billing in the promotion of a movie or theatrical production

Bart Marlowe had certainly reached the point in his career where he could be sure to topline every film he made.

top spin *(noun)* Entertainment: positive momentum, especially for a film or an individual's Hollywood career

The independent picture was starting to show some topspin, thanks to favorable reviews around the country.

total *(adj.)* Teen & College: complete; an all-purpose word used for emphasis

What a total jerk he is!

totaled *(adj.)* Teen & College: intoxicated

That guy who grabbed the microphone and started singing is totaled.

to the bone *(adv. phrase)* General: entirely, to the point of exhaustion

Sasha worked her fingers to the bone to finish her sister's dress in time for the wedding.

to the letter *(adv. phrase)* General: exactly

Do you have the budget worked out to the letter?

to the max *(adv. phrase)* General: as much as one can

I studied for that exam to the max.

to the tune of *(adv. phrase)* General: in the approximate amount of; usually refers to numbers or dollars

That new swimming pool will cost the town plenty of money, to

the tune of a million dollars.

touch *(noun)* Sports (Football): informal game of football in which tackling is not allowed and one is considered tackled when touched with two hands by an opponent
Let's get together Sunday for a game of touch.

touch and go *(noun phrase)* General: with an uncertain outcome
Ida had a bad reaction to the antibiotics she was given after surgery, and for a while it was touch and go.

tough *(adj.)* Teen & College: excellent
That was a tough suit that actor wore in that movie.

tough row to hoe *(noun phrase)* General: difficult job
Raising six kids in this day and age is a tough row to hoe.

toxic *(adj.)* Teen & College: amazing
The Smithsons just up and moved away over the weekend? That's toxic!

track *(verb)* Street: to talk
We've been tracking for a long time about starting a singing group.

track record *(noun phrase)* General: one's performance history
I've got a great track record with new talent, so expect a gold record.

tracks *(noun)* Drug World: needle marks found on the body of a person who injects drugs habitually
The police found tracks on Linda's arms and behind her knees.

trade dress *(noun phrase)* Advertising: colors or logo style that become associated with a product or company
The soda company's trade dress of red and white was recognized worldwide.

trade-off *(noun)* General: what one must give up in order to get something else
If I take that new job on the West Coast, the trade-off is that I have to give up my apartment in New York.

trade on *(verb phrase)* General: to use to one's advantage
Barbie had always traded on her good looks, but now she needed to use her head to get out of this mess.

trades, the *(noun)* Entertainment: entertainment industry's newspapers and magazines; Variety, for instance, is one of the trades
The young actress wasn't even surprised when she read in the trades that her agent had been arrested for fraud.

train wreck *(noun phrase)* Medical: patient with multiple medical conditions
The patient was such a train wreck that the doctor didn't

know where to begin in determining treatment.

transphotic *(adj.)* Sci-fi: faster than light (FTL), referring to space travel
After the transphotic shuttle deposited the passengers to the designated star base, it headed back to the mother ship.

trap door *(noun phrase)* Computerspeak: inadvertent or deliberate opening in a program that allows the user to skirt a system's security protection; usually created or discovered by clever, devious types wanting a shortcut past cumbersome security measures
Terence was able to get at the classified data by identifying the trap door to the FBI's secret files.

trash *(verb)* Teen & College: to destroy, make a mess of
We totally trashed my mom's car last night, and now I've got to spend the day cleaning it.

trash cash *(noun phrase)* Advertising: advertising leaflets that look like United States dollar bills and attract attention for resembling such
The sidewalk was littered with trash cash advertising the opening of a new computer store.

trashed *(adj.)* Teen & College: intoxicated
Jerry was trashed at his parents' anniversary party.

trash television *(noun phrase)* Entertainment: sensationalistic and tawdry programs that feature interviews, personality profiles, and reenactments of grisly events; also known as: tabloid television
The senator's escapades had been reported extensively on trash television.

tread water *(verb phrase)* General: to keep oneself from being overwhelmed by difficulty; from the swimming term for keeping oneself afloat
The small company was just barely able to tread water during the lengthy economic recession.

treat *(noun)* Teen & College: attractive woman
I'd sure like to meet a nice treat tonight.

tree hugger *(noun phrase)* Government & Politics: environmental activist or lobbyist; *see also:* duck squeezer
The tree huggers lobbying for the environmental bill wouldn't give up until they won.

Trekkie *(proper noun)* Sci-fi: completely informed and devoted fan of the entire Star Trek series of books, television programs, movies, and related products
Clarice was an unapologetic Trekkie who spent weekends watching reruns or attending Star Trek conventions.

trey *(noun)* Drug World: three dollars' worth of a drug, usually referring to just a small dose of crack

I only have enough green for a tray. Can I get some on credit?

trial and error *(noun phrase)* General: method of solving a problem by trying all possible options until one happens on the correct solution

Jason made it big in the stock market through trial and error.

trial balloon *(noun phrase)* General: test of the possible re-action to something

The bank floated a trial balloon on the new loan program they were thinking of launching.

trick 1. *(verb)* Street: to spend money on one's love interest

You've been tricking like a rich man, Rick.

2. *(adj.)* Teen & College: inter-esting and appealing

That old rug you got at the flea market is pretty trick.

trickle-down *(noun)* Government, Business: benefits al-legedly gained by individuals or groups outside of the primary group a law or policy was meant to benefit

While the top income bracket will benefit immediately from the tax break, it will be several years until the trickle-down takes effect.

trick of the trade *(noun phrase)* General: expertise gained from great familiarity with a field

Stay with me, kid. I know a lot of tricks of the trade.

trip 1. *(noun)* Teen & College, Drug World: experience, drug-related or not

I almost barfed when I got off that ride. What a trip!

2. *(verb)* Street: to tell a lie

You've been tripping me all along?

trip-out *(noun)* Teen & College: empty-headed, distracted person; *see also:* airhead

Although her friends thought her mom was a trip-out, Monique knew she was more of a mad scientist.

trippy *(adj.)* Teen & College: strange, in a positive way

Those are trippy pants; I like them.

troll *(verb)* General: to search for

Ned and his buddies were out trolling for bettys when they got into a brawl in a bar.

trots, the *(noun)* General: di-arrhea; *see also:* Aztec two-step and Montezuma's revenge

It's embarrassing to admit, even to a doctor, that you have the trots.

truck *(noun)* Teen & College: slow-moving person

I always get behind a truck in the bank line and end up waiting hours.

true blue *(adj. phrase)* Com-puterspeak: all-IBM computer-equipped office

The owner won't allow anything but a true-blue shop.

true-blue green *(adj. phrase)*

Ecology: describing a person who is a fully committed environmentalist

There are more true-blue green folks in the Pacific Northwest than anywhere else in the country.

trump card *(noun phrase)* General: secret plan or effort that is one's final hope for success

The agent's contacts in the terrorist underground were his trump card in finding the murderer.

try one's hand *(verb phrase)* General: to attempt something for the first time

I'd like to try my hand at oil painting.

try something on for size *(verb phrase)* General: to decide if one likes an idea or finds it suitable

Why don't you try this new itinerary on for size and let me know what you think.

tube 1. *(verb)* Teen & College: to watch television

I just tubed with the folks last night.

2. *(noun)* General: the television; short for boob tube

I saw a great show on the tube last week.

3. *(verb)* Medical: to die; *see also:* box and flatline

The accident victim tubed before we could do anything to save him.

tubular *(adj.)* Surferspeak: excellent

Those were some tubular burgers being served at that barbecue.

tude *(noun)* Teen & College: short for attitude

With a tude like that, she's not going to have any friends by the end of the summer.

tug-of-war *(noun)* General: struggle

The two departments are in a tug-of-war over budget allocations.

turf *(verb)* Medical: to pass along responsibility for a patient; also known as: punt, turf down, and turf over.

I saw that patient in emergency last night, but I turfed him over to Dr. Savage at County General.

turn a blind eye *(verb phrase)* General: to pretend not to see something

The woman had always turned a blind eye to her son's illegal activities.

turn a deaf ear *(verb phrase)* General: to refuse to hear something

The defiant matriarch turned a deaf ear to her family's pleas for help.

turn in *(verb phrase)* General: to go to bed

It's really late, James. Let's turn in.

turn one's back on *(verb phrase)* General: to refuse to help someone

It was amazing that Sal could

turn his back on his own friend.

turn on the heat *(verb phrase)*
Teen & College: to apply pressure
Mom has really turned on the heat to get Kerry to come home for Christmas.

turnover *(noun)* Sports: play in which possession of the ball is lost to the other team, either due to misplay or penalty
Whitley was responsible for four turnovers that day, and the coach was furious.

turn over a new leaf *(verb phrase)* General: to commit to improving one's behavior or attitude
I'm turning over a new leaf this fall and not eating any more sugar.

turn the tables *(verb phrase)*
General: to reverse a situation
Aurora cleverly turned the table on Ron and proposed to him before he could propose to her.

turn the tide *(verb phrase)*
General: to shift from a negative direction to a positive direction
The optimistic projections for the new year helped the struggling company turn the tide.

tweaked out *(adj. phrase)*
Teen & College: distracted, in another world; see also: space
I was tweaked out when the doorbell rang.

tweet *(noun)* Teen & College: teacher

When's the tweet going to be back?

twist 1. *(noun)* Bar: shaving of lemon peel
I'll just have a diet cola with a twist, please.

2. *(noun)* General: woman
Who's the twist with Barney tonight?

twist a braid *(verb phrase)*
Teen & College: to say good-bye
I've got to twist a braid because my father needs to use the phone.

twist someone's arm *(verb phrase)* General: to persuade someone to do something
I'm not supposed to go to the party, but I guess you could twist my arm.

twitcher *(noun)* Fantasy: mildly derogatory term for a participant in a role-playing game who gets demonstrably overenthusiastic for the game
There were a couple of twitchers in the neighborhood that the regular gang used only when they were short of players.

two bricks shy of a load *(expression)* General: in a diminished mental state
"That fellow's two bricks shy of a load," the waitress stated matter-of-factly.

two cents *(noun phrase)* General: one's opinion
Excuse me, but I'd like to put my two cents in here.

U

up-front exposure *(noun phrase)* Entertainment: initial investment in the first stages of making a film, referring to the initial exposure to financial risk in the process
When the producer brought the film rights to the as-yet unpublished novel, he had a feeling it was up-front exposure that would pay off.

ufology *(noun)* Sci-fi: belief in, and study of, reports of Unidentified Flying Objects (UFOs)
Barbara hardly had the interest in her job as a chemist since she got caught up in ufology last year.

uforia *(noun)* Sci-fi: avid interest in Unidentified Flying Objects (UFOs)
After the unmistakable sighting, the entire town was consumed with uforia.

ugly customer *(noun phrase)* General: violent, unsavory character
The ugly customer sitting at the end of the bar was beginning to frighten the patrons.

ultra *(noun)* Business, Salespeople: consumer who requires the best, most upscale version of everything they buy
"Oh, this one's mine," the salesperson exclaimed when the obvious ultra walked in the door.

ump *(noun)* Sports (Baseball): umpire
I swear the ump was working with his eyes closed last night.

Uncle Sam *(proper noun)* General: United States government
Don't forget, Uncle Sam will want to take a share of your profits on that deal.

Uncle Sugar *(proper noun)* Military: military's name for the federal government, short for Uncle Sugar Daddy, referring to the source of funds the military has traditionally received from the government
Yeah, all my kids got their teeth straightened, thanks to Uncle Sugar.

uncool *(adj.)* Teen & College: showing bad judgment, not good
That was very uncool of you to swear at the coach in front of the whole team.

under a cloud *(prep. phrase)* General: under suspicion
The pawn shop had been under a cloud with the authorities for a number of months.

under fire *(adv. phrase)* General: under attack
I don't work very well when I'm under fire all the time.

under one's belt *(adv. phrase)* General: in one's experience
After three cross-country tips, I have plenty of miles of driving under my belt.

under one's breath *(adv.*

phrase) General: spoken in a whisper, usually to oneself

Morton cursed under his breath while he stood in line at the bank.

under one's nose (prep. phrase) General: in an obvious place

The waiter searched frantically for his corkscrew and finally founds it right under his nose— in the pocket of his apron.

under one's thumb (prep. phrase) General: under one's control

Penny's got that new guy under her thumb already and he's only been here for two weeks.

under one's wing (adv. phrase) General: under one's guidance and protection

Mrs. Spofford took her new neighbor under her wing and showed her around town.

under the table (adv. phrase) General: secretly, usually implies illegally, as in order to avoid paying taxes

The restaurant proprietor was fined for paying the waitstaff under the table.

under the weather (prep. phrase) General: ill

I won't be coming to work today because I'm feeling a little under the weather.

unk-unks (noun) Military: unknown factors

The unk-unks of this plan may force us to shelve the whole thing.

unruly (adj.) Teen & College: grizzly, gory

The quarterback took an unruly hit in that last play.

unwelcome visit (noun phrase) Military: move into enemy territory

We made an unwelcome visit across the border last night.

up (adj.) Computerspeak: functioning or working again after malfunctioning, or being down

The floor manager breathed a sigh of relief when the technician nodded that the system was finally up.

up a tree (prep. phrase) General: in trouble

After losing the whole semester's lecture notes, Susan was really up a tree.

up for grabs (adj. phrase) General: available for anyone to attempt to take

The license for the popular cartoon character was up for grabs at the end of the year.

upgrade 1. (verb) Air & Space: to improve one's class of seating on a flight; for example, from coach to business class or first class

Since Doug knows the pilot, he's likely to be able to upgrade his seat.

2. (noun) Real Estate: improvement on a property

The buyers decided that the kitchen upgrade in the condominium wasn't worth the pre-

mium price being charged by the builder.

up one's alley *(adv. phrase)* General: perfectly suited to one's preferences or abilities
Unlike her colleagues, the reporter found the unusual assignment to be right up her alley.

up one's sleeve *(adv. phrase)* General: secretly kept in reserve until needed
I've got another plan up my sleeve if this one doesn't work out.

upper hand *(noun phrase)* General: advantage
You've got the upper hand, so take your time and play the game right.

upshot *(noun)* General: final outcome
So what was the upshot of your meeting with Henderson?

up the creek *(prep. phrase)* General: in trouble; also known as: up shits creek
I was truly up the creek, after I lost my flashlight and my map.

up the kazoo *(adv. phrase)* General: in plentiful supply
I've got paintings up the kazoo; it's a couch I need.

up the ying-yang *(prep. phrase)* Teen & College: too much or too many, an excessive amount
I've got babysitting jobs up the ying-yang this summer.

up to no good *(prep. phrase)* Teen & College: looking for, or engaged in, a physical encounter

I haven't seen Patrice for an hour. She must be up to no good.

up to par *(adj. phrase)* General: at the usual standard of quality
I wasn't feeling up to par when Milo asked me to dance so I said no.

up to speed *(prep. phrase)* Government & Politics: as current as possible
After he returns from his paternity leave, Ted will have to be brought up to speed on the developments within his department.

use one's head *(verb phrase)* General: to think clearly and sensibly
Use your head for once and stay away from those troublemakers at school.

utility player *(noun phrase)* Sports: player who is able to perform in a variety of positions; generally, refers to one who is adept at numerous functions
Constance is a real utility player at our regional seminars.

user *(noun)* Computerspeak: person who works on a computer but who doesn't know or want to know how a system or program works; *see also:* gweep
Margaret suddenly realized that not one of the users in her office could get them out of a computer jam.

user-friendly *(adj.)* Computerspeak: easy to use, with simple

instructions and clear options, originally referring to computers and programs, but now in general use
The map was so user-friendly that even a child could read it.

V

vanilla *(adj.)* General: plain and spare
I just want the vanilla version of the proposal.

veg out *(verb phrase)* Teen & College: to do absolutely nothing
I didn't work this summer; I just vegged out and played tennis.

vegetable garden *(noun phrase)* Medical: area of the hospital where comatose patients are assigned; *see also:* C & T Ward
Sandra was bothered by the soft music always playing in the vegetable garden at the end of the hall.

velvet *(noun)* Business: quick, painless profit
That deal Leo made uptown turned out to be velvet.

viable *(adv.)* Government: possible, a workable possibility; replaced "feasible" as the generic word of choice among government bureaucrats; *see also:* do-able
The senator termed the compromise on the bill as viable.

vibe someone out *(verb phrase)* Surferspeak: to behave in a cold manner toward someone
Wow, Josie just vibed me out on the beach.

-ville *(suffix)* Teen & College: place with a certain characteristic
That advanced math class is nerdville, U.S.A.

virus *(noun)* Computerspeak: program or instruction secretly introduced to a system in order to create havoc or cause permanent harm to the system and its data
Everyone had heard the rumor about the "Flintstone Virus," which could only be halted when "Barney Rubble" was typed on the screen.

vitals *(noun)* Medical: short for vital signs, including blood pressure, pulse, etc.
"What are the patient's vitals?" the emergency room technician demanded of the medic.

voice-over *(noun)* Advertising, Entertainment: television advertisement or piece of film featuring the voice of an announcer or narrator without the person's image ever being seen; also known as: V.O.
Blanche Whiting made her fortune late in her career, having found a niche doing voice-overs for salad dressing commercials.

voluntary enhanced exit program *(noun phrase)* Business: job elimination program offering certain employees attractive financial incentives for leaving their jobs

A few employees were able to take advantage of a voluntary enhanced exit program when the company was downsized after being sold; others were simply fired.

vulture *(noun)* Air & Space: bothersome commercial airline passenger

The two vultures in row eighteen have already asked for pillows, aspirin, blankets, and a foot massage.

vulture fund *(noun phrase)* Wall Street: investment fund that buys shares in companies deep in debt, with the aim of selling off the shares at a profit when the market improves

The brokerage firm's controversial vulture fund generated a solid profit for its investors.

W

wa *(noun)* Foreign (Japanese): team spirit, commitment to the common good of the team over individual achievement

The sports reporters were claiming that the team's wa was responsible for its dramatic turnaround.

wack *(adj.)* Teen & College: bad, undesirable

The new rules at the basketball court are totally wack.

wacked *(adj.)* General: crazy;

also known as: wacked out

Bob is really wacked — he went out and charged a new leather coat and he doesn't even have money for rent.

wag 1. *(noun)* Surferspeak: idiot

What a wag! He just asked me if I'm a surfer!

2. *(noun)* Government & Politics, News: spokesperson or commentator

I heard a Defense Department wag saying they would oppose any further budget cuts.

wail *(verb)* Teen & College: to beat up

*Marcia was **grounded** for wailing on her little brother.*

wait for the other shoe to drop *(expression)* General: to wait to see the consequences or next development of something

After Congress announced its plans to cut the deficit, taxpayers were waiting for the other shoe to drop.

wake-up call *(noun phrase)* General: attention-getting event or statement

The public's extreme negative reaction to his speech was the President's wake-up call on the tax issue.

waldo *(adj.)* Teen & College: out of it

I was just waldo after three hours of tennis.

Waldorf Astoria *(proper noun)* Crime & Law: solitary confinement in prison; *see also:* hole, the

"Whatever you do, don't send me to the Waldorf Astoria," the inmate complained.

walk the plank *(verb phrase)* General: to take the blame or punishment for something
Since no one would confess, T.J.'s father made him walk the plank for the broken window.

walk-in *(noun)* General: party that shows up at a restaurant or beauty salon without having made reservations or an appointment in advance
It took forty-five minutes for the walk-ins to be seated, but luckily they waited happily at the bar.

walking _____ *(noun phrase)* Teen & College: expert in a certain subject
You should ask Sky about that. He's a walking history book.

walking papers *(noun phrase)* General: termination from one's job; also known as: pink slip
I got my walking papers last week, so I may have to move back home to cut my expenses.

walk in tall corn *(verb phrase)* Wall Street: to be making a lot of money
Ellison's been walking in tall corn since he became a broker.

walk-on *(noun)* Entertainment: small part in a show or movie that requires minimal screen or stage time and very few lines
Julie was grateful to be acting, even if it was just a couple of walk-ons on the afternoon soap operas.

walk on air *(verb phrase)* General: to be elated
Trudy was walking on air after she received her college acceptance.

walk on eggs *(verb phrase)* General: to deal with a situation very carefully
I've got to walk on eggs with the bank or they'll call my loan in.

wall *(verb)* Street: to stand against a wall during a party instead of dancing
I just walled at Keesha's house last night. I didn't feel like partying.

wallpaper *(noun)* Computerspeak: long, complicated printouts that include much more information than necessary
Nothing's worse than the wallpaper generated by dense, sloppy programming instructions.

wannabe *(noun)* Teen & College, General: disparaging term for one who tries too hard to be like certain others
Rachel dressed like a Madonnawannabe.

war chest *(noun phrase)* Government & Politics: incumbent candidate's campaign coffers
The Senator's war chest was so formidable it had scared away many a potential challenger.

Ward X *(proper noun)* Medical: hospital morgue
"This one's headed for Ward X," the nurse advised the or-

derly, pointing to the body covered with a sheet on the gurney.

warm body *(noun phrase)*
General: person
We need to get some warm bodies at the candidate's rally tonight.

warts and all *(noun phrase)*
General: plain, ugly truth
I've told you everything I saw, warts and all.

wash down *(verb phrase)*
General: to drink liquids to make inferior food go down easier
This cake is so dry I've got to wash it down with some coffee.

wash one's hands of *(verb phrase)* General: to absolve oneself of blame or responsibility
I'm tired of wasting advice on you. I'm washing my hands of this whole situation.

Wassup? *(expression)* Teen & College: What's up? What's going on?
Wassup? I heard you got a job at the Burger Hut.

waste *(verb)* Crime & Law: to kill, also known as: chill, hit, ice, lay out, off, rub out, and whack
They're hunting Victor down for wasting a cop.

wasted *(adj.)* Teen & College: intoxicated; *see also:* trashed
Minnie was just wasted by the end of the concert.

wastoid *(noun)* Teen & College: disparaging term for one who spends too much time drinking or doing drugs

"Hey, I like to have a good time, but I'm no wastoid," Carl insisted.

watchdog *(adj.)* Government: person or organization assigned to oversee, monitor, or investigate the activities of a committee, agency, department, or other governing body
The Senate's new mining bill will be closely monitored by environmental watchdog groups.

watering hole *(noun phrase)*
Bars: bar
Archie could always be found at his favorite watering hole after work.

wave, the *(noun)* Sports: gimmick requiring sports spectators, starting at one end of a crowd to the other, to stand up and throw their arms over their head; the overall effect is like a big wave
The crowd did the wave so many times during the game that Jeanie's back hurt.

waver *(noun)* Teen & College: one who is into avant-garde music, black clothes, and New Wave interests
Bonnie was a waver and frequented the underground clubs to hear new music.

wax *(verb)* General: to defeat
Johnny got waxed on his first case as a lawyer.

way 1. *(adv.)* Teen & College: affirmative response; specifically meaning "Yes, it's true";

often used in response to: no way, which means "I don't believe that."

Bonnie's mother signed her up for the church youth group? No way. Yes, way.

2. *(adv.)* Teen & College: very

That bathing suit is way cool.

ways and means *(noun phrase)* General: method of raising money or otherwise accomplishing something

I'd like to find the ways and means to take a vacation this summer.

We're talking . . . *(expression)* General: I mean; expression used for emphasis

There were a lot of bugs out there—I mean, we're talking thousands.

weak *(adj.)* Teen & College: no good; *see also:* lame

Martine isn't allowed to drive to school for two weeks. Isn't that weak?

weapons system *(noun phrase)* Military: weapon; describing even a single weapon as a weapons system increases the perceived threat of the weapon itself

The soldier on watch wasn't relying on a sophisticated weapons system, just a rifle, a revolver, and a mortar gun.

wear kid gloves *(verb phrase)* General: to deal with someone carefully and tactfully

You've got to wear kid gloves

when you talk to outraged customers.

wear more than one hat *(verb phrase)* General: to have multiple responsibilities

Bill wears more than one hat in his office.

wear one's heart on one's sleeve *(verb phrase)* General: to show one's emotions easily

Denny wasn't one to wear his heart on his sleeve, but he was clearly upset when Brenda broke up with him.

wear the pants in the family *(verb phrase)* General: to be the head of the family

I'd like to know who wears the pants in that family!

weasel *(verb)* General: to connive; also known as: weasel out

Don't try to weasel your way out of trouble with me!

web issue *(noun phrase)* Government & Politics: campaign issue that brings together normally disparate interest groups in support of the candidate

The challenger's tax increase proposal was the incumbent's web issue.

wedge *(noun)* Teen & College: food

Let's get some wedge before we go to the play rehearsal.

wedge issue *(noun phrase)* Government & Politics: controversial campaign issue that can break up an opponent's coalition of support and win votes away

When the challenger announced that he would support a tax increase to reduce the national debt, the incumbent knew she had found her wedge issue.

weed *(noun)* Drug World: marijuana; also known as: bud, bule, bush, cali, collyweed, corn, cranny, food, ganja, grass, herb, hooter, marahoochie, muggle, ned, rad weed, smoke, tea, trom, and wisdom weed
"I'd like to get my hands on some good weed," the aging hippie said wistfully.

weenie *(noun)* General: weak, unassertive person; *see also:* butt, wimp, and wuss
You're going to let her get away with that? What a weenie!

weeper *(noun)* Entertainment: sad film or television program
There was nothing like a good weeper to bring in the film-going crowds during those gray, winter months.

weigh in *(verb phrase)* General: to let others know of one's opinion
The discussion was becoming heated, and Kevin was anxious to weigh in on the controversy.

weight of the world *(noun phrase)* General: great burden or responsibility
You look like you're carrying the weight of the world today. Is anything wrong?

weightism *(noun)* PC: discrimination against overweight people

The company was accused of weightism by a disgruntled employee who felt he had been passed up for promotion because of his size.

went toes *(verb)* Business: when an enterprise has gone out of business; *see also:* belly up and close doors
The combination video-frozen yogurt-tanning shop went toes in just six months.

wet blanket *(noun phrase)* General: one who hampers others' pleasure
Don't be such a wet blanket. Everybody else wants to go to the movies!

wet behind the ears *(adj. phrase)* General: inexperienced
The captain wouldn't let Waldo take the helm of the boat because he was still too wet behind the ears.

wet dog *(noun phrase)* Bars: wine that smells or tastes acrid
One sniff of the cork and Jane knew the wine was a wet dog.

whack *(verb)* Crime & Law: to kill; used most frequently by mob personnel; also known as: chill, ice, hit, lay out, off, rub out and waste
After Vito got whacked, there was a big battle over who would take charge of the operation.

Whatever. *(expression)* Teen & College: I don't care. Do whatever you want.
So you're making a roast chicken

tonight? That's fine. Whatever.

What is this, my birthday?
(expression) Teen & College:
Why am I so lucky?
*I got two letters from home
today. What is this, my birthday?*

What's the deal? *(expression)*
Teen & College: What does this
mean?
*So what's the deal, are we going
to the movies or not?*

What's the word? *(expression)* General: What's happening? also known as: What's the
good word?
What's the word? Are we playing tennis this afternoon or not?

wheel and deal *(verb phrase)*
General: to negotiate adeptly
*Gert's really good at wheeling
and dealing with the buyers.*

**where the rubber meets the
road** *(adv. phrase)* General:
most important test
*The resident had passed all his
medical exams brilliantly, but
the rubber would meet the road
when he operated for the first
time.*

whipped *(adj.)* Teen & College:
enthralled, enchanted, dominated
*She's got him so whipped that he
does her assignments and her
laundry!*

whispering campaign *(noun
phrase)* General: series of detrimental rumors
*The whispering campaign
against Keith probably cost him
a promotion.*

whisper stock *(noun phrase)*
Wall Street: stock believed to be
poised to experience considerable stock-effecting activity, either internally or externally
*Everyone in the firm agreed the
young broker **had a great ear**
for whisper stock.*

whistle blowers *(noun phrase)*
Government, Business: those
who take it upon themselves to
expose corruption, poor management, discrimination, etc., in
government or business
*Journalists these days pride
themselves as whistle blowers,
but some people think they go
too far.*

white bread *(adj. phrase)*
General: bland, ordinary
*Arlene was aware of how white
bread she seemed to her co-workers.*

white collar *(adj. phrase)* General, Business: working professionals at every level of
employment
*The increase in white collar
crime is surely a sign of the
times.*

white elephant *(noun phrase)*
General: burdensome item one
cannot easily dispose of
*What a white elephant that
Victorian lamp turned out to be!*

white hat *(noun phrase)* General: person seen as blameless in a
scandal or unfortunate situation;
as opposed to the black hat, who
is seen as being entirely to blame

The ambassador's assistant was the white hat in the smuggling incident at the embassy.

white knight *(noun phrase)* Wall Street: agreeable outside party who helps a company avoid a hostile takeover
The entertainment industry mogul was glad to be the white knight for his old friend's clothing company.

white-knuckle *(adj.)* General: terrifying
Boomer took the gang on a white-knuckle ride through town.

white knuckler *(noun phrase)* Sports: extremely close game
The game had been a real white knuckler, but the home team had finally won.

white lie *(noun phrase)* General: small mistruth used to get one out of a sticky situation
I told Polly a white lie so she wouldn't be hurt for not being invited to the party.

whitewash *(verb)* General: to portray something as not as bad as it really is
The candidate was accused of whitewashing his involvement in those questionable stock deals.

whiz kid *(noun phrase)* Military: mildly derogatory term used by military personnel to describe analysts or Department of Defense staff members who do more hypothesizing then hands-on work in the military
The officers could hardly dis-guise their disdain for the whiz kid who had scrapped their plans with his analytical mumbo-jumbo.

whole enchilada *(noun phrase)* General: entire matter
I'd like you to take over this project, the whole enchilada.

whole nine yards *(noun phrase)* General: everything, the limit
She gave me every excuse she could think of — the whole nine yards.

whore *(noun)* Wall Street: stock customer who hungers to buy only hot, new-issue stocks in order to sell them quickly at a tidy profit
*Parsons never wasted his time on **blue chip** stocks; he was too much of a whore for that.*

Why are you clowning? *(expression)* Street: Why are you insulting me?
What's your problem with me? Why are you clowning?

wicked *(adj.)* Teen & College: extreme
I got a wicked sunburn at the beach on Saturday.

wide break *(noun phrase)* Entertainment: maximum exposure for an opening film, measured in the number of screens where the film is viewed
It was amazing that the film failed in spite of its wide break, costly production, and superstar leads.

widget *(noun)* General: purposely unnamed item used in hypothetical discussions
If we produced 100 widgets an hour last year, how many more could we produce this year with better equipment?

wifeable *(adj.)* Technology: sexist term that describes products designed with a minimum of technological devices so as to appeal to (and presumably be usable by) women
The video system was touted by the manufacturer to its distributors as being perfectly wifeable.

wiff *(verb)* Sports: to miss the ball completely, in a sport where one wields a bat, club, or racquet
Little Sally was embarrassed to have wiffed each time she went to bat that day.

wiggle room *(noun phrase)* Government & Politics, Public Relations: safe margin surrounding a statement or policy that allows for qualification as conditions change
The counselor gave himself some wiggle room in describing the student's mediocre performance; it was well known his parents were major benefactors of the school.

wig out *(verb phrase)* Teen & College: to become extremely agitated
My dad wigged out when he saw my report card.

wig-wag *(noun)* Sports (Football): hand signals used to call a play from the sidelines
The quarterback read the coach's wig-wag and adjusted his instructions for his teammates.

wild *(adj.)* Teen & College: very cool
Josie's new room is really wild.

wild card *(noun phrase)* General, Sports: condition or event that could not have been predicted
The unseeded player's victory over the top-seeded favorite was a wild card in the big tournament.

wilding *(noun)* Crime & Law: random series of crimes committed by a gang of roving marauders; *see also:* wolf-pack crime
The youths were quickly arrested in the wilding incident outside the concert arena.

Willie Horton *(proper noun)* Government & Politics: mistake that will ultimately bring one's downfall; from the Republican's use of the image of convict Willie Horton against Democratic candidate Michael Dukakis in the 1988 presidential campaign
I don't want that twenty-year-old drunk driving conviction to be my Willie Horton, not after I've come this far.

willy-nilly *(adv.)* General: randomly

I'm not going to choose a doctor willy-nilly.

wilma *(noun)* Surferspeak: female idiot; refers to Wilma Flintstone from television's "The Flintstones"
What a wilma! If she cuts me off my wave one more time, I'll just run into her.

wilson *(noun)* Teen & College: nasty fall from a skateboard
Brandon had a wilson and broke his arm.

wimp *(noun)* General: weak, unassertive person; *see also:* butt, weenie, and wuss
Michael felt like a wimp for finishing last in the company race.

windbag *(noun)* General: one who talks too much without saying anything important
That old windbag could go on for hours.

window 1. *(noun)* Air & Space: the period of time during which a launch is possible, generally weather permitting
The shuttle had a very small window that day, as storm clouds loomed on the horizon.
2. *(noun)* Wall Street: period during which a limited stock offer is available
The savvy brokers were primed to pounce on the window for their clients.
3. *(noun)* Military: military opportunity
The enemy's defensive units were diverted, and our air strike

force was able to take advantage of the window.

window shop *(verb phrase)* General: to browse without intending to buy
I had the nicest afternoon —I window shopped up Hilldale Avenue.

windshield tourist *(noun phrase)* Travel: vacationing motorist who rarely stops to take in the sights
The souvenir stand suffered from a strong incidence of windshield tourism likely caused by its bad location along the desolate desert highway.

wind sprint *(noun phrase)* Sports: short, fast run
The team did innumerable wind sprints during spring training.

-winger *(suffix)* Government & Politics: of the extreme; used with left (leftwinger) and right (rightwinger) to describe a person on either of the far sides of the political spectrum
The congressman was known as a vocal rightwinger who wasn't afraid of a rough floor debate to promote his interests.

wing it *(verb phrase)* General: to attempt to do something even though one is unprepared or unqualified
I hadn't had time to study the script, but I decided to wing it and audition anyway.

wink at *(verb phrase)* General: to pretend not to be aware of

Spike's father always winked at his son's trouble at school.

winter blues *(noun phrase)* Medical: type of depression which strikes those who require sunlight to be at their healthiest mentally; also known as: seasonal affective disorder
Marguerite's family moved to Florida for half the year to fight severe winter blues.

wipe the floor with *(verb phrase)* General: to defeat decisively
The Cougars wiped the floor with the Bobcats at the state championship.

wired 1. *(verb)* Crime & Law: fitted with a microphone
Simpson was wired when she went in to negotiate with the kidnappers.
2. *(adj.)* Government, Business: when an assignment, contract, or grant is determined ahead of time to be given to a certain party or organization, rather than chosen from an open field of applicants or bidders
Don't even bother applying for that art grant; everyone knows it's wired.
3. *(adj.)* Drug World: under the intense influence of a stimulating drug
The youth was so wired he couldn't even concentrate on the conversation he was having.

wirehead *(noun)* Computerspeak: those for whom a fanaticism for computers is their only interest in life
The popular seniors completely ignored the table of wireheads that sat at the end of their lunch table.

wiseguy *(noun)* Crime & Law: operative of the mob; *see also:* goodfella
When the merchant refused to cooperate, some wiseguys showed up and smashed up his shop.

witch doctor *(noun phrase)* Medical: internist
This guy will need to see a witch doctor if those stomach cramps don't go away.

with flying colors *(adv. phrase)* General: very successfully
Ollie passed his citizenship exam with flying colors.

within bounds *(prep. phrase)* General: within the realm of what is considered proper
The sales force was encouraged to develop new business, only using tactics that were within bounds.

with it *(phrase)* General: informed and aware, the opposite of ignorant; *see also:* in the loop and in the know
The bartender knew every hot group on the horizon since he was very with-it regarding the club scene.

wolf down *(verb phrase)* General: to eat quickly
I wolfed down my lunch so I

could finish errands on my lunch hour.

wolf-pack crime *(noun phrase)* Crime & Law: robbery or assault committed by a roving group of troublemakers who randomly go from victim to victim; *see also:* wilding

The neighborhood had become terrorized by the surge in wolf-pack crime in the last few weeks.

wonk *(verb)* Government & Politics: to answer a question or criticism with a technical, detailed, brainy response which suggests nothing but expertise on the subject

What the official lacked in political polish, she made up for in the ability to wonk people until they were nodding in agreement.

woof *(verb)* Teen & College: to boast

Marlena was woofing about the new car her parents had promised to buy her.

woopie *(acronym)* Press: Well-Off Older Person; a person who is over sixty-five and financially secure

The woopie was the most common buyer of recreational vehicles.

word *(expression)* Teen & College, Street: I agree. Or, as a question, Do you agree? Is this true?

The principal's gone for two weeks? Word?

word of mouth *(noun phrase)* General: news or opinion spread from person to person

The word of mouth on the new Bart Marlowe picture is that it's terrific.

Word to my mother. *(expression)* Street: I swear it's the truth.

I saw Benji kissing Violet, word to my mother.

work both sides of the street *(verb phrase)* General: to pander to opposing interests in an effort to attract all

That candidate shamelessly works both sides of the street on health care issues.

works 1. *(noun)* Drug World: all of the implements employed by a drug user (pipe, syringe, cooker, etc.)

The police found a drawer full of works in the suspect's kitchen.

2. *(noun)* General: something in its entirety, everything

I'd like a hot dog with the works, please.

worm something out of someone *(verb phrase)* General: to convince someone to reveal hidden information

I managed to worm the guy's telephone number out of his roommate.

worth one's weight *(adj. phrase)* General: valuable asset; short for worth one's weight in gold

Terrence only worked part-time,

but he was considered worth his weight in the company.

wow them *(verb phrase)* General: to make a memorable positive impression

We were hoping to wow the execs with our idea for an ad campaign.

wrangler *(noun)* Entertainment: individual on a film or television set responsible for handling the animals or children that appear in the scenes

Monica was known as one of the best baby wranglers in the business.

wrap 1. *(noun)* Teen & College: female companion

How many wraps does that guy need to have?

2. *(noun)* Crime & Law: agreement to resolve one or more criminal cases in a single disposition

The lawyer attempted to make a wrap on the probation violation and the new weapons charges on behalf of her client.

wrap up *(verb phrase)* General: to finish

Let's wrap up this last matter so we can go home.

wrapped around one's little finger *(adj. phrase)* General: under the controlling influence of someone

You know you'd never defy her. She's got you wrapped around her little finger.

wreck *(verb)* Teen & College: to fight

The two players wrecked for five minutes before someone was able to break it up.

wrecked *(adj.)* Teen & College: intoxicated

I can't get wrecked tonight because I've got an exam in the morning.

write off *(verb phrase)* General: to dismiss the importance of, to accept the loss of

I had already written you off when you hopped on the train just as the doors closed.

wuss *(noun)* Teen & College: weak, unassertive person; *see also:* butt, weenie, and wimp

If you don't ask him out now, everyone's going to think you're a wuss.

WYSIWYG *(pronounced "wizzy-wig")* *(acronym)* Computerspeak: short for "What You See is What You Get," referring to a program that allows the user to see exactly on the computer screen what will be printed on paper

Unless you've got WYSIWYG, you usually have to use a bit of trial and error to determine your document's specifications.

X

X.O. *(noun phrase)* Seafarers: initialism for Executive Officer, the second in command on a Navy ship

The sailors couldn't stand their X.O., whom they found to be im-

perious and demanding.

Y

Yabba-dabba-doo! *(expression)* Surferspeak: generic greeting among surfers; from the television cartoon "The Flintstones"

Hey, look, there's Rocky! Yabba-dabba-doo, Rock-man!

yank someone's chain *(verb phrase)* General: to aggravate someone in a way that is particularly annoying to them

My crazy boss is doing everything he can to yank my chain!

Yar! *(expression)* Surferspeak: Cool!

Yar! What a great wetsuit.

yawner *(noun)* Entertainment: boring theatrical production

The widely touted musical closed after ten performances since critics agreed it was an unsalvageable yawner.

yellow stuff *(noun phrase)* Military: heavy equipment used in military maneuvers

Don't forget to budget for the yellow stuff, which we'll need to make the temporary base secure.

yellow ticket *(noun phrase)* Military: dishonorable discharge from the military

After being busted overseas on drug charges, Kyle got a yellow ticket from the Army.

yesterwear *(noun)* Street: same clothes as yesterday or last season

She's a bore, always wearing that yesterwear.

yips *(noun)* Sports (Golf): attack of nerves

I got the yips on the fifteenth hole and couldn't even get near it.

Yo! *(interjection)* Teen & College, Street: Hello! Hey!

Yo! What's happening?

yoked *(adj.)* Health & Fitness: describing great muscular definition

That guy in the weightroom is yoked.

You're the expert. *(expression)* Auction World, Salespeople: pseudo-flattering response to shoppers' queries regarding period, authenticity, quality, etc., of an item

"Look, this car has all the extras at half the cost, but you're the expert. I'm not telling you anything you don't already know."

You're thinking you're all that. *(expression)* Street: You think you're better than other people.

Just because you won the relay, you're thinking you're all that.

yuppie *(acronym)* Press: Young Urban Professional

The yuppies across the hall from me just got a new stereo system.

yuppie flue *(noun phrase)* Medical: general medical condition that can include mononucle-

osis, chronic fatigue syndrome, or Epstein-Barr syndrome
Please don't tell me I have the yuppie flu!

Z

za *(noun)* Teen & College: short for pizza
Let's borrow your mom's car and go get some za.

zap 1. *(verb)* Medical: to give a patient electroshock therapy
The doctors decided to zap the new patient when he did not respond to other treatments.

2. *(verb)* Computerspeak: to erase
*Could you just zap those two documents? I'll just keep **hard copies** in the file.*

3. *(verb)* Food: to cook in a microwave oven; *see also:* nuke
Zap those vegetables for a minute to get them steaming again.

4. *(verb)* Teen & College: to change television channels rapidly with a remote control; *see also:* channel surf
Dad's zapping in the living room looking for a ballgame on television.

zebra *(noun)* Sports: referee or game official who wears a black-and-white striped shirt
Darren ran into the zebra when he broke away with the ball and tried to head down court.

zenology *(noun)* Sci-fi: inter-

est in, and study of, extraterrestrial life forms
Charmaine had become somewhat of a celebrity zenologist on the television talk show circuit.

zero in on *(verb phrase)* General: to focus on
Let's zero in on a few promising leads and work on them for a week.

zero lot line *(noun phrase)* Real Estate: condition where a building abuts a property line
Though there was a zero lot line in the front of the house, there was a comfortable yard in the back.

zero out *(verb phrase)* Wall Street: to manage not to pay taxes without breaking the law
Smithers had the best accountant and tax attorney in town; he managed to zero out every other year or so.

zero-sum *(noun)* Government: no gain or advantage
The revised plan doesn't irritate the opposition, but for us it's a zero sum solution.

Z-gram *(noun)* Seafarers: blunt, to-the-point directive memorandum; named after the popular Admiral Elmo Zumwalt, who perfected the genre
The deputy attaché was relieved to see a Z-gram on her desk when she was assigned to handle the dignitary's visit.

zilch *(noun)* General: nothing

There's zilch going on tonight, so go home.

zip city *(noun)* General: nothing

I looked everywhere for the keys, but I found zip city.

zip fuel *(noun phrase)* Air & Space: extra high-energy type of jet fuel

The rocket needs zip fuel for the first stage of take-off to fight the pull of gravity.

zipper *(noun)* Surferspeak: wave that rolls in and breaks quickly

I had no chance to catch that zipper.

zit *(noun)* Teen & College: pimple; *see also:* zun

I can't believe I got this huge zit the day before senior pictures are to be taken.

Zoed *(verb)* Government & Politics: put in a vulnerable, unprotected position and irreparably harmed; from Zoe Baird, who was nominated for Attorney General by President Bill Clinton, exposed to brutal political criticism, and then had her name abruptly withdrawn from nomination; *see also:* hung out to dry and left to twist in the wind

The famed attorney was flat-tered by the Administration's interest in him for a political appointment, but he finally refused for fear of being Zoed.

zombie *(noun)* Drug World, College: person who smokes marijuana constantly

Brit had become such a zombie that his buddies had to force him to study for his finals.

zone *(verb)* Teen & College: to be distracted or to daydream; also known as: zone out; *see also:* space

I'm sorry. I guess I was zoning while you were talking to me.

zooed out *(adj. phrase)* Surferspeak: crowded

The surf's too zooed out for my taste. Let's go find another spot.

zorch *(verb)* Computerspeak: to make rapid progress

The system zorched when it sorted the thousands of records.

zun *(noun)* Teen & College: pimple; *see also:* zit

Is that a zun I see ruining your perfect skin?

Zup? *(expression)* Teen & College: What's up? What's happening?; *see also:* sappenin' and wassup

Zup, man. I haven't seen you for a long time.

ADVERTISING

antenna shop
auction fever
blurb
flack
guerilla marketing
handholding
infomercial
ink
overexposure
M.O.S
mush-core pornography
outsert
performance panache
plug
put on the map
ride the boards
roadblock
sizzle
snipe
teaser
throwaway
trade dress
trash cash
voice-over

AIR AND SPACE

A-okay
black box
deep space
dogs
dry run
go–no-go
no-shows

red-eye
upgrade
vultures
window
zip fuel

ART

cultural jammer
outsider art
po-mo
prop art
terrorist art

AUCTION WORLD

auction fever
lookers
new blood
You're the expert

BANKING

crank
points
teaser rate

BARS

amateur night
apron
back
baked
banger
barfly
barhop
beergoggles

bolt
booze cruise
bouncer
brewsky
chaser
chugalug
damages
dive
down a few
final-final
frontload
get stiffed
happy hour
happy camper
knock back
last call
long neck
meat market
neat
nightcap
nurse
on the rocks
shooter
splash
straight up
twist
watering hole
wet dog

BUSINESS

accelerated death benefits
antenna shop
baby bells
ball is in your court, the

beard
bearhug
black book
black knight
black market
blue collar
boiler room
bottoms-up research
broad strokes
cafeteria plan
cash cow
close doors
cold call
comfort zone
contingent work force
copreneur
dog
dog-and-pony show
dolphin think
dolphin safe
downsize
dump
end result
go belly up
golden parachute
golden coffin
golden handcuffs
gray market
green product
green marketing
greenback green
greenmail
handholding
hands on
hands off

CARTALK

rat boy
rock
roller
rope
score
shermed
sniff
snort
speedball
stash
steerer
stomp on
tab
tin
tracks
trey
weed
wired
works
zombie

ECOLOGY

biocentrism
dead time
eco-office
eco-tourism
green seal
green product
green marketing
greenback green
pointless pollution
sprout
true-blue green

EDUCATION

gifted child
interdisciplinary
K-12
multi-disciplinary
race norming

ENTERTAINMENT

above the line
actcom
alternative rock
angel
ankle
anticipointment
appointment television
arc
B-
backend money
backer
bankable
beat sheet
below the line
best boy
billing
blooper
biopic
bit
bit part
blow a line
blunt
bof
boffo
break
buck

garmento
grunge
look

FOOD

all the way
binder
bolt
branwagon
brown bag
damages
deuce
dive
empty calories
fat tooth
fluff and fold
foodie
free-range
garbage
get stiffed
graze
grinder
in the ozone
inhale
lite
menuese
microbrewery
munchies
mystery meat
new age beverage
no-shows
nosh
nuke
on wheels

pig out
pound
power breakfast/lunch/
    dinner
rabbit food
scarf
sinker
sponge
sprouthead
table from hell
take-out
zap

FOREIGN

aficionado
allegro
avant garde
bad hejab
bedienung
blitz
bon vivant
bona fide
bourgeois
carte blanche
connoisseur
creme de la creme
ersatz
finesse
forte
good hejab
Hasta la Vista!
kowtow
manana
nouveau riche

nouvelle cuisine
primo
soupe de jour

GAMBLING

one-armed bandit

GENERAL

10
86
a cold day in hell
ace in the hole
across the board
add insult to injury
add fuel to the fire
afraid of one's shadow
after one's own heart
ahead of the game
air dirty laundry
all bets are off
all ears
all of one's dogs aren't
    barking
all systems go
all the rage
all wet
along for the ride
any Tom, Dick or Harry
apple of one's eye
apple-pie order
apple polish
apples and oranges
armchair general
as the crow flies

ask for the moon
asleep on the job
at the drop of a hat
at sixes and sevens
at loggerheads
at sea
at pains
at one's beck and call
at one's fingertips
at heart
at death's door
ax to grind
back to square one
back-pedal
backseat driver
bad blood
bad egg
bad guy
bad-mouth
bad news, the
bag and baggage
ball of fire
ball park figure
bang-up
barf
bark up the wrong tree
barrel
basket case
bat an eye
be caught dead
bean counter
beat one's head against a
    wall
beat a dead horse
beat to the punch

GOVERNMENT AND POLITICS

wedge issue

whistle blowers

wiggle room

Willie Horton

-winger

wired

wonk

zero-sum

zoed

HEALTH AND FITNESS

cut

mall walking

pump up

roids

tight

yoked

HUMAN RESOURCES

downsize

interpersonal

KIDS

bug juice

flat tire

noogie

potatoes in one's ears

rad

MEDICAL

addiction medicine

advance directive

albatross

alternative dentation

Aztec two-step

baby catcher

banana

blade

big C

blue blower

blue pipe

bone factory

bounce back

box

BRI

butt up

C & C

C & T ward

camper

Code Blue

cold steel and sunshine

crock

deep fry

Dr. Feelgood

dump

dwindles, the

electronic cadaver

fanger

fascinoma

finger wave

flatline

fluids and electrolytes

gasser

gork

grapes

I.V.

ivy pole

jungle rot

MILITARY

Mark 1 Mod 1
megadeath
MFR
mick
milicrat
NOFUN
NUTS
o-dark-hundred
onload
overkill
pea shooter
Peacckeeper
Phase zero
program
retool
RIF (reduction in forces)
rug rank
sanitize
scenario-dependent
search and destroy
Secdef
second strike
selected out
selected
sigint
sign off on
soft
state of the art
Tank, the
threat tube
three-humped camel
ticket puncher
Uncle Sugar
unk-unks
unwelcome visit

weapons system
whiz kid
yellow stuff
yellow ticket

NEWS

Backgrounder
deep background
leaks
M.O.S.
sound bite
telepundit
wag

OFFICE TALK

burn a copy
circular file
desk jockey
paperweight
permahold
on-hold music
temp
work station

PC

animal companion
animalist
bias-free
biocentrism
cerebrally challenged
communitarian
cruelty-free

cultural genocide
exceptional child
developing nations
differently abled
disadvantaged
economically challenged
environmental racism
flesh
gender illusionist
generously cut
lookism
maintenance hatch
motivationally deficient
multiculturalism
nonsizist
person of size
pre-woman
race norming
sex worker
weightism

home in
infomercial
overexposure
latchkey kid
makeover
moonie
pink collar
preppie
sandwich generation
Silicon Valley
skippie
snow bird
spin
spin control
spin doctor
steel belt
sunbelt
thinking man/woman, the
woopie
yuppie

PRESS

afterboomer
baby boomer
Bible belt
boomer baby
buppie
couch potato
dink
Generation X
glass ceiling
golden ager
greenwashing
guppie

PSYCHOLOGY

dysfunctional
rebirthing

PUBLIC RELATIONS

damage control
flack
handholding
ink
overexposure
plug
put on the map
spin

TECHNOLOGY

TEEN AND COLLEGE

Metal mouth

Mickey D's

mint

Miss Thang

mobile

moby

mondo

money

monkey

monthly bill

mooch

mopped

mosh pit

mouth breather

mow

muckle

Muffie and Biff

munch on

munchie

mutant

my bad

N.I.

N.Q.

narbo

narc

nasty

nectar

nerd

nerd pack

new blood

newt

nibble at

nice do

nightmare

nitro

no comp

no biggie

No wire hangers!

No duh

nog

Not even!

Not!

nuke

__-o-rama

ob

obscure

-oholic

on a mission

on the rag

out of here

PMS monster

pain in the neck

Party on!

party favors

patrol

peeps

pessimal

pick up your face

pig out

pinner

pissed

plastic

played

player

polluted

pond scum

poser

posse

possie

pound

trip

trip-out

trippy

truck

tube

tude

tweaked out

twist a braid

uncool

unruly

up the ying-yang

up to no good

__ville

wack

wail

waldo

walking__

wannabe

Wassup?

wasted

wastoid

waver

way

weak

Whatever

What is this, my birthday?

What's the deal?

whipped

wicked

wig out

wild

wilson

woof

word

wrap

wreck

wrecked

wuss

Yo!

za

zombie

zone

zun

Zup?

TRAFFIC

big rig

bottleneck

broadside

bumper-to-bumper

carpool

clear shot

clip

commuter mug

dead stop

fender bender

greenlock

H.O.V.

jumpstart

rear-ender

roadkill

rubberneck

rush hour

slow-and-go

squeegee people

TRAVEL

Axtec two-step

Bed and Breakfast